BEATING BACK

by

Al Jennings and Will Irwin

qp

QUID PRO BOOKS

New Orleans, Louisiana

Published in 2012 by Quid Pro Books. Part of the *Journeys & Memoirs Series*, and a Quid Pro *Digitally Remastered Book*.™

ISBN 978-1-61027-916-1 (paperback)

QUID PRO, LLC
5860 Citrus Blvd., Ste. D-101
New Orleans, Louisiana 70123
www.quidprobooks.com

BEATING BACK

BY

AL JENNINGS

AND

WILL IRWIN

ILLUSTRATED BY
CHARLES M. RUSSELL

NEW YORK AND LONDON
D. APPLETON AND COMPANY
1914

CONTENTS

CHAPTER		PAGE
I.	INTRODUCING MR. JENNINGS	1
II.	THE LONG RIDERS	40
III.	TWO OUTLAWS	69
IV.	THE COUNTRY GROWS HOT	82
V.	THE LAST CAMPAIGN	96
VI.	THE END OF THE TRAIL	133
VII.	IN THE GRIP OF THE LAW	153
VIII.	CONVICT 31539	162
IX.	THE DEPTHS	182
X.	THE DAWN OF HOPE	198
XI.	PLANNING MY COMEBACK	219
XII.	THE SET-BACK	253
XIII.	BETWEEN TWO NATURES	272
XIV.	REHABILITATION	309

LIST OF ILLUSTRATIONS

FACING
PAGE

Al Jennings, the Long Rider, showing his actual
costume and equipment . . *Frontispiece*

Judge Jennings   6

"My temper suddenly flamed up, and I called
him a liar"   42

"I made him ride beside me as we galloped down
the right of way" 120

"We drove him ahead of us down the road" . 130

"I went straight at his neck" 180

"There, I broke the ice, and watered my nitroglycerine" 302

"The desire for rehabilitation inspired my actions" 322

BEATING BACK

CHAPTER I

INTRODUCING MR. JENNINGS

(BY WILL IRWIN)

I FIRST met Al Jennings in a New York club frequented by actors, painters and writers. Arriving one day for a late luncheon, I found the round table occupied by a congenial group, having a mighty good time. There was a stranger present; and I marked him on first sight as a Somebody. He was a little man, hardly more than five feet tall; he had a shock of bright auburn hair and a face, what with tan and sun-wrinkles over a ruddy skin, like a baked apple. I slipped into the vacant seat beside him. Someone introduced him as Mr. Jennings; he replied in a Western accent and turned upon me the beams of his personality. Here was one, you felt instantly, whom all men of good will would like on

1

sight, one to whom children and dogs would come running by instinct.

That face, as I studied it more narrowly in the next few minutes, showed certain extraordinary points. His fine, clear, steady eye was greenish blue. His wide brow ran straight down with no indentation—Greek fashion—into a small, cleanly-drawn nose which seemed somehow to lie close against his features, as though presenting no point of attack for an adversary. That conformation of the brow and nose, I have observed, is a common trait in pugilists, born soldiers, militant men of affairs, and fighters generally. James J. Jeffries and Battling Nelson possessed it in common with Theodore Roosevelt and Admiral Bob Evans. Under the nose lay a powerful jaw and the wide, firm mouth of an orator. The upper lip was cleft by a big scar; the upper canine teeth had been crowned with gold to support a dentist's bridge. Plainly, he had taken at some time a heavy blow which had crushed in lip and teeth. I was yet to learn that under his clothes he carried the following complement of scars: the souvenir of a rifle bullet in his left ankle; the mark of a steel-jacketed Winchester bullet in his left thigh; a pistol ball encysted in the muscles above his right knee; the track of a bullet across the front of both knees; a double scar where a shot had entered and left his right shoulder; and the white tracks of a knife wound which had traversed his left wrist.

How we opened conversation I do not remember; probably with some remarks about "God's country," such being the hailing-sign for Western people in New York. But we had not talked five minutes before he dropped a remark which sounded odd in an Eastern club. Irvin Cobb had been spinning a humorous story at the expense of the doctors. When the laugh died down Mr. Jennings turned to me and said:

"That sounds like a joke, but I saw as bad as that in the Ohio State Penitentiary; and it was no joke, either."

"Were you ever at the Ohio Penitentiary?" I asked, not getting, at first, the full purport of his remark. "I used to know a man who served a five-year term there," and I mentioned the name.

"I should say I did!" replied Jennings. "About my best friend, too. We were both on clerical work, and saw a lot of each other."

"What was your position?" I asked. "A guard?" And the second after I regretted that impertinent question. But Jennings swept away all regret by his answer:

"Hell, no! I was in for life—train-robbing."

3

He said this in a perfectly matter-of-fact tone, as though he were speaking of an old job at selling groceries. Then he turned the conversation to other and more commonplace topics.

It was some time yet before I understood the deeper meaning in this conversation. Harris Dickson, it appeared, had introduced him at the club, and had, by special request, explained to his host at luncheon the old record of this Mr. Jennings. I, however, was a newcomer; and I must know. So Jennings had taken the first opportunity to tell me, as he has told every man, woman and child to whom it can possibly make any difference in the eleven years since, with a new suit on his back and a ticket to Chicago in his pocket, he stepped out of the penitentiary.

However, we had scarcely left the table when Dickson called me aside to explain him in a hurried biography. This was Al Jennings, successively cowboy, land boomer, and lawyer; afterward train-robber, bank-robber and life-termer in the Federal Penitentiary. Released and pardoned through the successive mercies of Mark Hanna and Theodore Roosevelt, he had gone back to Oklahoma, the scene of his old operations, and, with his record on his sleeve, he had started to take up again the life which he left for the high road. Meeting squarely and without flinching those obstacles which society sets across the path of the ex-convict, he proceeded to build up a law practice. Finally, just ten years after he left the penitentiary, he made a reform campaign for prosecuting attorney of Oklahoma City, fought the politicians of both parties blind, and lost in the end by a small vote—so small that most Oklahomans believe he was really elected. "His campaign speeches, as they report them there, were the greatest in political history," said Dickson. "He'd tell them about his past, prison and all, until he had them crying like penitents at the mourner's bench. Then he'd add: 'There, I've told you every thing I ever did. Now, suppose those machine fellows tell what they've done? In case their memory goes back on them, I'll supply a few details right here!'"

How, by successive stages of acquaintance, I came to be the editor of Al Jennings' autobiography is aside from the mark. Two or three times, indeed, he has tried to write this story for himself. One of his manuscripts, "The Long Riders," shows acute observation of life and a real talent for description. But Jennings has never found time, in those full and busy years since he left prison, to learn the art of writing. "The Long Riders" fails to tell a story. He is, however, a master in the art of talk, whether from the platform or from an easy-chair. That narrative gift which often freezes within him when he sits before white paper, flows limpid when he lights a cigar, crosses his feet, and engages the eye of his *vis-à-vis*. So it came that on my advice he talked off this autobiography to me, with a court stenographer—under orders to make him forget her presence—"taking" his conversation. I have only rearranged, pruned, edited, suggested, and supplied, with what skill I have, the lack which everyone must feel in all literal transcripts of conversation—the fuller meaning given by intonations and gestures.

Nevertheless, it has seemed best for the editor of this frank, unabashed story to write the first chapter, in order that the reader may better understand the man. In doing so I must be as frank with Jennings as Jennings, in the later passages, will be with himself.

Alphonso J. Jennings, then, was born in an abandoned Virginia schoolhouse during the worst days of the Civil War. He came of the proud, belligerent, Southern slave-holding stock—"the best blood of Virginia," and all that. His father, Judge Jennings, is remembered by old settlers of Oklahoma as a perfect type of the ancient Southern colonel, even

INTRODUCING MR. JENNINGS

to the goatees. He followed in his lifetime nearly all the learned professions—he was successively schoolmaster, physician, Methodist clergyman, lawyer, editor, and lawyer again. In the end he settled down to the law. That was the family talent; his four sons who survived to manhood all became lawyers. He had in him, apparently, that typical restlessness of the West which does so much to explain his son, Al Jennings. Whenever he reappears in this narrative he is practicing law in still another town.

Al, youngest of the four sons who grew up, was born in the midst of alarms. When the Civil War broke out, the elder Jennings had started a plantation in Tennessee. He enlisted as surgeon in a Virginia regiment. In 1863 Longstreet and Rosencranz were conducting that series of operations which led up to the battle of Knoxville. The elder Jennings perceived that there would be a clash near his plantation. He advised his wife to take the slaves and live stock and go to her mother in Virginia. Incidentally he called the turn; on the night of the battle he used his own house as a field hospital. Mrs. Jennings was forced to stop on the road, and at an abandoned schoolhouse in Taswell County, Virginia, Alphonso was born. The two armies closed in about them. All travel became unsafe. So she

7

stayed at the schoolhouse in Taswell County, awaiting the issue of the war.

It was a year and a half before Mrs. Jennings knew whether her husband was dead or alive; for there were no mails in the South of war times. When the surrender came, and the roads were filled with returning Confederate soldiers, she used to bake apple "pop-overs" and give them out at her front gate. One day she saw a gray uniform on the road, and ran out, pies in hand—to meet her husband. He brought the news that, after the surrender, her brother had been killed in a duel with a fellow officer.

From that time the Jennings family shared the common fate of the impoverished South. They solved the problem by moving North to Marion, Ohio. There the old soldier heroism in Dr. Jennings remade his fortune. The cholera epidemic came. While other physicians were running away, while two of his own children lay dying with the disease, he stayed at his post and served the sick night and day. When the refugees came back, he found himself in possession of all the practice he needed.

To us, however, the significant thing about these first years in the North is the position of the Jennings boys in boy society. The murderous antipa-

INTRODUCING MR. JENNINGS

thies born in the Civil War were still alive; and in
these things children exaggerate the feelings of their
elders. Life, it would appear, was one long war, the
Jennings boys, with their clannishness, their hot
temper, and their Southern pride, against this hostile Northern world.

It began, I believe, before Al Jennings was old
enough to fight, when the Goodall boys, Northern
cousins, called Ed and John Jennings "Secession-
ists" and "poor white trash." That last aspersion
was what hurt. Before the war they had belonged
to the slave-holding class; but now the jibe at their
poverty fitted. John scaled the fence "and repro-
duced the battle of Manassas," says Al Jennings.
The war went on; the Cornell boys, the Lowes, and
the Pulleys were drawn into the feud. As soon as
Frank and Al could wield their little fists they took
their part. Frank was rather timid in the beginning. "At times he was able to kick a cotton-tail
rabbit out of his way, so he could get along faster,"
says Al, "which seems strange to me now, because
he grew up to be the bravest man, the most dependable in a tight place, that I ever knew." Al himself
entered heart and soul into this warfare. "Give us
the boy and the man will take care of himself," said
the Jesuits, and "the thoughts of youth are long
thoughts." This fighting childhood does much, I

9

have no doubt, to explain the Al Jennings of thirty.

Only one other incident of this period bears on the story. At the age of seven, Al Jennings tried to experience religion and failed. There was a big camp-meeting in Marion; his father, still preaching in the intervals of his medical practice, sat on the platform. Something about the meeting touched the religious chord in the nature of that little boy on the back seat. When the presiding elder asked all who wanted salvation to hold up their hands, Al, quivering with eagerness, gave the sign with the rest. The deacons, passing through the congregation to bring up the penitents, never seemed to notice his little hand, though he thrust it almost into their faces. Doubtless they felt that he was too young; but it appealed differently to Al. He thought they were picking only "prominent citizens" and pretty girls. Hurt to the quick, he ran away from meeting and went apple-stealing. Having filled his clothes with green apples, he complicated his crime by going swimming on Sunday. While he was splashing in the pond, a drove of razor-back hogs found the clothes and the apples. When he came out, his waist and breeches were torn to ribbons. With a small boy's modesty, he waited neck-deep in the pool until dark, and sneaked home naked. When the storm had passed, Al Jennings found in himself an illogical but

10

instinctive bias against religion, which persisted into his mature years, and which was intensified by the growing skepticism of his father, who left the church soon after.

When Al was eleven, his mother fell sick. They started her back to Virginia, but she died on the way, leaving four sons and a younger daughter. All the sons figure in this story—John, the eldest; Ed, Frank, and Al. The two latter were less than two years apart in age, and passionately attached to each other. Their lives, through prosperity and adversity, crime, punishment, and rehabilitation, ran parallel all the way.

The year after his mother's death found the family at Manchester, Ohio. Here a trivial quarrel with his father stirred up the blazing temper which Al was beginning to develop. He lay awake all one night, nerving himself to what he meant to do; before daylight he sneaked out of the house and stowed away on a river steamer bound for Cincinnati. So he followed the rule of runaway American boys by taking the final step at the age of eleven, and by starting West. Crawling out at Cincinnati, he found work for three nights as super in "Ticket-of-Leave-Man." At the end of the run he rode a blind baggage to St. Louis. A little, freckle-faced, red-headed boy, probably dowered already with a

11

winning personality, undoubtedly pert and "fresh,"
he made friends with a saloon-keeper and earned for
a week a precarious living by sweeping out the saloon. The Jennings boys were all musical; the elder
brothers played in the town band at home, and had
given little Al some instruction on the trombone.
When he learned that the variety theater next door
needed a trombone player, he applied for the job.
The very nerve of this child must have appealed to
the leader, for he gave him a chance. Little Al had
always read his trombone score in the treble clef,
while the music they furnished him was written in
the bass. Nevertheless, with the confident courage
of eleven, he went ahead and "faked" his part for
three days, until a grown-up musician with a union
card displaced him.

That night he swung onto a brake beam and rode
to Kansas City. There he worked a while as errand
boy for a packing-house, lost the job for imperti-
nence, and wandered to the outskirts of town, where
he fell in with a "boomer outfit" going West to New
Mexico. This, remember, was the summer of 1875.
The tide of rough immigration was still setting
westward, and the plains were perilous with Indians
and robbers. The "boomers," pioneer settlers who
traveled in covered immigrant wagons, used to form
caravans for mutual protection. They took him in

as a kind of roving annex to the outfit; thence, for a whole summer, he slept on the ground, chased horned toads, fought or played ball with the "boomer" children, and had his meals at the common "chuck-wagon" of the caravan.

They had reached the vicinity of Trinidad, in the heart of the Colorado cattle country, when the "boomers" quarreled and separated, leaving him behind. So he found himself alone on Commercial Street, Trinidad, with a quarter in his pocket and a hollowness in his little stomach. He met a Mexican bootblack who wanted to retire from business, and exchanged the quarter for a box and brushes. He was swindled, it appeared; the people of Trinidad did not care how their boots looked. All day he ranged the square without making a cent. And then came the vital meeting, which probably turned the whole current of his life.

"A big, broad-shouldered, blue-eyed fellow came across the street," says Jennings. "I thought then, and I think now, that he was one of the finest, handsomest men I ever saw in my life. I never looked into a straighter, clearer, blue eye. He was wearing all the regalia of a dude cowboy. His boot heels weren't bigger at the bottom than a quarter; they slanted forward; and they seemed fastened to the sole at about the instep. I said:

" 'Shine?'

"He stopped and looked me over, and grinned.

" 'Well, Bub. I reckon you can paste them a little,' says he.

"I went to work. It was the first pair of boots I'd ever blacked, except my own, and I made a bad job of it. I did pretty well on the vamp, but I never touched the heels. When I'd finished he stood screwing his boots around so's he could look at them, and said:

" 'Bub, don't you think you can paste 'em a little right thar?'

"I was tired and hungry, and naturally pert. I don't remember what I said, but I probably used words that a little boy has got no right to know. Instead of kicking me over as I deserved, he just looked down on me, and smiled, and said:

" 'Bub, you've sure got a temper. Where's your paw and maw?'

" 'Ain't got none,' said I.

" 'Who were they?' he asked.

"I didn't answer. The truth is, I didn't like to lie—never did like it, for all the other things I've done in my life—and this whopper tongue-tied me.

" 'I reckon you ain't interested,' he said, after a while. 'Well, I ain't got no right to ask you any such questions. I don't tell people where I'm from

14

myself.' That was true, as I learned afterward. He was a refugee from Kentucky—a case of killing. Whether Stanton was his real name I don't know yet.

"Then he talked to me quite a little, sizing me up, I suppose, before he said:

" 'Bub, don't you want to come along with me? My name's Jim Stanton, and I'm foreman of the 101 outfit. I'll teach you to ride, and give you a job.' "

The old West was sudden. Having determined upon the adoption, Jim Stanton proceeded with the affair in royal fashion. He bought a little saddle, borrowed a pony, and took Al out to the ranch. As they rode up, a half dozen cowboys were lolling among their saddles on the porch.

"Hello, Jim—where did you get Sandy?" one of them called. From that time on, so long as he rode the range, Al was "Sandy."

Jim Stanton did the job with a whole heart. He taught his apprentice to ride; he educated him in the customs of the range; most significantly he bought him a 45-caliber Colt's, the great Western side-arm, and taught him how to use it. Within a few weeks Al had learned enough to become "horse-wrastler"—that member of a cattle camp who takes care of the ponies. Like any boy, Al loved to see a horse go; and he got the habit of bringing in the

15

herd blown and lathered. Jim Stanton spoke to him sharply about it. After the manner of resentful and independent boyhood, Al replied by running them harder next day. Then Jim Stanton put his foot down.

"Sandy," he said, "I ain't goin' to tell you any more 'bout running them horses. Next time they come in wet I'm going to take it out of your hide. We'll put the chaps on you so you won't sit down for a week." This was a rough punishment used in cattle camps on men who had become obnoxious. It consisted in stretching the victim over a wagon tongue and whipping him with a strap like a schoolboy. Al accepted the challenge. That night, by Jim Stanton's orders, he was thrashed thoroughly and effectively. Then the 101 outfit took his gun away, lest he be tempted toward violence, and left him alone to think it over.

The disgrace burned in; and it roused his first impulse toward violence. The next day Al did not take out the horse herd. He moped about the camp, refusing to speak to the men or to eat at the ranch-house. He got his meals at the kitchen door and walked the range, all the time planning how to get a gun and nerving himself for what he intended to do—kill Jim Stanton in front, man-fashion.

"Of course, I know I couldn't have done it—I

16

loved him too much," says Jennings, "but I thought I had to, just the same. After three days, Jim Stanton came over to where I was mooning. He said:

" 'Bub, you got to take your bumps if you're ever going to be a man. Let's call this off.

"I said nothing. I was dying to make up; but my pride held me back. Jim kept right on:

" 'Sandy, I'm going cow hunting. Don't you want to throw in with me and go along? And, when we get to town, I'm going to buy you a new bridle, with tassels on it.'

"It wasn't the offer of the bridle which melted me, so much as the excuse it gave for swallowing my pride. All at once I put my hand in Jim's, and the quarrel was over. From that moment, as I know now, I grew up. I never was a child again."

Jim Stanton, in fact, became a second father to the little refugee. Even yet Al Jennings speaks of him with an affection near to tears.

Those were the high times of the middle seventies, when half the Western domain, still unfenced, was pasture for the herds of long-horns—wild days, those, and glorious, if rough. Away from the settlements and frontier cities there was no formal law. Each man carried his own law "in leather on his hip," his own hangman's rope on his saddle-horn.

17

The rules of the game were unwritten, but perfectly understood. By his own right arm a man defended his family and herds. An insult to honor called for death—but in a man-fight, face to face, with all opportunity for both contestants to draw. Assassination, however, was murder, to be avenged by the friends of the dead with their guns, or by the community with a riata.

When a man was killed in fair fight over what the community considered a sufficient cause, the killer went unmolested. In the neighborhood of towns the law made a show of prosecuting these "affairs." But community feeling was dominant there, as on the ranges. If the community felt that the killer had his quarrel just, and if he had slain fairly and in front, the old, overworked plea of self-defence got him off. In fact, the book law of the towns often worked less justice than the gun law of the ranges, since men with pull and influence might escape the penalty for crimes condemned by the community at large. All that was the dark side to a glorious man-life, filled with young vigor, mirth, cheerfully accepted hardships, and adventure.

In this life Al Jennings grew from a little, stubby boy to a little, compact youth. Before he was fourteen he had become a fullfledged cowboy, earning a man's pay of seventy-five dollars a month and "found." It was not uncommon to see a boy thus doing a man's work on the ranges. For, once he had learned to ride, a boy was a light mount, putting no great burden on his horse. Roping is more a matter of skill than of strength; if your loop falls true, the trained horse does the heavy work.

From the time he got money of his own he bought books and read incessantly. At first Jim Stanton got him his literature in Trinidad; when that resource was exhausted, he sent East. Al devoured Scott and the other standard romanticists; he developed a passion for history, and especially for the campaigns of Napoleon. Most of the 101 cowboys were scant of book learning; and Al took to reading aloud around the camp fire or the ranch-house table. Scott, and all writers of his school, were the favorites; he read the camp-fire circle "The Lady of the Lake," "Marmion," "Ivanhoe," and "Kenilworth" from cover to cover.

"I remember," says Jennings, "that I tackled 'The Child's History of England' once. When I came to the place where King Alfred burned the cakes, one of the boys spoke up and said:

" 'If I'd have been a king I'd 'a' dealt her a swift kick in the jaw—treating a king like that!' When I fell asleep, they were still arguing whether any

19

man, even a king, had a right to kick a woman in the jaw."

A tragedy rang down the curtain on this scene of his life. Sometimes in the spring roundup the branding outfit missed a calf. When, next spring, the "long yearling" was discovered running beside a cow—presumably its mother—it belonged, by custom of the range, to the outfit whose brand the cow bore. In the spring round-up after Al was fourteen the 101 outfit found such a maverick beside one of the cows of the O X—the next ranch. Jim Stanton found, however, that it had a "blotched" brand, which looked to him like 101. Sometimes, just as the brand was pressed down, the calf would give a jerk, producing one of these blotches. The O X outfit did not agree; they flatly claimed the yearling. Jim offered to skin the calf and prove by the inner skin, which always caught the first impression of the iron, that this blotch was a 101 brand. The claimants from the O X refused, and rode away in a violent rage. Many of the tougher ranches employed a "killer" to take care of such troubles. That afternoon the killer of the O X, a Mexican or half-breed, rode up to where Jim Stanton was tying a thrown steer, shot him dead from behind, and rode South out of Colorado.

He must have been a minor hero of the plains, this

Judge Jennings

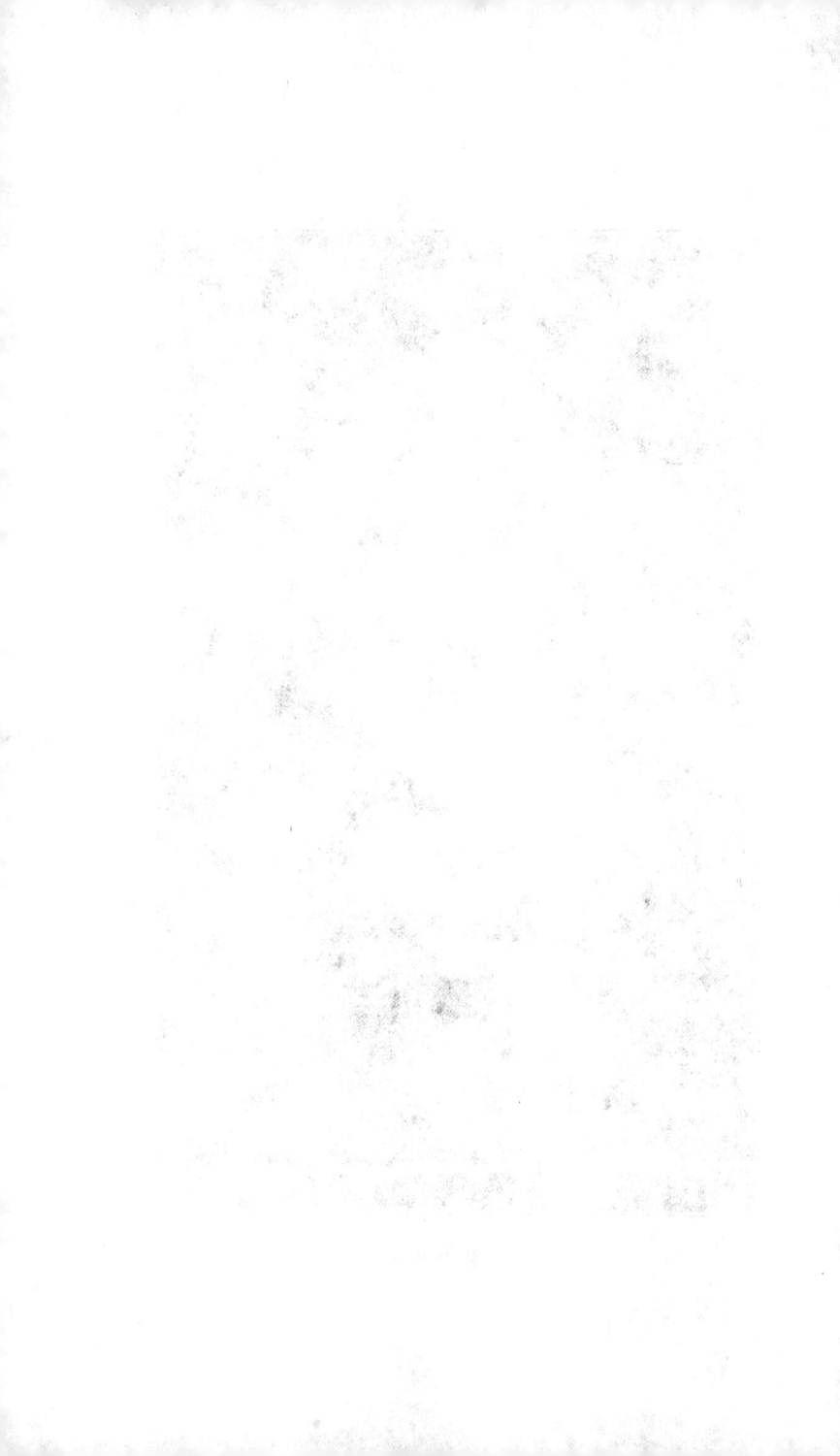

INTRODUCING MR. JENNINGS

Jim Stanton; only an extraordinary personality could have inspired what followed. For a party of 101 cowboys swore an oath to get this killer. They started South, taking Al along, on the trail of the murderer. They never told him their purpose, considering him too young for such desperate work; but he came to understand. All summer they traveled, working from ranch to ranch, finding, losing, and refinding the trail. And in the fall they located their man on the Rio Grande. They rode to the ranch-house in the late afternoon and waited, their horses still saddled. At sunset the killer rode into the corral. Al, standing beside his horse ready for instant action, saw the avengers ride leisurely toward their man, saw him reach for his hip—and tumble from the saddle with two bullets in his head. The 101 outfit whirled and galloped westward. There was no pursuit, there was no complaint to the law—no further trouble of any kind. The outfit by the Rio Grande doubtless decided that the "killer" deserved what he got. So things often went under the gun law; and the deepest-dyed conservative must admit that there was a certain real justice in this manner of regulating society.

The avengers rode on into New Mexico. There, for two years, Al Jennings worked at his trade from ranch to ranch. He was almost a man now, and bore a man's part in this rough life. He still carries a pistol bullet encysted in the muscles about his left knee. He got it from a stray shot, on a night when drunken cowboys were shooting up the town. His left wrist is crossed by an old scar. He got that from a knife in an affray with the Mexicans.

All this time he had been reading; and, when he was sixteen, ambition dawned. He wanted an education; he wanted to follow his father's profession of the law. By a curiosity of memory, he cannot remember how he knew that his family was living in West Virginia. He had held no communication with them; for all he knew, they thought him dead; yet in some manner which will not come back to mind he had learned. With a few dollars in his pocket, he started East. When he reached Cincinnati, he found himself penniless. He went to the same old Valk's Theater where he had been a super when he first ran away, and got a place in the "army" of a French melodrama. Between acts another super told him that the run finished that night, and warned him that the big, bullying "super-captain" would try to cheat him out of his pay. The curtain was no sooner down than Al demanded his dollar.

"Come back to-morrow night; the run ain't finished," said the captain. Al felt that he was lying, and said so. The quarrel grew warm. The captain had no means of knowing that this short, slight boy wore under his red uniform a Colt's forty-five in a shoulder scabbard. So he felt safe in knocking him down.

Lying on the floor, Al drew and fired. The captain dropped in his tracks. The stage became bedlam. Al, his revolver still drawn, retreated to the dressing-room, pulled his coat and trousers over his costume, and ran through the stage entrance down the alley. He reached the railroad yards unpursued. A freight train was just pulling out. He swung onto the brake beam; and so, with one or two changes of trains, he came back to his family in West Virginia.

I asked Jennings whether he felt any special remorse over this shooting. He searched his soul before he said no, only considerable apprehension—for he realized that the East had a different view on such things. His conscience was clean enough. That was the way they settled such matters on the range. A big man who cheated and assaulted a little one must expect to be shot. His father, of course, saw it in a different light. He had always been afraid of what Al might do in a temper, and he told him so with emphasis, while he took steps to find just what had happened in Valk's Theater. The super-captain had not died, it appeared. The ball had passed cleanly through his shoulder, and he was at work within a week.

So, by contrast, Al settled down to read law. The next summer, feeling his restlessness upon him, he played solo alto in the band of an old-fashioned wagon circus. And that autumn his family, through Judge Virgil Armstrong, secured him a "cadetship" —equivalent to a scholarship—in the University of West Virginia.

In equipment and experience this was probably the strangest freshman who ever presented himself for matriculation. He had never received a day's instruction in grammar. He knew hardly any geography. He could add and subtract, but the multiplication table was to him as logarithms. On the other hand, he had a wide general acquaintance with English literature, carried universal history at his finger's ends, and knew almost enough law for admission to the bar. West Virginia, though loyal to the Union, had to bear with its secessionist sisters the heavy after-burden of the war. The State University was still struggling to keep its head above water, and took students on almost any terms. For two years Cadet Jennings divided his time between the grammar school of the preparatory department and the legal department.

Perhaps it is worth while to record one event of

INTRODUCING MR. JENNINGS

these school days, not only for its light on character, but because it had such a strange parallel in his
later life. Wild and restless, bored with the quiet
of the academic life, Jennings founded the "U. of
W. V. Guerillas," a set of rough, surreptitious mis-
chief makers, who delighted to overturn outhouses
and break up class dances. The authorities knew
that Jennings was the ring-leader, but they lacked
absolute proof. Whenever he was called to account,
Al, like a good lawyer, would refuse to affirm or
deny the charges. Finally, on a Christmas Eve,
the Guerillas stole four bags of powder and loaded
them inside an old cannon which stood on the square
of the campus. They wadded the charge with rags,
shotted it with broken bricks, and touched it off with
a fuse. The discharge blew the cannon from its
carriage, and broke the surrounding windows.

The next morning Al found himself on the carpet
before Major Lee, a fine and respected soldier.

"Jennings," said the Major, "I believe you dis-
charged that cannon."

"If you believe it," replied Cadet Jennings,
"what's the use of me talking?"

The Major looked him over.

"Jennings," he said, "you've got the makings of
a man in you. You've never lied to me, and I like
that. You're an able boy, and it would hurt me to

expel you, but this can't go on. Why don't you settle down and go to work? I like you, and I wish you'd play square with me." Suddenly Cadet Jennings found himself shaking hands with the Major and promising to abide by the rules. From that time he was a model student. By the end of the year the Major made him Lieutenant in the cadet battallion.

Two years of this; and then, having the general principles of law in his head, he grew impatient of looking to his family for support. His father and brothers had yielded to manifest destiny and gone West. He joined the band of the same old circus, with the idea of getting to his family and making a little money on the road. The solo cornet player fell out; Al secured the job for his brother Frank; the two played all summer in the mining camps and cattle towns of Colorado.

In the course of that tour he witnessed a tragic and desperate piece of heroism which, even after all the melodrama of his bandit days, remains in his mind the bravest thing he ever knew. The circus train was running from Longmont to Boulder. They carried an exceptionally tough and drunken gang of canvasmen. The boss canvasman was a brutal fighter, who ruled by the power of his two fists. His forces had been sneaking away to get drunk. That night he swore a mighty oath that "they wouldn't run out on him again," and padlocked from without the door of their bunk car. Then he himself crawled into the car from the little, high window at the end. There was a barrel of gasoline on the floor. Some canvasman, smoking against orders, dropped a match into it. In two minutes the car was a furnace—and the only outlet that little, high window.

The boss stood under the window, his clothes afire, throwing man after man out to safety, until the rescuers from without caught his arms and pulled him through. Burned beyond human semblance, he fought to get back. When his last breath left him, there beside the tracks, he was still fighting.

Finally, Al and Frank settled down at Coldwater, Kansas, a new town, and were admitted to the bar. His first case is a picture of old procedure in the West. A woman had been thrown off from her claim by an Englishman. She brought action. His father, Judge Jennings, held the brief for the plaintiff; Al took the case of the Englishman. Judge Jennings cast some aspersions upon the British attitude toward woman. This stirred up the Briton. He rose and started for the elder Jennings. The trial judge and the jury united in restraining him. Young Al, very nervous, grew personal in his summing up. He knew his father, he

said; and the old gentleman had a genius for making
black white. He urged the jury to disregard his
father's eloquence and give their verdict on the
merits of the case. "And father reared back," says
Jennings, "and gave me the hardest tongue-lashing
I ever got in my life. He fairly made me crawl inside. He took every one of my faults and laid them
on the table. He asked them what they thought of
a boy who'd talk that way to his old father when he
wasn't yet dry behind the ears? The jury gave me
the verdict, but they did it because they were sorry
for me."

Young Al, still quivering under his lashing, told
his father two days later that he was going to quit
the law.

"Why?" asked his father. "You won, didn't
you? And I gave you that roasting on purpose to
teach you that when you face a court you've got to
keep your temper and stand for personalities."

Al had acquired some property, and was doing
well at law, when Fate and his own folly hurled him
into another phase of life. While with the circus
he had learned that he was a natural sprinter. He
has been timed for the hundred yards in 10½; he
might have done "even time" had he ever received
expert coaching. An old professional sprinter
named Foss—let us say—appeared in Coldwater,

traveling under an assumed name. He scraped acquaintance with Al. They ran against each other; Foss could beat him six yards in a hundred. Then Foss confided to Al the business which brought him to Coldwater. There was a sprinter in the next town who thought he could run. Foss had come incognito to get a match. Strangely, Al Jennings, for all his experience, had never heard of the "cross," the simple, primitive game which has discredited professional foot-racing. He bet all his money on Foss; growing more enthusiastic, he hypothecated family property to bet. The race came. Of course Foss stumbled just after the start, recovering himself, and made a vain, plucky effort to catch his man at the tape.

"We were so astonished," says Al Jennings, "that nobody thought to shoot him."

Humiliated, in debt to his family, Al left Coldwater. His next stop was Boston, Colorado.

You will look in vain for Boston on the map. It was one of those boom towns with which the pioneer business men of that era shook dice against Fate. If they won, they had the foundation of a future Denver or Oklahoma City; if they lost, the place reverted to primitive wilderness. Boston lay in the middle of a rich cattle country; but that was not the basis of its bid for prosperity. Las Animas, in which it was situated, is a large county. The boomers of Boston planned to divide the county and have Boston for the county-seat. They put up a tenthousand-dollar hotel and a street of stores; they laid out a town site and grew rich on paper trading lots; and they pooled all their ready money in a fund to corrupt the Colorado legislature, which was in those days easily corruptible. The firm of Jennings Brothers—Al and Frank—kept a store, opened a real estate office, and pooled their funds with the rest.

Boston shared in the disorder of all towns in the cattle country. The cowboys used to come in from the ranges on Saturday nights and shoot up Main Street. On one day Boston had three funerals due to violence. A settler shot his neighbor. Since it was cold-blooded assassination, a band of the tougher citizens—the Jennings brothers had no part in this—lynched the murderer. That same afternoon an extremely drunken cowboy of bad reputation came into town and tried to kill his enemy. A bystander, drawing just in time, killed him. The one clergyman in Boston refused to bury the cowboy. Al Jennings, always a friend of the cattle element, conducted the services over him.

"Told all about his virtues," says Al. "Didn't take long."

INTRODUCING MR. JENNINGS

There was another wild night, when Judge Jennings, by his courage and eloquence, kept a drunken mob from committing a lynching, before the bottom fell out of Boston. The legislature, as expected, voted for the division, and the creation of "Vaca County," with Boston as county-seat. But the governor vetoed the bill. A fire swept away most of the houses. A band of cowboys rode into town and "shot up" all that remained—which finished Boston. Over the town site now grow the alfalfa fields, and there is a watering trough on the foundation of the ten-thousand-dollar hotel.

That brings us to 1889, in which year Oklahoma was opened for settlement. To understand the rest of this story, you must understand fully the civic condition, in that year and the following years, of the territory which is now the State of Oklahoma. It was then divided into two parts—Indian Territory and Oklahoma proper. The Territory had long been the home of the Five Civilized Tribes. The legal system was dual—Federal law, with certain special provisions to fit Indian necessities, and the strict, often curious tribal laws which the Indians administered among themselves. The whites occupied this district only by a kind of courtesy. Some had married Indian women, and so became lords of principalities in Indian lands. Certain stockmen leased ranges from the Indians, often for trifling payments. Further, there was the element known contemptuously among cattlemen as "nesters." These pioneer farmers were also leasers, usually agreeing to clear the land in return for a five-year tenure.

Oklahoma proper, the other end of the present State, had been held by the government, practically untenanted, for future use of the Indian tribes. By 1889, however, the Indian population had so dwindled, and the "boomers" had grown so insistent, that the government threw it open for settlement. That was the first and greatest of our land rushes. The settlers lined up on the border. At the sound of a gun they rushed, the first comer to any tract seizing it by right of arrival and holding it, often, by force of arms.

The formal law of the land came early into Oklahoma. Within a few years it was a settled and orderly district; now, less than a quarter of a century later, it is as though the old West had never existed in those prairies.

Until recently things went differently in Indian Territory. Held back from close modern settlement by its curious legal status, largely inhabited by Indian tribes which were civilized only in the relative sense, it became, in the next few years, the refuge for the "bad men" of the West, and for those who

could live only under the gun law. The cattle business was changing. The range was shrinking every
day. Under old conditions, a man got his seventy-
five or a hundred dollars a month for work which
required nerve, resource, and continual dalliance
with danger. Now, a line rider at thirty dollars a
month did the comparatively safe and monotonous
work of keeping up the wire fences. Those who
could breathe only under old conditions drifted to
the Territory.

There were four strata, roughly speaking, in
white territorial society. First, the townspeople,
living under Federal law about as people lived anywhere in new Western towns. A large part of them
held employment, in one way or another, under the
Federal government. The territorial police were
represented by the marshals, men of nerve and daring, under whom were the deputy marshals, a
strangely mixed body. Some of them had both honesty and courage. Some had neither. Some, as will
afterward appear, were actual accomplices of the
criminals whom they took pay to hunt.

The "nesters" formed a class by themselves; generally they were the sport of the third class, the cattlemen, and the prey of the fourth class, the outlaws.

The cattlemen and outlaws had a loose affinity

for each other. Here and there was a ranch which existed only as headquarters for outlaw raids. The boldest cattlemen protected the outlaws; even the more moral or timid usually ignored them and minded their own business—unless their property was molested, when they resorted to private vengeance.

So the outlaws—train robbers, bank raiders, brand blotters, horse thieves, and vendors of whiskey in a district where whiskey selling was a crime—could depend on the country to assist and conceal them. It was as in the merry days of Robin Hood, when the outlaws shared their gains with the peasantry, and the peasantry made return by misleading the sheriff of Nottingham.

A fair country it was, and is even now, when the nester has conquered, and the old days are utterly gone, and all Oklahoma, the Indian Territory included, has entered the sisterhood of States. We had no finer tract in our national domain than that which we gave these Indians. It rolls in gentle prairies, riotous with long grass and flowering shrubs. It is traversed by low hills and little mountain ranges covered with native forest. It is shot with clear streams, widening here and there to little lakes. This story, however, has nothing to do with scenery; the pertinent fact is that these hills, water courses, forests, and thickets adapted themselves wonderfully to the uses of gentlemen in perpetual act of escape.

To the Oklahoma rush came Al Jennings, uprooted from Colorado by the explosion of the Boston boom. He wanted no land; he had his fill of that. He regarded Oklahoma simply as a good country to work up the practice of law. Frank, who will figure largely in the rest of this story, remained in Colorado, and became deputy county clerk in Denver. Now approaching thirty, he seems by all accounts to have been a stalwart and attractive man. Unlike Al, he was not only athletic, but big and powerful. Without Al's temper, he nevertheless was all cool nerve. Once the fight was crowded on him, he made a mighty efficient fighter with either fist or gun. Al, after six months of roving in the new Territory, finally hung out his shingle at El Reno. He grew popular; after Canadian County organized itself, he became, almost without opposition, its county attorney. Ambition awoke; he says that he gave an honest administration, and I have heard nothing to the contrary. But as government came into Oklahoma, so did politicians; and this lone wolf of a man got on badly with them. Failing of renomination, he went to Woodward, Oklahoma, where his father and his brothers, John and Ed, were practicing law. For a few months he was adrift there, waiting for something to turn up.

Here we have him, near that middle course of life's road concerning which Dante sang; and I have tried to record only such incidents in his early life as will explain what happened later. Physically, he had grown to be a little dynamo of strength and a greyhound of speed. His hundred and twenty pounds were all muscle and force. Of every rough, manly art which the West knew he was master. Not only could he ride; he was a real horseman—which means something more than mere riding. In pistol shooting of the kind useful under old conditions he figured as an adept. The crucial point in that kind of shooting was not marksmanship, but quickness on the draw. Al shot by "fanning" a single-action Colt's 44, with the trigger filed away. Used in that manner by an expert, a single-action gun was faster than a double-action. He shot a rifle from under his arm by sense of direction. In a rifle gallery he would have looked like a novice, but he was deadly on moving objects inside of the two-hundred-yard range.

In his infancy he had found a hostile world arrayed against him, and learned to battle for his rights. In the significant and vital years of childhood he had lived a man's life under the gun law. Servant of the formal law though he was, a feeling of the sanctity of private vengeance probably rested at the bottom of his thought; and in our crises we act not upon the ethics of our formal training, but upon the impulses of our unconscious natures. He still believed—at bottom—that vengeance of a private wrong was his own private matter. Thirty years had not cooled his hot, desperate temper.

Nor was he in other and slighter respects at rights with the morals of this modern world. Though he did not recognize it then, he admits it now. He had played the game of commerce, in his boom days at Boston, as the old boomer of the old West always used to play it. He had trafficked in worthless town lots; he had helped corrupt a state legislature. If he administered honestly the office of county attorney, it was partly because he cared less for money, in that period of his life, than for a political future, and partly because he had an ingrained sense of his duty toward his pals—represented in this case by the people of Canadian County. To desert a friend, to go back on an ally, was the blackest sin of his decalogue.

Such a complex nature as his cannot be expressed by any formula or set of formulas. But one other factor does something to explain it—his Southern blood. The historians of the old West have, it seems to me, ignored the part which the Southerner played in making that curious, manly, half-civilization which grew up in the West and Southwest during the fifty years after the war. Burning with the chagrin of defeat, convinced of the justice in their lost cause, stripped of their slaves and property, born or reared among the hideous disorders of a devastating war, they brought West not only their courage, their chivalry, their sentiments, but also their belief in the duello as a corrective of social disorder, and their resentment against the transition from a feudal state to an industrial one. To this type Al Jennings had bred true. Not least of all its traits, in him, was the passionate clan feeling which led, by the road of tragedy, to the overturn of his whole nature.

Jennings expressed all this to me in another way. He was talking of his ancestors. The first American Jennings, family tradition holds, was William, a brother to Sir Humphrey Jennings, once an official at the Court of George III, later a founder of the English iron trade and the unconscious cause of that chancery suit which Dickens made immortal in *Jarndyce vs. Jarndyce*. William Jennings was supercargo of a trading vessel owned by his brother. Just before the Revolution some insult of the government turned him against Great Britain. He sailed forth on the high seas and began to prey on British commerce. The colonies, when the war broke out, gave him a commission, and rewarded him, when the war was over, by a land grant in the valley of Virginia. He was great-great-grandfather to Al Jennings. Through his mother's family Al inherits a streak of royal Stuart blood.

"That high, proud, overbearing blood has a lot to do with the way I acted," said Al Jennings. "When such people are picked on they believe in their bones that it's right to tear up the whole earth to get even."

Here the historian rests; from this point the story will be an autobiography, expressed in many of the crucial passages exactly as he talked it off to me in Oklahoma City, with the stenographer alternately chuckling and sobbing over her notes.

CHAPTER II

THE LONG RIDERS

WHEN I tell how the events of a single night transformed me from a lawyer to an enemy of the law I shall fail, I suppose, to convince Eastern people and all others brought up in a regular, ordered state of society. To understand, such people would have to know the game as we played it in the old West. It will be all the harder for me to convince them, in that the beginning of my story involves feelings too deep and sacred for expression on paper. Further, the decision in the case of Oklahoma Territory *vs.* Jack Love and Temple Houston prevents me from giving fully my side of the tragedy. I must keep to the facts, bare though they may seem.

After I lost my county attorneyship at El Reno I drifted for six months, dividing my time between the towns and the cattle ranches, while I looked for a good location to resume the law. My family had settled at Woodward, a new Oklahoma town, where father was county judge and Ed and John were practicing. I was paying them a visit when Ed got a large and interesting case.

Frank Garst had brought eighteen hundred head of C-Dot-G cattle into Oklahoma and put them out to pasture on a range held under fence by Jack Love. When the time for payment came, Garst and Love had a dispute over the pasturage fees. Garst consulted Ed, who found that Jack Love held no title to that pasturage—he had fenced government land. By advice of counsel, Garst refused payment and moved his cattle. Love sued out an attachment; and on this process Garst and Love locked horns in court. Ed was Garst's attorney of record, while Temple Houston represented Love. The trial, which I witnessed as a spectator, became very bitter. Ed won a complete victory—he had all the law on his side. Both Love and Houston took the decision hard.

A week later Ed defended some boys for stealing from a box car. Being busy, he asked me to assist him at the trial. There we bumped again into Temple Houston, who was assisting the prosecution. Jack Love, for some reason or other, was a spectator at this trial. Houston, by sneers and indirect references, showed that he was still bitter. His attitude got on my nerves. My temper suddenly flamed

41

up, and I called him a liar. He replied by calling
me another liar, with additions; then he jumped toward me. Ed came between and slapped his face.
Court adjourned in great confusion. The town of
Woodward knew all about the bad blood between
Jack Love and Temple Houston on one side and the
Jennings brothers on the other. Moreover, Love
and Houston were notoriously handy with guns,
while I myself had some such reputation. So every
one expected shooting before morning. Nevertheless, after my father talked to me and showed me
that I had put him in a ticklish position, I cooled
down a little and promised to patch it up. However,
Temple Houston was drinking heavily that night
and in no condition to hear reason. I told father
that I'd catch Houston at the courthouse door next
morning, present my apologies and await his. In
the mean time home was the only place for a Jennings. Meeting Ed on the street, I asked him to find
John and bring him in. Then I went home and lay
down to wait for them. It was a hot night and I fell
asleep.

I was awakened by some one calling outside:

"Judge! Get up quick! Your boys are killed!"

I ran to the door. John was just coming through
the gate, bleeding.

"I am all right," he said in a low tone, "but go to

42

"My temper suddenly flamed up, and I called him a liar"

Garvey's. Houston and Love have killed Ed." How I got to Garvey's saloon I don't know. A crowd surrounded the place and the barroom was deserted. But the back room was full. I shoved people aside and got to Ed. He had been shot twice—once in the back of the head, once over the left ear. I took his head in my lap, and there he breathed his last.

Before they took me away the change in my nature had come over me. Looking down into Ed's face, I swore to give up everything and kill those two men.

The day after we buried Ed, Frank came from Denver. He found John delirious, trying in his ravings to tell us how it happened. My father sat beside him, dumb with grief. Frank felt exactly as I did. He told me so.

But our father was county judge. Knowing what we had in mind, he begged us for his sake to let the law take its course. There was a special reason at the time. John's wounds had become infected. He lay in danger of his life. Father asked us whether, with one of his boys dead and another dying, we wanted to pile a new tragedy on him. At last we promised.

We did not dare trust ourselves in Woodward, where Love and Houston, as soon as they got out on bail, would offer continual temptation. As things stood I was certain that justice was going to fail us, and I determined to put myself clean away from temptation. The night when the doctors pronounced John out of danger, Frank and I saddled our horses, took what money we had, and rode away toward Southern Oklahoma, intending to establish among the outlaws some base from which, if the time ever came, we could make our raid and kill those two men. From that time forth, as I know now, we were outlaws in spirit. The rest came as gradually and easily as sliding down hill.

We went first to the Morris ranch. There I made my first friend among the bandits—one Jim Hughes, a rough, game man, formerly an outlaw. Ben Hughes, a brother of Jim, and one Jud South were in the Federal jail at Fort Smith, charged with killing an Indian deputy marshal named Naked Head. Jim Hughes asked me, as a lawyer, to help his brother out. I had never intended to practice law again, but I could not refuse this favor to a friend. We rode into Arkansas, camping out as we went. Concealing my true name, I assisted his attorney of record, and got both men acquitted. All this drew me one stage deeper into outlaw society.

Also it led to an adventure consummated months later when I myself was on the dodge. Ben Hughes had for cell mate in the Arkansas jail one Jim Cash,

a robber, charged with murder. The case against
him was so strong that he never stood a chance, and
he went to the gallows. The condemned man told
Ben Hughes where he had buried seven thousand
dollars in stolen money—gave him a map and full
directions. The next spring a party of us—all
wanted by the law—went hunting for this buried
treasure. We camped, leaving a negro to guard our
horses. The map was perfectly plain; we found
the place according to directions, and began to dig
under a flat rock. Before we had got down a foot
we heard a shot. We grabbed our guns, crawled
to the bushes, and surveyed the camp. It looked
peaceable, and we rushed in for our horses. We
found the negro rolling and moaning with pain. He
had got to monkeying with a loaded revolver, and,
not understanding guns, had shot himself in the foot.
We were patching him up when we spied a body of
marshals looking for gentlemen answering to our
description. When the subsequent episode was finished we found ourselves miles from the treasure and
afraid to go back. If that seven thousand dollars
ever existed, it may be there yet. And there it will
stay, for all of me.

However, this treasure hunt happened long after
my return to Indian Territory. At the time John
Harless owned the Spike-S ranch—so called from its

brand—near the junction of Snake Creek and Duck Creek in the Creek nation. Harless was a cattleman with a habit of rustling other people's live stock. The Spike-S ranch, in fact, was a rendezvous for "long riders," as we used to call them—train robbers, bank robbers, and raiders. These people were aristocrats in the territorial underworld, looking down on plain horse thieves, brand blotters, and whiskey peddlers. The rode the best horses in the country, for their lives depended on the speed and endurance of their mounts. I cannot fully describe the people whom I met at the Spike-S, because in this story I will give away no secrets but my own. Some were men of good education, driven out from society, as I had been, by tragedy. Some were born killers. Some were products of the Eastern slums. But they were all distinguished by their nerve and daring, which accounts, I suppose, for the fact that the horse thieves and whiskey peddlers, together with a great many people who never turned a criminal trick in their lives, would always protect them against marshals.

The Spike-S was one of the most beautiful ranches in the Territory. Mrs. Harless had planted a flower garden and a peach orchard; Harless had put up a big red barn which was a landmark. Three or four miles south lay a little mountain range, wooded with chestnut and cedar trees, and to the east a heavy thicket covered the bottoms of Duck Creek. Once in the mountains, you could laugh at the marshals, and no man who wasn't an outlaw or a friend dared enter the thicket—it was too good a place for an ambush.

Jack Love and Temple Houston had not yet come to trial when Frank and I determined to locate on the Spike-S. I borrowed three thousand dollars from a friend, and invested it in cattle with Harless. So for a few months we hung around the ranch, lending a hand with the cattle and studying outlaw customs. During this period the boys pulled off two or three jobs. I knew exactly how they were done, and I was always invited to go along; but I laughed and declined. The outlaws told me they would get me yet. They were right.

In January, 1896, I learned that my father was at Tecumseh; and I rode down to see him. When he came to the door he seemed surprised and dazed.

"My God, Al!" he said, "what are you trying to do? Do you mean to disgrace our name?"

I asked: "What do you mean?" and he answered:

"Don't you know that they are hunting you for train robbery? That Norman job." A train had

47

been held up at Norman a few weeks before, though I didn't know it then.

Of course I denied the charge. He asked me why I didn't give myself up and stand trial. I wouldn't, for several reasons—mainly my difficulty in proving an alibi, in case they framed up testimony against me. For when Father told me the date of the robbery, and I ran back over the past few weeks, I realized that I had spent all that day with the outlaws on the Spike-S. None of those men could be dragged alive into a court of justice.

Father and I parted bad friends. I rode all that night, with my hatred for the world swelling in me. Next morning I pulled up at a little country store to buy some crackers and cheese for breakfast. Three or four heavily armed men stood about watching me. Whether they were marshals or long riders, I did not know nor greatly care. I finished my breakfast, mounted, and started away. I hadn't ridden two hundred yards when the whole crowd opened on me with Winchesters. My horse went down dead, and I got a bullet in the right ankle.

Bad as my temper is, I have never known such anger as I felt at that moment. It is literally true that I saw everything red. I jerked my Winchester from the scabbard and ran toward them, firing blind—trying to mow them all down with one shot.

THE LONG RIDERS

If they had been real killers they could have got me a dozen times, for all my shots were going wild. As it was, they and the storekeeper ran into the timber. I rushed through the store looking for some one to kill. It was deserted.

There, in the spirit of a fellow who misses a man and kicks his dog, I committed my first crime. They took me for a criminal. Very well, I would show them! I smashed the cash drawer with the butt of my gun, robbed it of twenty-seven dollars and fifty cents, mounted a horse which stood hitched by the door, and rode away. I hadn't thought of my ankle until I saw my stirrup dripping with blood. I found a puff ball, which is first aid to the injured in the West, and managed to stop the bleeding. When I rode into the Spike-S, they tell me, I was as pale as a sheet. I don't know yet whether it was from loss of blood or from anger. The boys were eating supper around a camp fire. I told them what I had done.

They didn't appear surprised. I can see yet the cynical smiles on their brown faces. The worst killer of the lot spoke up, and said:

"Pretty soon the law will be looking for a little fellow about the size of you!"

"They can look!" I said.

"I guess you'll join us now!" said the killer.

"I'm with you until doomsday," I said.

I had forgotten Frank, until he found me alone out behind the barn.

"Do you mean it, Al?" he asked.

"I sure mean it," I said. "You can do what you please."

"Then I'm with you, Old Sox," he said. To the end Frank followed the game mostly because I was in it, and he wouldn't leave me. He never had a real liking for outlaw life, and he tried at intervals to make me quit. Not that he wasn't game—he is the bravest, coolest fighter I ever knew.

Four days afterward we went on our first train robbery.

I started this story with the intention of telling every crime which I ever committed. There is no reason why I shouldn't, if I were the only person to be considered. The statute of limitations has run on my offences, and I couldn't make my old reputation worse by setting down everything I know. But, as I think over these affairs in detail, I keep coming on other people's part in them. Not one job but involves some man who has given up the game and gone to live far away, unsuspected by his neighbors, or some woman who is happily married and out of touch with outlaw society. So I must be indefinite about the actual robberies in those early days. In the last few months of my outlaw years I did things which involve me alone or which have been aired, to the smallest bit of evidence, in court. These I shall relate in order.

But I can tell about that first robbery, because it never came off. As usual, we had learned from private sources that a large sum was to be shipped into the Territory by express. We picked out a siding where the train must stop for water—but we took no chances on its running past. We planned to make the flagman signal for a stop, and to build a barrier of ties across the track, so that the engineer, seeing them, would slow up. Five of us went on that job.

It was a pitch-dark night. We crossed the railroad to a small grove which looked like a black smudge against the skyline. In the densest part of the thicket we tied our horses. The boys took off their coats and closed about me with the garments spread out, while I lit a match and looked at my watch. The snapping of the lid, as I shut it, sounded to me like a cannon shot. It was forty minutes until the train was due—little time enough to complete our arrangements. In absolute silence, except for the clinking of our spurs and the creaking of a new cartridge belt, we reached the railroad tracks and passed on to a bridge.

BEATING BACK

I was all nerves and apprehension—I admit that now. I remember looking up to the sky and seeing a long, black cloud which obscured the stars and seemed to follow us as we walked. I felt uneasy about that cloud. I stopped to look at it. Then, realizing that I had fallen behind, and fearing that the men might josh me, I pushed on. Now a dread of cowardice took possession of my soul, and I rushed ahead of my comrades. Then a weakness came over me. It seemed that my joints must surely give way beneath the weight of my body. As I looked down through the ties and saw the stars dizzily reflected in the black, swirling water, I had a sinking heaviness in the pit of my stomach. It was such an amazing heaviness that I couldn't see how I could go further. I made a misstep, and my leg slipped between the ties. Some one gripped me and got me onto my feet. The action steadied me. The clouds kept following. The iron bridge rods above looked like prison bars. I finished with my eyes straight ahead. We made a turn; before us was the tub-like hulk of the water tank, and near it the light of a window pierced the darkness. What if a sheriff with his force were waiting behind that light?

We halted and held a conference in whispers. Two of my companions sneaked away. They came back, supporting between them an old Irishman, who staggered dizzily and begged them to "go easy" with him. When they halted him before us, I could hear his teeth chattering. In fact, we had to joke with him and reassure him before he gathered enough nerve to take orders.

"You stand here," our leader said. "If she whistles for water, do nothing. If she don't, you stop her."

The Irishman started to take his lantern out from under his coat. Some one shoved a gun in his face, and he nearly collapsed, so that we had to let him light his pipe, under cover of our bodies, in order to get his nerve back. Meanwhile two of the boys had laid a half dozen ties across the track where the engineer would see them by his headlight.

Then came the rhythmic quiver of the rails. The train was on time.

The leader ordered us to our places. I was to take the opposite side of the track and begin shooting at the windows as soon as she stopped.

I got my place. The tree-tops suddenly flashed yellow. A fiery eye had dodged round the curve. With the first flash of their headlight the gang disappeared as though by magic—every man had dropped to the ground.

The regular clicking of the wheels over the rail joints came to me as I lay there. It seemed to me that this vibration had become communicated to my body. My nerves twitched with it, my flesh quivered with it. My scalp tightened on my head, and I couldn't keep my revolvers from shaking in my hands. What would happen in the next few minutes surged through my mind—curses, commands, shots, shattered glass, cries, perhaps bloodshed, even death.

The lantern began to swing. The train did not slacken its speed. The Irishman signaled madly and for his life; still it went on. There was a blaze of windows in my face. It passed me, raising a sucking wind. Then I saw Little Dick rear up beside me, waving his revolvers and yelling so that I heard him over the racket:

"My God—the women and children! She'll be wrecked!"

That was the first I'd thought of our barricade, and it froze me to stone. The cowcatcher struck the ties, tossed them this way and that, and the train went on, unharmed. I learned a lesson there. Never again did I build a barricade before a train. We were not out to slaughter the innocent.

The killer of our outfit wanted to shoot the Irishman, believing he'd given a secret signal for the train to go by. We closed about him and tore him away. It wasn't the Irishman's fault. You could see by the way he swung the lantern that he was sincere.

THE LONG RIDERS

I never quite understood this affair. It doesn't seem possible that the engineer could have failed to see both the signal and the barricade. Most likely he had received a tip somehow that we were after the treasure, and had taken a chance.

When we went on our next job, I was leader of the long-rider gang which operated from the Spike-S. Just how that came about I can't exactly tell, unless it was a matter of the trained mind. When it came to the pinch you could count on them for courage and action; but few of them—except Frank, of course—could go very far in mapping out a raid. As a lawyer, I was accustomed to look at any proposition from every side. I could not only plan a robbery, but I could prepare get-aways and alibis—provide for every contingency. A train robbery needs a directing head as much as a battle. From the time when we started on a raid until we eluded the marshals and scattered with the "dinero," I had absolute authority over my gang.

After all, one train robbery is much like another. There are two ways of going at it. Under the old method, used always by the Dalton boys, two of the gang mount the forward end of the baggage car a station down the line. When the train starts they crawl over the tender, hold up the engineer and fireman, and force them to make a stop at the point

where the rest of the gang is waiting. But if the
trainmen have a heavy consignment in the express
car, and therefore expect to be robbed, they watch
that baggage platform; you risk a complete fizzle.
We used another method. We picked a point where
the train had to stop for water, or else we held up
a signal man and made him "flag her." As soon as
the train stopped, part of the gang would begin a
fusillade from both hands in order to cow the passengers and the crew. If a passenger shoved his head
out of the window, we would smash the glass over
his head. In the meantime two of the gang would
attend to the engine, one keeping the engineer and
fireman covered until the other turned water into
the firebox. When that was done one remained with
the trainmen, while the other went back to help in
the actual robbery. Though we sometimes went
through the passengers, the express safe was always
our real object—we never robbed a train unless we
had a tip on a large sum of money. There isn't
very much in robbing the passengers. You can't
watch them all. At the first fire the big wads of
money and the valuable jewelry generally go under
the seats or behind the steam pipes. Mostly, you
get only watches, trinkets, and small change.

Occasionally the express messenger showed fight,
but a few bullets just over his head always stopped

him. Then, with one of my coolest men, I would attend to the express safe. Sometimes we made the messenger open it; generally we blew it with giant powder. We'd empty the contents into sacks, fan a few shots around the train for a warning, and get to our horses.

People were so dazed that they acted like trained dogs. Really, robbing a train is easy. The element of surprise favors the robbers. The hard and dangerous part comes afterward, when the trainmen start up the marshals and vigilantes, and the whole country seems roused against you. I've seen a district alive with armed men an hour after the robbery. We generally held together for a day or so. Then, when we'd got clean through the cordon, we'd scatter, making an appointment, often for months ahead, to meet for the next robbery. Generally I'd pass the intervening time among the cattle ranches in another part of the Territory. Frank used to loaf around among the nesters. When we found him again, he'd be comfortably settled down in a farmhouse, smoking a corncob pipe, helping the women wipe the dishes, and singing at the melodeon of evenings. He could eat into the bosom of a family quicker than any other man I ever knew.

I understand that people are digging all over the Creek nation for the buried treasure of the Jennings gang. I buried my treasure all right, but not that way. It used to run through our fingers like water. First, a big wad went to the territorial or railroad official who had informed us of the shipment. We had our friends to take care of—they were mostly poor. We thought nothing, when we were flush, of throwing down a hundred-dollar bill on the table. Most of the valuables we gave away— gold thimbles and brooches to the little girls, gold watches to the older people. I don't know just where the rest of it went—mostly, I suppose, I dropped it on Broadway or Wabash Avenue; for I used to vary life on the ranches by going East. When the time came for the next job we were always broke.

Our chief trouble, barring the escape from the marshals, was in reassembling. We didn't dare use the mails. Most of us went under assumed names. I usually traveled as "Mr. Edwards," and Frank as "Mr. Williams." Sometimes, when you heard of a chance for a robbery and wanted to gather the riders, you had to hunt for a fortnight. You knew nothing about them except their regular haunts, and even then you were hardly ever right. One such hunt I shall always remember for its finish.

We had scattered at the 22 ranch, after a hot pursuit by the marshals, and I was knocking around among the horse thieves and ranchers on the Chickasaw, when I heard news of a chance for a reasonably good haul. I knew where I could lay my hands on the rest of the boys, but I wanted especially a certain long rider whom I'll call Webb. He was a very reticent man, and I knew little of his past, except that he came from the East and had a good education. Between jobs he had a gentle and sentimental nature. In action he was absolutely deadly.

The last heard of Webb—so "Mex," one of our long riders, informed me—he was at "Perky's" on Mud Creek. He described "Perky's" place as a little long house with a stone chimney which had fallen away from the wall and been propped up by a log. Mud Creek was a dangerous country for anyone connected with the law. A good many deputy marshals had been killed there for prying into matters which didn't concern them. Perky himself was a horse thief.

I found at last the house with the leaning chimney. A man was digging in the little cotton patch— striking a few strokes, then looking round. I asked him if he was Perky. He said:

"No, I never heard of such a fellow."

I was sure of him nevertheless; so I told him I was looking for Webb.

He said: "Who Webb?"

I answered: "Just Webb."

59

He shook his head.

"Did you know Mex?" I asked.

He stopped digging right there, and asked: "Do you?"

"Sure. I just left him on Winter Creek," I said.

"I reckon I know who you are now," he said. "I thought I did, and then I waren't certain. You're Al, ain't you? Webb was here yesterday."

I was so eager that I got too sudden. I asked: "Where did he go?"

He grew suspicious again, and said: "If you're Al, you oughtn't to ask me that question. By ——, I don't know whether you're Al or not!"

"I can tell you just how he looks and what he was riding," I said.

He said: "Any fellow can do that. You get down and come in. We ain't got much, but the old woman can scare up something." It was an hour before I persuaded him that I was really Al Jennings. Then he told me that Webb had gone on to San Baker's. At Baker's they said that he had left the day before, without telling where he was bound. We seldom informed anyone of our movements.

I was up against it. I simply wandered round in circles, asking questions, until an old-time cowpuncher told me that Webb was sparking a nester girl over on the Spavinaw.

THE LONG RIDERS

To make a long story short, I hunted for four or
five days, never more than a few hours behind my
man and never finding him. Finally, I heard that
a horse thief named Ike, present whereabouts unknown, might have the information I wanted. And
a certain John Barrows, of the same occupation,
offered to guide me while I looked for Ike. We rode
to a little cabin in a clearing.

A pack of fox hounds came out, barking, as we
drew up at the front gate. Presently a head slid
through the window, and this was the conversation
as I recall it now:

"Howdy, John," said the head. "Won't you light
and come in? I didn't know who you were, first off.
Then I seed it was you. Got anything to swop?"

"No, I reckon I ain't got nothin' to swop to-day.
Ed, this man is from Mex, an' he wants to see Ike.
I fetched him down, as I reckoned you'se about the
only man who knowed where Ike was."

In silence Ed whittled for a time on a splinter
which he had cut from the window sill. Then he
spat impressively on the ground, and afterward
gazed in utter helplessness at his dusty cotton patch,
choked with brown weeds.

"Don't know how I can get off, John," he said.
"My crop was about took with the consarned weeds,
an' was awful backward, an' I've been layin' off for

61

some time to go horse huntin'. I reckon I'll have to swop that mare if I ever get her again. She's breachy, and there ain't no fence can hold her. You'uns get off." He turned his head up toward the sun, and continued: "It's most too late in the day t' start now, but I reckon I can go to-morrow." We stayed with him that night. It was morning before Ed offered to take John's place and guide me to Ike. We started; we had gone five or six miles when we saw a man picking lazily among the cotton rows. Ed called:

"Howdy, Izard! How's your crop turnin' out?"

With alacrity Izard dropped his basket, approached, and perched on the fence.

"My cotton ain't what it oughter be," he said. "'Spect I've done let it go too long. I'm powerful crowded with work, an' jes' ain't had time to turn round."

"Folks well?" asked Ed.

"Nothin' to brag of. Little Izard's had the agey, an' the baby's awful colicky. I ain't so powerful pert myself. Rest of 'em's so's to be around, 'cept my woman, an' she ain't had a well day since we left Texas. Your folks well?"

"Jes' tol'able. Seed anythin' of a little bay mare fourteen an' a half hands high, blazed face, wire cut on left shoulder?"

"Yours?"

"That's the calculation."

"Wet?" (Outlaw slang for "stolen.")

"Sure!"

"Any brands?"

"Yes, only they're blotched. Looks kinder like this."

Sliding from his horse, Ed squatted down on his spurs in the road and began to trace the design. Izard followed the stubby, rope-stiffened finger. Finally he said:

"Ain't seed her, Ed. Want to swap her? I'll give you a powerful good swop, sight unseen."

"What's your swop?"

"The one *I'm huntin'*."

Then they negotiated. Ed wanted Izard to throw in a pig. Izard said that he'd even up if Ed would throw in a pup which he could get from his brother Jim. They closed the transaction there, the horses to be delivered when found.

Izard rose to his feet, squinted at the sun, and said:

"It's most noon, fellers. Ain't got much to eat, but, sich as it is, you're welcome."

"Jest ain't hardly got time," said Ed, faintly and politely; but just the same he sidled up the path to the house. By the time we'd finished our fat bacon, corn bread, and white butter we had learned for certain just where we could find Ike.

Ike lived much like the others. Before he came in from the cotton patch Ed had pumped Mrs. Burton to find if there was a horse trade in sight. As soon as Ike arrived he and Ed fell into horse-swapping negotiations, which lasted half an hour. When he was left alone with me, Ike grew communicative. I asked why he didn't settle down on a good farm. He said:

"Well, brother, us fellers has got to make something off our horses, an' o' course that don't let us stay long enough in one place to get a crop. Neighbors is so peart to go pryin' into a feller's business."

But he couldn't direct us to Webb. He passed us on to still another settler. "You'll find him," he said, "in the Cherokee country, t'other side of Grand River. He put in a crop there this year," he added incidentally.

All these men, in fact, were horse thieves by profession and horse traders by avocation, planting a crop, as my host had hinted, only for a blind, and moving on when the country got too hot. Keyed up as I was for another big job, they both amused and irritated me, but without their assistance we long riders could never have existed. They did not know who I was, did not care to know. It was

64

enough for them that I was neither a marshal nor an informer, but like themselves a member of that strange, secret order which must keep itself fortified, by mutual help, against the law.

And at the ranch in the Cherokee country—where Ed stayed to bring off another horse trade—I ran hot upon the trail of Webb. He was due that night at a nester dance on Col. Rowe's ranch. I kept out of sight all the afternoon, and rode up to Col. Rowe's at sunset.

A function of this sort was a great occasion among the nesters. The country cotillon leader who organized the dance used to mount his horse, ride up to the houses of the social lights in the community, and call out:

"Goin' to be a dance over to Rowe's Saturday. Want you-uns to come. We done got the fiddler all right. You-uns tell all you see." And he would fade away in a cloud of dust.

Before sunset the guests were arriving. The boys romped in on horseback, whooping and riding "slanting." Some had pulled down their trousers over their boots and put on neckties; and some hadn't. The girls came in wagons. They wore bangs low over their foreheads and blue or pink ribbons round their waists. Most of them were pretty, but all looked as though they'd never worn a corset

65

in their lives. These were quiet, law-abiding people,
though now and then the whiskey-peddling element
would get mixed up with them and start trouble.

After the crowd began to gather I rode away, for
deputy marshals sometimes attend such dances.
When I returned, after dark, a crowd had gathered
around a bonfire in the front yard, and the fiddle
was going inside. I tied my horse and crept to an
open window. There, beside the fiddler, stood Webb
in a plain black suit, just looking on. I tried to at-
tract his attention; but he was watching the girls
and listening to the fiddle.

The quadrille had gone three or four figures, and
the perspiration had started, when there was a
whoop at the door and the local bad man, very drunk,
burst in waving his six-shooter and announcing that
he was a wolf. The dance stopped. The women
screamed and crowded into the corner; some of the
more timid men followed them. The bad man stood
weaving on his feet, yelling:

"You be ——— ——— good and quiet. I've
come to take charge of this here dance!" He threw
up his 45 and fired a shot into the ceiling. One of
the lights went out, and the floor cleared, leaving
him in possession.

The desperado did a shuffle in the middle of the
floor, his double spurs ringing. Then he spied the

little man in the black suit who stood over by the music. When he turned that way the fiddler nearly fell over backward.

"Say, can you dance?" yelled the bad man.

Webb answered quietly: "Yes, I have danced!"

"Then," said the bad man, "hit the middle of the floor quick, or I'll build a blaze around you that will send you to hell!"

Webb answered in a voice so quiet that I didn't know until afterward what he said, which was:

"Brother, you're taking the wrong view of things here. These people have come to enjoy themselves. Why can't you let them have a good time?"

The desperado made the mistake of taking Webb's low-toned voice for cowardice. He swung round, started to throw down his gun—and there was a flash and a roar. I dove through the window, just as the other light went out. When I reached Webb he was striking a match. The desperado lay on the floor dead.

"Got him an inch from the eye," said Webb. Then he called to the crowd:

"Drag this fellow out into the yard and go on with the dance. He won't bother you any more." As a matter of fact, they did go on with the dance. Rowe's people scrubbed up the blood; when we galloped away the fiddler was at it again. No one tried to stop us, because everyone felt that the desperado had got his deserts.

Next day—as I learned later—the marshals arrived with a warrant for the arrest of this very desperado on a charge of whiskey peddling. They took the body to town, announced that they had killed him while he was resisting arrest, and collected the rewards for his capture.

CHAPTER III

TWO OUTLAWS

AFTER the affair at Col. Rowe's we assembled in our camp on the Spavinaw. Waiting for us there was a long rider whom we called Arizona or "Zonie"—I never knew him by any other name. He had been with the gang when I joined it at the Spike-S. His past was a mystery. We only knew that he had the appearance of a Southern mountaineer—tall, wiry, tow-haired, and blue-eyed. He was illiterate, hard, silent, and a constitutional killer. He had neither caution nor discretion, and none of the higher sense of things. In going on a train robbery I used to fear him as much as the marshals—I felt that it was only a question of time until he would interpret some little notion as resistance, and take the excuse to shoot. He gloried in slaughter. The only times he ever talked much were when he described some of his old affairs. None of us liked him; we kept him with us partly because we had to hang together, and partly because of his absolute nerve. On his side, he had never liked Webb

—resented Webb's refinement and sensibilities, I suppose.

When Zonie heard what Webb had done, he sidled over and for the first time opened conversation with him.

"I'm sorry I wasn't there to see you bust that fellow," he said.

Webb answered: "Those things are to be regretted."

"Well, I'd have shot him as he came through the door," said Zonie. After that, he accepted Webb as a man who had won his spurs.

Yet, before we separated forever, we understood Zonie better. It came about in this way:

We had pulled off a job; we had made our escape after a specially hot pursuit; we were dividing the loot in a cabin where lived the mother of a long rider. One of us sat cross-legged before the fireplace, arranging the gold and currency in five equal piles. And beside the fireplace the old woman—a sympathetic soul who never bothered herself about her son's business —was performing a surgical operation. A marshal had got Zonie through the forearm, and had escaped by a miracle with his own life. The bullet was still in the wound, and the old woman, pushing her steel spectacles down from her forehead, started to extract it with a knitting needle and a pair of scissors.

During this operation Zonie showed by an occasional click of his teeth how much she hurt him. As we ran over our winnings, and packed away the money, I noticed that he was talking freely with her—an unusual thing for him. Before supper he proposed that we give the old lady a little present. Each of us threw a hundred dollars into the pile, and handed it to her with a presentation speech. We made a lively supper party. Everything had turned out well, and we were flush. Zonie spoke up and told about some of his train-robbing experiences—especially the time when he took a Bible and a pair of brass knuckles from the reticule of an old lady. "She was so fond of them knuckles," said Zonie, "that she wore them to church of a Sunday." And all this time he was clicking his teeth with the pain of his wound.

What I had rather suspected became plain to me when we prepared to ride away. I was in the dark hall buckling on my spurs; and I overheard a conversation which I record as well as I can after eighteen years. I didn't begin to listen purposely, but when it started I couldn't help myself. Zonie was saying to her:

"My mammy would be about as old as you and maybe older. I never seed her or pop either. They was took off with yaller fever down in Mississippi, an' I was sent to the poor fahm. After I got to be a chunk of a boy a woman took me away. She 'lowed I was big enough to pick cotton. I was powerful glad to go, for they was always whoppin' me at the fahm, but it was no better whar I went. Them folks kept right on beatin' me, until I didn't have any sense. One day 'Lige—that's the man—knocked me down with a stick of wood, an' when I kim to it was night, an' my head was hurtin' me powerful bad. I made up my mind to run away. Crawlin' by the door in the dark, my hand hit the butt of the old shotgun. I'd help cut the slugs to load it for geese, an' I knew it was loaded yet, for we hadn't killed no geese. With that gun in my hand I couldn't stop myself, I hated 'Lige so bad. Mammy, that night I killed 'Lige and ran off. An' I've been bustin 'em ever since."

I had looked upon Arizona with aversion, regarding him as an intractable man without pity for any creature except his horse. And here the first sympathy which a woman ever showed him had stirred up a hidden goodness in his nature. I could see his face in the fire light. It looked positively soft.

The old woman broke the silence.

"Arizona, you haven't been much took care of," she said.

"Mammy," he said, "you're the only human being

that ever treated me white. Even the boys I ride with don't like me," which was true.

The old woman took both his hands in hers, and said: "I've had three boys killed by the officers, and my husband was killed in Texas a long time ago. Arizona, you can be my boy, same as my own." She reached up, and kissed his cheek.

He didn't reply, I suppose because he had no words. He just turned away, pulled his hat down over his eyes, and chumped out through the door.

We rode into the mountains, camped, made sure that all pursuit was over, appointed a place to meet for the next job, and prepared to scatter. But before we left I told the boys one by one about that conversation, and suggested that we might be kinder to Zonie in future. So, as we parted, each man took his hand and shook it warmly. He seemed greatly puzzled. Then he said in a jerky voice:

"Fellers, I don't savvy. Yer ain't goin' to quit the trail, are ye?"

"Oh, no!" said I. "We meet, according to appointment, at Jamison's on December twenty-fifth."

"Then what're ye pumpin' my hand fer?"

Bill happened to be impulsive. He broke in and told.

Zonie turned to his saddle, and mounted. "I

reckon you think I'm soft," he said. "So-long—I'll meet you at Jamison's."

I never remembered until long after that the twenty-fifth of December, on which we had agreed to meet, was Christmas day. There are no holidays on the trail. Frank and I approached the Jamison ranch that night in a downpour of rain, with the mud up to our horses' knees. We found the cotton patch in the darkness, and made out the clumps of trees which marked the house; but there was no light. Hitching our horses to the rail fence, we approached afoot, on our guard lest the darkness meant an ambush.

As we climbed the low fence separating the yard from the cotton patch, Frank stopped short. He stooped over; I heard him give a little "ugh!"

"It's a man—dead!" he said. "I struck his face!"

By sense of touch, I found that Frank was right. The face under my hand was cold and rigid.

We crawled up to the house. There was no sound except the water dripping from the eaves. Frank knocked; no response. Frank lifted the wooden latch, pushed the door ajar; no one stirred. He gave a stronger push; the door yielded slowly, as though held by some pressure within. We entered together. Almost at my first step I stumbled over something flabby. Though it took all my nerve, I lit a match.

Zonie was looking straight up into my face, with the stare of the dead. His long, yellow hair lay in a wet wisp across his forehead, and there was a blotch of red foam between his white teeth. Otherwise he appeared as though he had grown tired and dropped down to rest.

It was some time before we decided to risk a light. When we had a good blaze in the fireplace we saw the marks of an awful fight. Zonie's Winchester and revolvers were empty, and empty cartridge shells lay all about him. The body in the yard was Jamison's; he, too, was riddled. Who did it, or just why, I have never known. The killers were probably vigilantes—marshals would have carried off the bodies to get the reward. Our tardiness had saved the rest.

So there was the end of Zonie, the killer. How many notches he had on his gun I never knew—a great many, I suspect. The cruelty which he had undergone in youth, and perhaps a brain lesion from that blow on the head, made him the wild man he was. With other surroundings he might have lived and died a friend to the law. Again and again, in later years, I heard the same story from convicts. It is my firm conviction now that heredity counts little, and environment much, in making a criminal.

BEATING BACK

During my early years on the trail we had a boy called Elmer in the outfit; and, as I look back over my past, he is one of my chief regrets. His father had been shot dead in a bank raid just before I went to the Spike-S. After I became leader he heard of his father's death. He came up to join us—a tall, blond boy of seventeen with a face like a girl's. He found the outfit at the Verdigris River, assembling for a job. I hadn't yet arrived. They told me afterward that when one of the boys said, "I seen your father killed," Elmer's lower jaw twitched, and he turned his back on the crowd. When I came they had already agreed to take him along.

I didn't like that; he was too young. While we made preparations to start I thought it over. If I ordered him away he would never go—I knew the breed. So I approached the subject indirectly by asking him if he'd attend to a few things around the Spike-S which I hadn't time to look after—told him I'd pay him with a slice from the job. "I know you aren't a quitter," I said. "Your father was game—everybody knows that."

If I had stopped there I might have persuaded him. My mistake lay in pressing the point further.

"In the end," I said, "this is a losing game. Sooner or later it winds up with stripes or bullets or hemp, and all along it's hell and high water."

TWO OUTLAWS

He felt that I was challenging his nerve. That set him in his determination, and I couldn't budge him. The boys had said he could go. If I refused, he'd follow anyway. I remember he kept answering me in a phrase he'd picked up from Arizona:

"I'll be in the first set!"

I gave up in time. After all, it was his own lookout. He went with us; and he played his part like any of the rest. Yet he was always on my mind. Again and again I tried to make him leave. He always came back to the same argument: "What was good enough for pappy is good enough for me."

We were riding away from our next job, when Elmer showed the stuff in him. That ride brought nothing especially exciting; yet I have always remembered it, while others which involved danger and narrow escapes faded from mind. We finished and started away at about midnight, beginning, as usual, leisurely enough. The country was not yet roused, the marshals were not yet abroad, and we wanted to warm up our horses. For a few miles we took it at an easy fox trot. Then, as soon as they were warm and breathing properly for the long dash, our horses voluntarily broke into the measured cadence of a gallop. I was riding Black Dick, a magnificent, big, standard-bred; and every one of our mounts could distance, in a long or short race, anything which the marshals owned. The black fences and trees, barns and houses swam past us. When we came out of the thickly inhabited district, we began to double back or to zigzag by unfrequented paths, in order that our trail might be tangled or lost.

By and by the fence posts were gray instead of black. The cocks in the distance began to call from farmyard to farmyard. A coyote took up the noise; the eastern sky turned the color of wood ashes. We drew rein at last beside a thicket—a dark and sinister woodland in the dawn after that cold autumn night. Our clothes were heavy with dew, our blood chilled. For a few minutes we went stamping about to get life into our stiffened, swollen muscles. It is little wonder that we ached all over, for we had come fifty miles in less than five hours. Then we began the operation which we never neglected, however sore and weary we might be. We unsaddled, spread out our saddle blankets, knelt on them, and thoroughly rubbed down the legs of our horses. Their delicate muscles must be patted and kneaded like those of a trained athlete; for upon them our safety depended. Only when we had finished with the horses did Mex speak up:

"Say, kid, how about the grub?" In our excitement we had eaten hardly any supper. With the work and exposure of the night, we were ravenous. Elmer had been ordered to bring along rations for one meal.

Elmer turned his saddle over, and shook out his blanket. The package was gone! We could see where a worn saddle string had broken. The gang swore in concert. Elmer offered to go back and look for the package; but we couldn't have that. I was most concerned of all. It might be a day before we dared approach a house; and on empty stomachs the men were likely to get careless and quarrelsome. I had a card up my sleeve, however. I'd packed a few "terrapin" (hard biscuits) into my saddle bags. I divided them, refusing to take any myself. With the long riders, as with sailors, it was the commander who must bear the brunt of hardship. I told them that I'd eaten my share.

We had mounted and started, when Elmer rode up.

"I reckon you didn't really have no biscuit," he said. "You take some of mine, or I'll sling 'em away." I saw that he meant it, and we divided.

Elmer never rode with our gang again. We scattered; when I came back I discovered that he had thrown in with a low chain-harness thief named John Foster. I found Elmer, and told him that Foster had neither decency nor nerve; that they would surely get into trouble. But Foster held some sort of fascination over the boy, and then went away on a little raid of their own. When they reached Pottawatomie County they held up two Frenchmen in a cabin. The Kid was watching one of them in a corner, while Foster tied the other to a beam. Elmer's man started to run. Elmer shot him; Foster got rattled and cut the other man's throat. After that they ran wild down the country, robbing wherever they saw a chance. The finish came in Texas, where they made an attempt on a bank. The Kid entered by the front door and held up the cashier; Foster took the side door, where one of the bank officers was sitting at a table. Instead of making him throw up his hands, Foster hit him over the head with his revolver, and the gun went off. Elmer thought this meant a general fusillade, and he shot the cashier dead. They grabbed all the money in sight and mounted. A battle started in the streets; Foster's horse was killed. He mounted behind Elmer, and they got away to the river. It was swollen and dangerous. They found another horse. Elmer rode into the stream, and called to Foster to follow; Foster was afraid, and Elmer would not leave him. While they were debating the posse overtook them. Elmer wanted to open fire and die in his tracks, but Foster weakened, as I would have expected. He said that he knew everyone around there, and his pull would get them out of trouble. They surrendered without a shot, and were taken to Wichita Falls by Captain MacDonald and his rangers. That night the citizens broke into jail and hanged them to a telegraph pole. The leader asked Elmer if he wanted to make a statement.

He said: "Tell my stepfather I died game." Then, as they hesitated, because he was so young, he added: "Pull your old rope—I don't care!" That was the end of Elmer.

I became mixed up with this affair in a curious way. The people of Pottawatomie County laid the murder of the two Frenchmen to an outlaw named Smith, who had no hand in it whatever. They were searching high and low for him when I came through, riding away from a job. I had lost my mount—the thing I rode was more like a sheep than a horse. I had lost my Winchester; I had only one revolver and five cartridges. While I was in that fix a body of marshals took me for Smith and chased me. I had no chance to outride them. I doubled on my tracks, rode into a thicket, plunged over the bank into the South Canadian River, and ran into a quicksand. I thought for a minute that it was all over with me, and while I struggled I heard the posse riding down the road only a few yards away. The horse and I got out by rolling, but it was a close call.

CHAPTER IV

THE COUNTRY GROWS HOT

ALL this time Frank and I had not forgotten the intention which drove us out on the trail —to kill Love and Houston. I was at the Spike-S, already an outlaw and cautious about showing myself in towns, when the news came that they had been acquitted on the ground of self-defense. That verdict stands in the records of Oklahoma Territory; so I can say no more about my side of this case. As things turned out, I had only made my revenge more difficult by taking the trail, but I waited my chance.

I thought the chance had come when a telegram reached me at the Spike-S ranch, both address and signature under assumed names.

"Temple Houston is attending court at Guthrie, if you care to discuss any matter with him," it read. Houston it was who fired the first shot into Ed. I prepared for action. I was always trying to keep Frank out of dangerous enterprises, so I said nothing to him about the telegram. Instead, I confided

in Little Dick, who was eager to go along. We rode
all night, fifty miles, into Guthrie, avoiding every
place where I might be known. On the way I made
my plans. I was to ride up and kill Houston wherever I found him; Dick was to keep off the crowd and
help me escape. I did not intend to assassinate him.
I would give him a chance to draw. Though he was
very fast with a gun, I felt I could beat him to it,
especially since the man who is doing the hunting
always has the best of a gun fight.

As I rode down the street I heard my name called.
I turned and recognized Marshal Ed Nix, whom I
knew. Though he understood that I was an outlaw,
he had no pressing reason for arresting me; besides,
we were good friends. I rode over and shook hands
with him.

"Al," he said, "I know what you're here for, and
it won't do."

I assumed not to understand. To throw him off
guard, I let him take me to his house. There he
held me in talk for some time. When I was free, I
wandered about town, avoiding everyone I knew and
inquiring of strangers as to Houston's whereabouts.
I learned at last that he had taken a northbound
train a few minutes after I met Nix. In order to
prevent trouble and befriend me, the marshal had
warned him by messenger.

BEATING BACK

Three or four times more Frank and I made dashes into the towns after one or both of these men. Once, at Woodward, Houston passed me on the street. But he was walking with his wife; before I could get him alone, he had been warned. Once, by visiting El Reno during the Democratic Convention, to which both Love and Houston were delegates, we put our liberty in danger. The same thing happened there—some one telegraphed up the line; they dropped off the train a few stations above, and never entered El Reno. Always some mutual friend frustrated us, until the time came when we carried so heavy a price on our heads, and were so busy dodging marshals, that we could not show ourselves in the towns.

To be perfectly frank, there was still another reason. You can never know how hard it is for a man with any sensibilities to determine on a deliberate killing and carry out the determination. Those hunts for Love and Houston took all the nerve and resentment that I had in me. Yet, in the period which the law gave me to think over my career, this failure was for a long time my greatest regret—I had left undone the very thing which I broke with society to accomplish.

And yet not long after I gave up the search for Love and Houston I did take part in a killing. It was not murder, as either the law or the Territory defined the term. It was a fair fight, forced upon me.

We were assembling for a raid; and, although we didn't know it, the beginning of the end had come. In spite of our assumed names, our secret was out. The "Jennings gang" had become notorious in the Territory. Every robbery of every kind was attributed to us—we never did or attempted a quarter of the things that are laid at our door. After each job the marshals became thicker and more zealous, and the pursuit longer. Our margin of safety had shrunk; because of the danger old friends had begun to refuse us hospitality. There were heavy rewards on our heads; and certain pseudo-friends, as we know now, had arranged to betray us for money. A significant incident put me on my guard. With one of my old acquaintances I had a little hailing sign. Whoever saw the other first used to draw his gun, "throw down," and "get the drop" on the other. Then we'd laugh and shake hands. One night, after a long absence, I knocked at his door; when he opened it I playfully poked my gun under his nose. His hands went up, but, instead of laughing and lowering them when he recognized me, he backed into a corner and begged me not to shoot. I saw the point. I kept him covered until he confessed that he was planning to hand me over.

BEATING BACK

It was in such times that I rode into the Cherokee Nation with Webb, the man who shot the desperado at the nester dance. The night was stormy, alternating between rain and snow. We had not eaten since morning. On the windward side my clothes seemed frozen to my skin. We saw a light and rode toward it, willing to take any desperate chance for food and warmth. It was a little, one-room log house, in a grove of scrub oaks. I knocked. No one answered. I pulled the string which raised the latch and entered. I nearly jumped back again when I found the place inhabited. In the corner sat two women, one of them holding a baby. On the other side of the fireplace crouched a boy with black, beady eyes. He was about ten-years-old size, but his face looked older.

I explained as politely as I could that we were cold and hungry, and would pay any reasonable price for supper. It was some time before anyone answered. Finally the woman holding the baby said:

"We ain't keepin' a tavern." Eastern people cannot understand, I suppose, that such a refusal of hospitality was almost a crime under old Western conditions. In the remote districts every house had to be a tavern in emergency, or there could be no travel. That excuses what we did next.

THE COUNTRY GROWS HOT

I talked to them for some time, and got no answer, before Webb lost his patience. He walked over to the cupboard, and opened it. They had plenty of coffee, bacon, butter.

"We'll pay you for this," I said, "but we've got to eat." Webb proceeded to fry bacon and make coffee. The women, still silent, went over to the corner and crawled into bed, all dressed. As we cooked and ate, they watched every movement with eyes as big as saucers. Webb, utterly worn out and made drowsy by the heat, stretched himself out before the fireplace, and fell asleep. I had nearly forgotten about the boy until he rose, stretched, yawned, and said:

"Well, I reckon I better be ridin'," and went out through a side door. Until then I had taken it for granted that he belonged to the cabin. I hesitated, wondering whether to stop him—and hesitated too long; for a moment later I heard a horse galloping away. I grew nervous. I shook Webb and whispered:

"I don't like this. That kid's gone for somebody." But Webb said that was only one of my hunches and turned over for another nap. Weary though I was, I couldn't sleep; at last I woke Webb, and insisted that we had better get away.

He was just rising when we heard a footstep outside. We dropped to our stomachs, ready for trouble. The door flew open. Three men sprang in.

I can scarcely remember the details of that fight, everything was so sudden. It seemed that the bullets came with the men—and they came as fast as double-geared lightning. Flashes, roars, shoots of pain—that's all until two of the men were down, and the third staggering away, his hands to his head. Webb was down, too—a great hole torn in his side. A single bullet had gone into my biceps and come out through my shoulder. Wounded although we were, both of us rushed to our horses. As I left, I looked back. The two women were still sitting up in bed, their eyes like silver dollars. Apparently they had neither moved nor spoken.

Getting into our saddles was agony. We made it at last, rode all night in that freezing rain, swam Grand River by way of extra torture, and reached in the morning a friendly house where we had our wounds dressed.

I wondered for a long time why we heard nothing of that affair. At last I learned through underground sources that these people were outlaws—horse thieves and whiskey peddlers. They took us for marshals!

After the last job of this period of my career, the Territory grew still hotter. When we had outrid-

den the marshals and split out, Frank and I determined to leave the country for a while. We were
cagey about New York and Chicago; we'd been there
before. So, with the proceeds of the latest robbery
in money belts under our shirts, we went to New Orleans. I happened to remember that a man whom
I'd known intimately at the University lived in New
Orleans; and I looked him up. Jack, as I will call
him, knew about my career. Nevertheless he invited
me to his house. I felt that I couldn't go under false
pretenses; but I also felt that he was a man whom I
could trust. Therefore I told him everything. He
still wanted me to come; so we were introduced to his
mother and sister, I as "Mr. Edwards" and Frank
as "Mr. Williams." We resembled each other so little that no one would naturally take us for brothers.

The family introduced us to their friends—the
pleasantest, most hospitable people I ever met. Immediately we were flooded with invitations—that's a
way they have in New Orleans. Frank and I bought
full outfits of society clothes. Every evening we
went to a dinner or a dance, wearing the loot in
money belts under the bands of our trousers, and 45-
caliber Colt revolvers in shoulder scabbards under
the left-hand flap of our new dress coats. Sometimes I had to manage a lot to conceal that gun from
my partner in the waltz.

BEATING BACK

Our friends had treated us so well that we determined to give them a little pleasure trip. Chartering a yacht, we took a party of seven to Galveston. Jack, his sister, Miss Margaret, two of her girl friends, the two hosts, and an elderly aunt, who didn't know that she was chaperoning outlaws. At Galveston Jack and Miss Margaret had friends who gave us a ball at the old Beach Hotel, afterward destroyed by the tidal wave. Here, also, we wore our money and our revolvers.

I was talking to Miss Margaret in an alcove, when I felt a light touch on my shoulder. I looked up and saw an old friend. He had been on our end of the game, but had gone back on it and become a Wells-Fargo detective. He said, loud enough for Miss Margaret to hear:

"Look out! This place is surrounded!" Then he passed on down the lobby, making a bluff at looking for some one.

I excused myself and crossed the floor to Frank. He was waltzing with one of the young women who had come with us from New Orleans. I said in Spanish:

"Look out!" He waltzed carelessly for another turn around the hall; then he joined me in an offhand way and asked:

"What's up?"

THE COUNTRY GROWS HOT

"Place surrounded," I said. "Come to the alcove and bring the girl."

When we reached the alcove, Miss Margaret was waiting.

"I heard what he said, and I know who you are," she said. "You're Al Jennings. They're trying to capture you and Mr. Williams."

"How do you know?" I asked. I thought that Jack had broken his promise to me, and even in that tight place I was irritated.

"We have an old photograph of you in your cadet uniform," she said. "My brother has forgotten that he showed me the picture and told me about you long ago. I've been thinking—get Mr. Williams and Emma. I believe I have a plan for us to get away."

I thought that "us" curious until she laid out her plan. I saw the beauty of it at once. We went to the cloak room for our coats and wraps. On the front piazza we four held a laughing dispute as to who should pay for the supper. Then Miss Margaret said in a good, loud voice:

"I'll tell you! We'll race for it! The last couple to touch the rosebush by the front gate has to pay." We all laughed, and agreed. After one or two false starts for a bluff, I counted "one-two-three!" and we raced past three detectives who just stood grinning at our antics. When we were safely away from the hotel, we bade the ladies a hurried good-bye, and took stock.

It looked dangerous. Galveston stands on an island. A causeway forms the only approach to the mainland. The foot passage and the railway station would surely be guarded. The one avenue of escape was by sea. Frank remembered that he had seen a disreputable old tramp steamer in the harbor. We squinted across the dark water and made out her lights and her hulk. Still in our dress suits and high hats, we explored the beach until we found a little yawl. We broke her lock, and rowed out to the steamer.

We pulled alongside, and held a parley with the watchman. The crew came peering over the rail—the strangest mongrel set I ever saw—everything from Carib to Malay. It was some time before they would let us see the captain. When we got him alone, we offered him fifteen hundred dollars if he would take us away to his next port of entry.

We had struck a great piece of luck. Among all the ships which entered the port of Galveston, this was the crooked one. The captain, a drunken Dutchman, carried on a general roving trade to cover up his operations in smuggling brandy and bananas. When he saw our fifteen hundred dollars he pulled up without clearance papers and sailed away for Trujillo, Honduras.

This was my first sea trip, and it bored me. The captain was pickled in brandy, and I took to drinking with him. There followed the one period in my life when I ever fell for alcohol. At Trujillo I conceived the notion that I'd like to vary our brand of liquor. Still in my dress suit, and still quite drunk, I went ashore and met another American, a fugitive like ourselves. He joined the expedition.

We touched at Rio; we parted company with the tramp steamer at the La Plata. From there we rounded the Horn in another boat, taking in most of the South American ports, reached San Francisco, doubled back to Mexico City. And suddenly we found those money belts nearly empty. We were practically broke when he reached the Texan border and parted from our friend of Trujillo, with whom we had traveled all the way.

I was now almost at the end of my long-rider days. Before I go on with the rest, I would better tell just how I felt about my old trade. My bitter hatred of the world had dwindled a little, and a love for the excitement and adventure in the game had grown up. I liked the plotting, the taste of danger,

93

the thrill of escapes. I liked the half-savage out-door life.

I felt no special remorse. I knew, of course, that it could not go on forever. Some day I should be cornered and killed. Until then I would take things as they came and enjoy life. That other and more horrible death—by lynching at the hands of the vigilantes—seldom occurred to me as a possibility. I was always alert; I seated myself when indoors with my back to the wall, and came to attention at the slightest sound. I had entire confidence that no one would ever take me alive. "A short life and a merry"—that was the whole idea. I had broken with society. My finish would be sudden and unexpected; why should I bother myself by wondering whether it would come late or soon?

Only once did I feel differently. A girl figured in that case. Her parents were ranchers, the best kind of Southern people; and she had been to a university. When I first visited them, they entertained me without question. When I came back her father met me at the door. He had been appointed a marshal, and he knew who I was. He did not try to arrest me, but he made it plain that I mustn't visit them any more. The girl came to me in the orchard, and I gave her my father's copy of Burns, which I had carried ever since I broke with my family. Be-

94

fore we finished our talk the marshals attacked me,
and there was a running fight. When I had got
clean away I saw against the moonlight a tall tree
with a branch hanging across the road. My spirits
were at their lowest ebb, and you can understand
what I fancied. This was the only time that I ever
entertained the idea of such a death as poor Kid
Elmer's.

Frank never enjoyed the game as I did. Mostly,
in fact, he hated it. But he was deeply involved,
and he wouldn't leave me. From time to time he
begged me to quit. He had such a spell before we
crossed the border into Texas. Finally I agreed
that, if he'd go back to the Territory with me, I'd
make one last campaign, pull out with my winnings,
and abandon the life for good.

We crossed the border in August, 1897. And the
next four months were like a return from Elba.

CHAPTER V

THE LAST CAMPAIGN

AFTER Frank and I returned to Texas from our South American trip, with our money belts flat, we knocked about the Mexican border for a few weeks, trying to find just how things stood in Oklahoma and watching for a chance to make a little travel money. We were staying at the Southern Hotel, between the two plazas in San Antonio. There we met an old outlaw friend who had gone into the cattle business, but was still willing to turn a trick. He told us that the general store at a German settlement, some fifteen or twenty miles away, did a banking business among the farmers. On Saturday the safe was always full of money, and the storekeeper took none of the usual banking precautions.

We laid our plans. We found that the place never kept open in the evening. As we were robbers, not burglars, it must be a daylight job. On the next Saturday morning we three rode over there on horses which the rancher furnished. Frank and

THE LAST CAMPAIGN

I hitched our horses and knocked around among the Germans, treating to beer and getting the lay of the land. When the crowd had thinned out a little we drifted over to the main store. The rancher kept out of sight in the outskirts of the settlement. There were a good many people buying at the counter when the storekeeper opened the safe.

On my signal the rancher began to shoot into the air. That made the crowd rush outside to see what was going on. Frank and I proceeded immediately to business. There were three or four Germans left in the place. We had some trouble in convincing them of our sincerity. One big German in particular was talking about what ought to be done to those shooters in the street, when Frank put a blue-barreled forty-five under his nose. He wanted to argue the question, and Frank had to jab him in the stomach with the muzzle before he would keep still and hoist his hands. Then we ran through the safe, tucked the bills into our pockets, and walked quietly out of the store, locking the door behind us. The crowd outside was still talking over those mysterious shots. We brushed through them unobtrusively, reached our horses, and rode. The rancher was waiting for us out in the open country.

He was a man well known in the community, and

no suspicion ever attached to him. As for Frank
and me, we made a clean and safe escape by doing
the unexpected. Once away from the settlement we
gave our horses to the rancher, who led them home;
and we took a train into San Antonio. The Germans had seen us arrive and depart on horseback,
so the posse searched the roads and hills. No one
thought of watching the trains.

On that job we cleaned up about sixteen thousand
dollars, or more than five thousand dollars apiece.
As I have said elsewhere, Frank and I had planned
to make one last campaign and leave the road. To
salt a little money down appealed to us as a good
idea. So, holding out a few hundreds for expenses,
we invested the remainder in cattle with the rancher,
our accomplice. We never saw that roll again. He
promptly sold out his property, pocketed our
money, and moved to Mexico.

The posses were still scouring the plains and sand
hills around the German settlement when Frank and
I took the train from San Antonio to Oklahoma. In
the house of a horse thief on the Washita we looked
over the situation. Our old crowd had changed.
Arizona had been killed by the vigilantes and Elmer
lynched. Mex had pulled out for other fields. He
was wiser than we; he understood that the law was
coming into the Territory, and that our hand was

about played. Where Webb had gone I have never found, even to this day. Bud, Bill, and Little Dick were still in the Territory. We found them at last; we five met, first at the Spike-S and later at a ranch near Shawnee.

The other boys had already planned a job—to rob a bank at Shawnee. I saw at once that I couldn't let this go through, for two reasons. First, the cashier of that bank—Cash Cade by name—had been a warm personal friend in the old days. Second and more important, my father was now judge of that county. In case of capture we would embarrass him terribly. He was troubled enough as it stood. Although we kept writing home to tell him that we were doing nothing illegal, he knew better, and so did his enemies.

I kept the second objection out of sight, but I did argue that Cash Cade was my friend, and I couldn't rob him. Bud, Bill, and Little Dick said that I talked like a fool; men in our business had no friends. The argument grew warm and personal. Finally I saw a line of escape.

"He's so good a friend," I said, "that I can always borrow money from him."

"Just you try it!" said the others.

"All right, I will," I said. So I wrote to Cash Cade about as follows:

99

BEATING BACK

I am here in the vicinity of Shawnee. Rather hard up. Would like to have as much as $25. Will return it to you some time.

I didn't sign it, but I gave it to a certain boy who was friendly with our gang, telling him to deliver it to Mr. Cade in person and to say that Al Jennings sent it. The boy came back with the twenty-five dollars. Then my comrades threw up their hands. That ready generosity of Cash Cade saved the Citizens' National Bank.

Soon afterward two propositions came out of the air. They were among the many tips given to us from time to time by certain men in business or public life who had no hesitation about sharing the profits of robbery, provided they themselves ran no risk. The first concerned a $90,000 shipment of currency on the Rock Island line. That was the job which afterward got us into trouble.

Owing to circumstances over which we had no control, the second never matured. A deputy marshal, a man of considerable influence in the Territory, knew all about a certain payment made regularly to one of the Five Tribes. He sent us a blind message; we rode to town by night for a conference. While the rest of the crowd stayed in the hills to watch the horses, Bud and I went to his house on foot.

THE LAST CAMPAIGN

His wife answered our knock. We had been roughing it for some days, and our appearance was not prepossessing. She gave a little scream and closed the door. Bud, who knew her, laughed, opened it again, and told her not to worry; we only wanted to see her husband on a business matter. "I think he's in the back yard, milking," she said. "I'll go fetch him."

"Don't bother," I said. "We'll go ourselves." And we hurried to the back yard to forestall any treachery—he was formerly a friend, but friends change, and we didn't want to run against a cannon. At the back door we met her, making for the barnyard. She laughed and looked foolish. There was plenty of suspicion on both sides—yet he had a straight business proposition.

He grasped our hands effusively and nervously, and explained at once that he had alias warrants for our arrest, but never intended serving them. In fact, the day before he had led a posse down to Hominy Post looking for us and expecting not to find us. Then he sent his wife inside, and we squatted down on our spurs among the cows while we talked business.

The government, knowing that the Jennings gang was operating again, intended to take no chances with this Indian payment. The agent who usually carried the money was to follow the regular route, our friend the deputy marshal guarding him, with an empty box. Meanwhile a lone messenger in a buckboard was to go by a new and unfrequented route with the money. The deputy marshal described the line of travel minutely. To get that hundred thousand dollars would be like falling into the river and coming out with a bucket of fish.

Declining the deputy marshal's invitation to stay all night, we rode back and laid our plans for my final campaign as a long rider. The Rock Island money was coming through about the first of October. We would pull off that robbery, scatter, and meet again at the Spike-S on December first to mature plans for the robbery of the Indian payment. By that time, if everything went well, we would have more than thirty thousand dollars apiece. Then, keeping my promise to Frank, I would give up the trail. But God disposes.

Those two big jobs had blinded us to the state of the country. If it sizzled when we left for New Orleans, it boiled now. The rewards for us—dead or alive—were so large as to tempt our best friends. I began to notice that people in our debt, people on whom we could always count, had become distant. Nevertheless we cut straight across that hostile country, making for a point near El Reno, where the Rock Island track crosses the Choctaw. That seemed to us the best place for our hold-up, and we wanted to spy out the country in advance. My sister Mary, who was married to a farmer, lived in that region. For the first time in my outlaw days I lodged with her, and from her house Bud and I rode by night to the Choctaw crossing, leaving the rest of the gang camped near Mary's house.

The place looked desirable. There was no settlement in the immediate vicinity—only Indian allotment land. The roads were good, and open. All trains had by law to stop before they made that crossing. Picking out a good place to hide our horses, we secreted ourselves in the willows to see the Rock Island express come through and watch the ways of the trainmen.

Just before train time we were astonished to see a lone engine sweep down the track without whistling, without even slowing up at the crossing. This disturbed us greatly. We made up our minds that some settler, seeing us in the region, had informed the railroad; and we called the turn. When the train passed, nearly two hours late, events confirmed our fears. The coaches were all dark—not a light anywhere except the locomotive headlight—and the train ran straight past the crossing at forty miles an hour.

We mounted and got away, feeling uneasy. We were eight miles from my sister's house when it occurred to me that we would be foolish to ride there after night. The marshal might be already holding the house, waiting for us. I discussed matters with Bud. He shared my suspicion. I then and there made up my mind never again to stay with my relatives. We dared not approach in the darkness, and the rest of that night we hid in a straw stack.

At dawn we approached Mary's farm by a side road, hitched our horses under cover, and sneaked to the place in the willows where the boys had been camped. They were gone. Three hundred yards away a man was plowing. By his motions I recognized my brother-in-law. We crawled to a point where we could survey the creek. The boys and their horses were nowhere in sight, but we saw innumerable horse tracks. The marshal had certainly been there; yet the sight of my brother-in-law peaceably plowing reassured me. I crossed to the high bank of the creek, and started toward the house. I'd no sooner poked up my head than my brother-in-law came dodging through the corn patch, half bent. When he got within speaking distance, he said:

"For God's sake, get out! The orchard is filled with marshals."

"Where are the boys?" I asked.

THE LAST CAMPAIGN

"They skipped during the night," he said. "Our neighbor to the north was fishing in the creek yesterday. He saw them and tipped off Pat Nagle at Kingfisher." Nagle was the marshal for that district.

"Where have the boys gone?" I asked.

"They didn't tell me—Mary knows," he answered. I went back to Bud. He was getting pretty ringy—said we were going to be shot down like rats in a trap. Thinking as fast as I could, I realized that I must get information about the other boys; besides, I was terribly worried over Mary. So, when we reached the horses, I told Bud to go down the section line and turn west. He said, surprised:

"Aren't you coming?"

I said: "No, by ——, I am going to the house."

He said: "You'll commit suicide!"

"Makes no difference," I said; "I'm going to see Mary and find where the boys are. If you hear anything, don't stop, but ride!"

I mounted Roan Dick, a big, splendid thoroughbred, and started for the house on the dead run. By luck the gates were open. As I approached, my sister came out of the kitchen door, waving her apron to make me go back. I can't describe how I felt at that moment. Tired, hungry, hunted, and surrounded, I was in such a white heat of desperation that an army couldn't have stopped me. I must see her and talk to her for the last time. I put steel to Roan Dick and went up in a clatter. As I dismounted her baby ran to me with his arms out. I took him up. Then I thought of the danger. I was about to put him down when it occurred to me that no one would shoot at a man with a baby in his arms.

"They're in the wheat fields, just beyond the orchard; they've been there all night!" she cried. Then she told me that Frank and the rest had gone to a friend's house near El Reno.

I bade her good-bye and swung into the saddle. She was crying bitterly. To ease her mind, and to make her think I had abandoned all sentiment, I laughed and quoted the lines of the popular song:

"Just tell them that you saw me, and they will know the rest."

Sure enough, that put her in a better humor. She laughed through her tears. But she was crying again a moment later when she begged me to give up that life, and wondered if she would ever see me again. I said, "Sure! I'll be back in a few days. Tell Pat Nagle if he doesn't treat you right I'll ride into Kingfisher and kill him." I mounted, stretched out over Roan Dick's neck and gave him all his thoroughbred speed, expecting to draw a vol-

ley. None came. Whether the posse had knocked
off for breakfast, whether they were expecting me
to approach from the north and didn't think to
watch the house, or whether they had an attack of
nerves, I don't know yet.

Bud was waiting for me on the section line. We
turned west, intending to make a wide circle round
that orchard where the marshals were waiting. Out
of the brush came a man in soldier leggings. He
carried a 38-caliber revolver in a cartridge belt.

"What are you doing here?" I asked.

"I'm going fishing on John's creek," he said. He
was a sight more astonished than I.

"Where's your pole?" I asked. "Expect to shoot
the fish? You're a rat of a marshal." A plowed
field lay in the other direction from the orchard. I
ripped out a gun and told him to hit that field quick;
if he looked back, I'd cut him in two. When I saw
him last he was making very fair time, considering
the going. I was in a devilish humor that morning.
The sense of being hunted, of having no place to
turn, had combed up the worst in me. Hurried as
we were, I stopped to make a visit of discourtesy at
the house of a preacher named Shannon, who had
been roasting me. He wasn't at home, so I left
word with his wife that he'd better shut up, or I'd
visit him again. By now teams and pedestrians be-

gan to appear on the roads. All the people we met just pulled up when they saw us. I had never known a country so thoroughly suspicious.

Further, we were almost in sight of El Reno—the place where I'd served as county attorney. I stood every chance of being recognized. It seemed best to lie low for the day. We entered the farmhouse of a German family, where we got breakfast and feed for our horses. The Germans talked little, but the farmer and his two sons sized us up in their stolid way. Bye and bye they went to plowing. We climbed to the roof of a small shed and stayed there all day, watching both the plowmen and the approaches to the farm. No one bothered us. At dusk we had supper with the Germans, paid our shot, and rode on. We got around El Reno that night and joined the rest of the gang.

From there we got in touch with our source of information. As we thought, the Rock Island people had been informed of our presence in the country. Unknown to us, there was quite a sum of money on the very train which Bud and I had chosen for observation. Upon receiving the tip, the conductor had stopped at Wellington to put off the money and take on marshals. The posse was waiting behind dark windows to open fire at the first sign of trouble. However, so our informant said, the big consignment of ninety thousand dollars would come through, according to program, at about noon of October first. That meant a daylight job. If you remember that date—October 1, 1897—it will save much future explanation.

We decided to make the real attempt in another district, and we camped in the timber along the Canadian, while we spied out the land forty or fifty miles from El Reno. On the line between Minco and Chickasha runs a high divide. The town of Pocasset stands there now, but in those days the only human signs were the track, a section house, and a siding. There the train could be stopped by signal and forced to turn onto the siding, where we could watch the track in both directions against a surprise.

On the night of September 30th we moved camp to a point near Minco, and at eleven o'clock on the morning of October first we rode to the section house and proceeded to business. We had determined to disguise ourselves. Among my things I had an old bearskin saddle pocket. I cut eye holes in it, and before we approached the section house I tied it over my face and lower hair—my hair is so red that a glimpse of it serves for an identification. The other boys intended to use their handkerchiefs as masks. They were not so particular as I, for they hadn't lived in this region.

109

BEATING BACK

Slipping the mask down to my neck, I waited at the section house with Bill and Dick, while Bud and Frank went to capture the section foreman, who was bossing a gang of laborers some distance down the track. There were no men at the section house, only two women and two children. The younger of these, just a baby really, came toddling out on the porch. I picked him up and began playing with him. We were having a good time, when I heard some one coming through the house. I slipped up the mask as a woman stepped out to the porch. She screamed; the baby broke and ran. I explained that she need have no fear; she wasn't going to be harmed, only she'd better go inside and sit down. She grabbed up the child, and flew.

"She was foolish to run that way," I said to the boys. "A violent man might have taken a shot at her."

"Well, what do you expect?" said Little Dick. "You'd better keep that mask hid when the engine comes along, or it'll run and hide. You look like hell." So we joked along until Frank and Bud arrived with the foreman. He had been informed of what we intended to do, and he took it coolly—said he didn't care if we left his folks alone.

"Well, just stay in the house," I said, "and don't poke your head out. In the excitement of these moments something might happen." Just then the baby, who had broken away from his mother, came running out to me. Frank picked him up and swung him about until he cackled with delight. Then he wanted to take that thing off my face— showed symptoms of crying about it. To appease him I gave him a quarter, the last I had in the world. We certainly needed that ninety thousand dollars.

It lacked only a few minutes to train time, when a man came down the track on foot—a stockily built fellow of the laboring type. Frank slipped out, had a few words with him, and led him inside. When he saw me in that mask he began to paw the air. He was an Irishman and excitable. We told him to stand by the section house and keep his head in, and he followed program all the way.

Now it was train time. We had taken the keys from the section foreman. Frank unlocked the switch and threw it onto the siding, where stood two or three sand cars. This operation, of course, set the automatic signal which showed the engineer that he was headed onto the siding and must stop. The track began to sing, and the train came in sight. As it approached the switch, it showed no sign of slowing down. Frank sprang to his feet, waved his arms, and pointed to the signal. If the engineer had

111

ignored that, Frank would have thrown the switch onto the main track and let the train go past, rather than have a wreck. But we heard the wheels begin to grind, and saw the sand fly. The train took the siding and stopped just short of the sand cars.

Then we turned loose, as usual shooting at the roof, and smashing a few windows over the heads of the people who looked out. Rushing down the line with my Winchester, I commanded the engineer to hit the dirt. He landed on all fours beside the track, rose up, and offered me his watch. I told him to keep his old clock—all I wanted of him was quiet. On the other side, Bill was attending to the fireman. I turned the engineer over to Bill. Just then firing commenced far down the line. Some of the passengers had started to escape by the rear platform, and Frank was keeping them in. As I ran back to see about this the door of the express car opened, and the messenger appeared with a sawed-off shotgun. Raising my Winchester, I tore loose just above his head and split from the door jamb a sliver which nearly slapped him in the face. He jumped to the other side, got the same reception from Bud, and shuttlecocked over to my side again. By now he had dropped his shotgun. I covered him and ordered him to jump. He landed flat, rolled into the gutter, and ran at me, yelling:

112

THE LAST CAMPAIGN

"Don't! Don't!"

I never saw such terror in a human face. I was afraid he'd run over me, and I poked my Winchester square into his chest. He stopped like a cow-pony.

"You're greatly excited," I said. "Stand there by the engineer and await orders." He obeyed as though he were in a trance, and started to walk straight over Bill. We grabbed him and threw him into the line.

Now the passengers were tamed, and Frank had "killed" the engine by turning water into the fire box. I proceeded to the business of the afternoon. There was a big safe in the corner of the express car, fastened to the floor by steel bands. It had no combination in sight. How it opened, I couldn't see. Beside it stood a little, ordinary "way safe," used to transport express packages which came aboard along the line. Without question that big safe contained the ninety thousand dollars. Dynamite was the only way. I had brought along five sticks òf giant powder, with caps and fuses, for that very emergency. I called for the messenger, and I had to help him climb in. He began yelling:

"I can't open it! Don't kill me. I can't open it!"

I said: "Shut up. I know you can't. You aren't going to get hurt. Quiet down now! Open that way safe." He couldn't even take the keys out of his

113

pocket. I had to reach in and get them myself, which I remember because the operation was very obnoxious to me. We opened the way safe and dumped all the contents into a canvas bag, not stopping, to look over the haul. I took two sticks of dynamite, cut a fuse about three inches long, and put it on the upper edge of the big safe. Then I ordered the messenger to help me lift the little way safe on top of that, so as to blow the explosion downward. As we heaved it up, I dropped my end, for it was very heavy. The messenger almost fainted. Bud kicked him out of the car, and himself helped me with the safe. I lit the fuse, and we jumped. Almost immediately there came an explosion so heavy that it puzzled me. It blew off the whole top of the car. It covered the right of way with splinters. It scattered the way safe into a thousand pieces. I jumped back through the door. The atmosphere was choking—why, I didn't understand until I got the smell of tobacco. A cigar shipment in the corner had been blown into dust. There was a hole in one corner of the big safe, large enough so that I could see inside, but not large enough to reach the money. The door still held. I looked about for the rest of my dynamite, and turned sick.

I'd made my slip—I'd played the fool. When I jumped, I'd left my three sticks of dynamite on the

floor of the car. They'd gone off in the general explosion, tearing a great hole in the flooring. I was
out of material.

I grabbed an axe and hacked with all my strength
at the hole in the safe. It was a puny effort. I
didn't make a dent. My little mistake had cost us
ninety thousand dollars.

There was no time to cry over spilt milk. I
jumped down and broke the news to the boys. We
hadn't a cent, as I have said, and we'd forgotten
about the contents of the way safe. We determined
to rob the passengers for expense money. That was
a reckless thing to do—how reckless, I didn't realize
fully at the time. I had been county attorney at El
Reno. The day coach was full of El Reno people.
For a man of my peculiar stature, build, complex-
ion, and color of hair, a bearskin mask is no great
disguise. Up to that time only the trainmen had
seen me.

Nevertheless I called the engineer and told him
to line up the passengers on the right of way. Bud
asked:

"What's the idea?"

"There are two towns in sight," I said. "We can't
afford to be inside making a slow search with the
possibility of some one surprising us." Before I
got forward the passengers were piling out and lin-

ing up against the wire fence. I glanced down the
line, and it looked like Old Home Week. There
were Hon. W. I. Gilbert, Dudley Brown, Father
Hall, the Catholic priest at El Reno, Rev. Dr. Hamilton, a Protestant clergyman, and a dozen others
whom I could call by name. As I started along
their front in that bearskin mask their hands rose
automatically.

It took some time to get them all off. Just as we
were ready to begin, I saw a woman hesitating at
the car door. I told her to hurry. She said:

"If you please, sir, my husband is sick. I can
hardly get him off."

"Then go back inside, and no one will trouble
you," I said.

"I'd much rather get off, if you will let me," she
said. But she staggered, so that I helped her into
line.

Everything seemed ready, when I heard a whoop
behind me. A negro woman, very fat and very
frightened, had started to get off backward after
the fashion of her sex. It was two or three feet
from the last step to the bank. She had one foot
on the step and was reaching with the other. Her
face was turned over her shoulder, and her eyes
looked like moons.

I said: "Jar loose, mud hen!" She saw me and

116

my mask for the first time. She let out a screech,
loosed her hold, and tumbled over on the bank. And
no one laughed except Bill. It surely was a serious
moment on both sides.

The passengers, still reaching toward heaven, were
squirming this way and that, trying to rest their
arms, which had got tired from keeping the same
position. I told them that they might lower their
hands. Some accepted the permission, some felt
safer as they were, and some would jerk up their
hands like mechanical toys whenever I looked their
way. Bill, Dick, and I watched the approaches and
kept order, while Bud and Frank took up the collection. By now the sick man had crawled out and
joined his wife. He was lying on the ground. Bud
ordered him to his feet. I interfered, and his wife,
reaching toward the bosom of her dress, said:

"I'll give you freely all I have." I shook my head
at her, and ordered Bud down the line. I learned
afterward that she had four hundred dollars.

We had nearly finished when Little Dick came
along, carrying a bunch of bananas in one hand and
a jug in the other. He was a peculiar man, this
Little Dick. He'd ride for days without speaking
to a comrade. He was addicted to drink, and, when
he got a little of the stuff in him he'd stay where
he was, regardless of consequences.

117

"I got some bananas for our dinner," said Dick, "and this smells like some real good old stuff. I haven't tasted it yet."

"Let me smell it," said I. It was whiskey. I gave the jug a swinging lick and broke it against a car wheel. I wanted no liquor in the gang, then or afterward. The danger of a train robbery is not the act itself; it is the events of the next few days.

"You think you're damn smart!" said Dick. For a moment I thought he'd shoot, he was so mad.

"Get to the horses!" I said. Away off in the distance I'd seen some men on horseback. The situation was growing ticklish, and I hurried the collectors along. Frank had just reached Father Hall. He had just fifty cents, which he handed over, saying: "I am only a poor priest." Frank gave it back and five dollars more. The next man in line was Dr. Hamilton, the Protestant clergyman at El Reno.

"I am a minister of the gospel, too!" he said. Frank looked him over. "You look more like a tinhorn gambler!" he said. "Shell out!" Dr. Hamilton and I have laughed over this since. The fact that he doesn't look like a clergyman cost him seven dollars and his watch.

As soon as Frank finished, I got the passengers back into the train and gave them some parting ad-

118

vice; then we broke for the horses. After we were gone, I understand, the train crew and Bill Gilbert chopped up a platform to start a fire in the engine.

We ran past the section house. I was still carrying the bananas. The mistress of the house stood at the window with the child in her arms. I passed a cluster of bananas to the baby. The woman cried:

"Don't you touch those nasty, stolen bananas! They'll choke you!"

"My good woman," I said, "you're excited. He'll never know the difference!" I peeled one and handed it to the baby. The last I saw of him he was eating with one hand and waving good-bye with the other.

As we mounted a man came riding full speed over a rise. I threw my revolver down on him, commanded him to halt, and made him ride beside me while we galloped down the right of way. He was an old cattleman named Black, whom I'd known at El Reno.

We five masked men and our captive passed the section gang, which had been resting not more than four hundred yards away all during the robbery. When they saw me they began digging very assiduously. We cut a fence with our wire nippers and crossed into a pasture. I was really suffering from that bearskin mask, what with the heat and the fumes of tobacco, and I took the risk of removing

119

it. Here the cattleman began begging us not to kill him. I said:

"You're in no danger. We're keeping you with us so you won't give any information."

He said: "You're perfectly welcome to what money I have."

"We don't want your money," I said. Then, sizing him up, I decided to take a chance. "I know you," I said. "If I let you go now, will you forget the day's transaction?" He promised and rode away to Chickasha. He kept his promise, as the old-time cattleman had a way of doing. In the subsequent proceedings his testimony would have saved the Territorial authorities a great deal of trouble.

Within an hour the whole county was in pursuit. The details of that afternoon's riding would be only repetitions of escape after escape. The first thing we did when we crossed out of the thickly inhabited country was to drop a match into the dry grass. This started a prairie fire, which obliterated our tracks and checked pursuit from one side. In Cold Springs Cañon I called a halt to water the horses and look over the loot. When we went through the contents of the way safe we found seventy-five hundred dollars in express packages. We hadn't counted on that; it put new heart into us. Twice, as we lay there in the cañon bodies of officers ap-

"I made him ride beside me as we galloped down the right of way"

proached so close that we could hear their voices.
We waited in the cañon until dark, and made our
way to a friendly house. We had just finished supper, when our host was called to the gate. Fifteen
or twenty marshals stood there asking the way to
Bob Moore's place on the Washita.

"What's the trouble?" asked our host.

"The Jennings gang has held up a train. We
hear they're making for Moore's," said the leader.
We waited under the windows, prepared for trouble
in case they came in; but they rode on. And then,
after a conference, we split up. Frank and I doubled back through the cordon to El Reno, figuring
that they would never look for us there. And a
little after ten o'clock I put into operation a plan
which had been growing in my mind all day.

As soon as the town lights went out, Frank and I
mounted and rode due west to Shawnee—nearly
eighty miles, as the road goes, between ten o'clock
on the night of October first and daylight of October
second. Waiting in the outskirts until the county
officials should be settled in their offices, I rode into
town and called on Mr. Pittman, the district attorney of the county. His mouth flew open with surprise when he saw me.

"Pittman," I said, "I've been hearing a lot of
fool talk about my robbing trains and going on the

121

dodge. I'm tired of it. I intend to surrender, face the music, and clear myself. I've a few things to settle up first, then I'm coming in. This is October first; two weeks from to-day, October fifteenth, I'll return. Have your officers ready." And as I left his office I repeated:

"Make a note of it—this is October first, and I'm coming back on October fifteenth."

According to expectation, Pittman was so excited at seeing me and hearing of my intentions that the date impressed itself on his mind only as an inconsequential detail. He never thought to look it up at the time, and when I had use for him it was fixed in his mind—wrong.

Frank, who had been showing himself to friends about town, joined me, and we rode a few miles by unfrequented roads to Tecumseh, the county seat. Going to the saloon of Ike Renfrow, I got him to send for Bob Motley, the sheriff, my father, and my brother John. Motley was my friend; I knew he wouldn't arrest me without a warrant. To them I talked just as I had to Pittman, getting the false date—October first—into their minds. Everyone was delighted, and no one thought to verify my statement of the date. This made a perfect alibi, for the robbery had occurred eighty miles away at noon of October first.

THE LAST CAMPAIGN

When I returned to Indian Territory, I found the country still boiling. The pursuit hadn't died out after two or three days, as it used to when I first went on the road. Again and again in those last few months that fact impressed itself on me, and I continued to ignore it. Frank had split off by himself, as usual, but Bud, Bill, Little Dick, and I were soon forced together for mutual protection. From the 22 ranch, which was under surveillance and unsafe, we rode into the Osage Nation. Passing ourselves off as marshals, we got a night's lodging from a member of the Indian police named Freeman. In the morning we dodged a cordon of marshals, and reached a friendly cow camp. Everyone was out. We were just getting dinner, when a nester knocked at the door. At the gate three others were watering their horses. They had Winchesters tied to the saddle horn with strings, nester-fashion. You could have riddled them before they got those guns loose.

We were making ourselves at home—Bill and I reading, Bud taking a nap on the bed, Little Dick cooking dinner. The nester, never suspecting us, asked if we'd seen any hard-looking characters.

"The Jennings outlaws are around here somewhere," he said, "and we've took the road to clean 'em up."

The thought of these men hunting us without warrant of law raised one of my old, desperate rages. I walked over to him.

"Do you know these outlaws?" I asked.

"No," he said, "but we're sure going to take them in if we find 'em."

"Then here's your chance!" I said. "We're the outlaws."

He acted as I thought he would—staggered back with one hand before his face.

"I didn't mean you no harm," he said when he got his tongue. "I didn't know you was the fellows."

"Have you a wife and children?" I said. "Then get back to them and thank God I've got a little mercy on them. You aren't worth killing—going out for people who don't bother you." The posse ran like sheep. The leader was keeping his eye on me as he mounted, and he missed the stirrup with his foot five or six times.

This was no place for us. We hurried dinner, and started down the road. Watching everything, I saw a mark across the wagon track where a man had evidently dragged his foot. In my circus days, I remembered, the advance crowd, when they wished to notify the main caravan of a bad road, used to mark it in such a manner. I spoke to the boys about this. They laughed at me, but I insisted on turning into the prairie. A long time afterward I learned that

THE LAST CAMPAIGN

I was right. The marshals were riding ahead. They had taken with them a horse thief, who didn't dare refuse for fear of giving himself away. He had managed to dismount and leave that sign. Otherwise we should have ridden into an ambush.

For the next few days it was ride and dodge, ride and dodge, tired from continual travel and loss of sleep, often hungry, always in a high state of irritation. The posse of citizens, each commanded by a deputy marshal, had spread fan-shape over the whole county. Bud Ledbetter, the famous marshal from Muskogee, had gone out after us; and, when Ledbetter started a hunt, he was after the man, not the mileage. Once a settler with whom we risked staying over night almost betrayed us. Once we rode straight into a camp in the darkness. While we debated whether to run, to attack, or to wait, I saw by certain signs that these were hunters, not marshals. They turned out to be highbrows from Massachusetts—one a Harvard professor. I rode in among them, impersonating a deputy marshal, and demanded their hunting permit. When they'd dug that up from the wagon, I asked severely:

"Have you any whiskey among your effects?"

To bring whiskey into Indian Territory was a violation of the law. The Harvard professor stammered as he declared that he hadn't.

BEATING BACK

"Don't you lie to me, young man," I said, and out came the jug. I lifted it.

"Here's to you," I said. "We aren't marshals. We're outlaws!" At first they were scared. Then their manners, which were distant, reserved and Yankee, thawed out. They asked us to supper. We accepted, and everyone had a good time.

We tried to put up again at the 22 ranch, and found that country still dangerous. We tried to escape toward Arkansas, and were beaten back. By now we looked like scarecrows. No one had shaved for a fortnight. The brush and rocks had torn our clothes into rags. My trousers became so frayed that they wouldn't stay in my boots. That fix was uncomfortable; further, the state of our clothing marked us for identification. We decided to raid the store at Cushing, now the heart of the oil country, but then a little settlement.

The storekeeper knew Bud and Bill. Therefore, they stayed outside in the timber, while Dick and I rode into town late at night. The merchant slept in the rear of his store. We knocked at his window, asking him to get up.

"Bob Jones, across the river, is dead. We want to get some burial clothes for him," I said. He came to the front door, half dressed. When he saw me in my tattered clothes and my Russian anarchist red whiskers, he backed off like a crawfish. I displayed my guns carelessly, and said:

"My dear fellow, we want four suits of clothes with chicken fixings, nothing more. If we get them, all right. Otherwise I'll break your neck. Dick, engage this person in conversation while I look around." I was puttering among the shelves and showcases, trying to get an exact fit for all our party, when I happened to glance over my shoulder. The storekeeper had his eye on me, and Dick was nowhere in sight. Chagrined and annoyed to think that Dick would desert me while my back was turned, I whirled on the storekeeper, asking:

"Where did that man go?"

"To the other end of the store," he said.

"Let us go down together and seek him," I said, getting sarcastic, for I was as mad as the devil. There stood Dick rummaging round the shelves and saying pleasantly: "I can't find 'em anywhere!"

"What are you looking for?" I asked.

"Brown cigareet papers," he said.

I didn't dare begin to express myself for fear I'd lose my self-control. I only told him to hurry up.

"Soon's I get them cigareet papers!" he said.

The storekeeper found them, and Dick—in the midst of a robbery mind you—handed the man a quarter, remarking:

"Six bunches for a quarter anywhere in the U. S. A." That was Little Dick all over. He didn't want much, but he wanted it right away, and he'd risk his life to get it.

Before we reached the timber we heard a Winchester pumping into the air for a signal to rouse the town. A new pursuit was on; for days it was hide and seek again.

Once we stopped at a log house and bargained with a woman for dinner. As she started to fry the bacon a "dominicker" rooster ran past the door. My mouth watered. We hadn't eaten fresh meat for a week.

"If you'll cook that for dinner I'll give you a dollar," I said.

"Mister, he's the only chicken I got, but all right," she said. "You-uns got to help catch him." He was an athlete of a rooster. We must have chased him half an hour before we began shooting. At that we always missed him, and finally the woman herself laid him out with a block of wood. We bought him for dinner, but we had him for supper. It took six hours to cook him.

She was alone in the cabin with two small children, a boy and a girl. I asked what had become of her husband.

"Him and me had a fight this mawnin', and he's

done gone," he said. "It was over. the boy. He p'intedly hates that child. He ain't hisn, he's mine. You see, he ain't got no paw."

We had just set down to eat the dominicker when the husband came back—a big, stocky fellow with a bull neck and a brutal face. I bade him good day; he didn't answer, but stepped up to the table and roared:

"There's that ——— ——— brat eating again!"

The woman fired up and said: "You just shut your mouth. You told me you was goin' to leave. I don't see why you don't stay leaved."

At that he made to strike her, and I interceded.

"This is my place!" he said, and struck again. I pulled my 45 and knocked him down with the barrel.

"Bill," I said, "take out this critter, hog tie him, and sting him a little with your quirt." While the husband was yelling for mercy outside, I asked the woman:

"Do you care anything about this man?"

"No, sir," she said. "I jest p'intedly don't."

"All right," said I. "We'll see he doesn't bother you again."

"I wisht you would," said she.

We passed the hat and left her a few dollars. Then we tied her man's hands together behind him, hitched a rope to him, mounted, and drove him ahead of us down the road. Whenever he let the rope go slack we'd take a few shots in the direction of his heels. By this time we'd gone three or four miles he couldn't run any longer to save his life. I let him get his breath; then I gave him a lecture on treating women. And I finished:

"I am going to give you a chance for your life. Take it on the run. If you fall down or look back or show that you aren't going your best, I'll kill you. If you ever go near that woman again, I'll hear about it; and I'll bring the boys and hang you to a black-jack limb." He ran zigzagging like a log wagon, but he beat all records for rough ground.

The hardships began telling on us all, and Bud developed the first symptoms of a sickness which later nearly carried him off. We made Red Hereford's place on Duck Creek, where we saw Bud put to bed. By now the country seemed quieter. We thought the marshals had called off the chase. But we didn't know Bud Ledbetter. He'd changed his tactics, that was all. Nevertheless we managed to scatter in safety, first making an appointment to meet at the Spike-S on December first in order to rob the lone messenger of that Indian payment. For two or three weeks I kept under cover at a friendly

"We drove him ahead of us down the road"

ranch, leading a monotonous life for a change.

When I came out of retirement and started to keep my appointment at the Spike-S ranch, I had some experiences which should have warned me that the country could never hold us any more. If there were two men in the whole territory on whom I depended, they were Sam Baker and Red Hereford. I stopped at Baker's on my way out. His wife told me that he had gone to find us boys. Her manner made me a little suspicious. When, presently, Baker came in he seemed cordial enough, but he asked where we were going, approaching the subject indirectly. Curiosity about the other fellow's whereabouts wasn't etiquette in our set.

The next night I made Red Hereford's with Bill, whom I'd met on the road. There, also, the atmosphere had changed. It wasn't what he said—it was his manner. When he started for the barn to feed I went along.

He said: "You needn't mind," and I said:

"Oh, it's a pleasure, I assure you." All the way I kept at his elbow, my hand on my gun. Back in the house I never left him for a moment. When bedtime came I insisted on sleeping with him—in all my clothes, even my spurs—and constantly I made indirect remarks about what I'd do to an informer in case of attack. I was right in my surmises, as I

learned afterward. That night Bud Ledbetter and
Paydon Talbot lay out on a spur of the mountain,
not five hundred yards away, waiting for Hereford
to flash a light back and forth at a window, as a
signal for attack.

CHAPTER VI

THE END OF THE TRAIL

WE rode to the Spike-S on the evening of November 30th, 1897, a day ahead of the appointment. The weather was a good setting for the drama of the next day. A dry storm had come on. The north wind blew cold and icy, whirling immense billows of dust across the prairie, befogging earth and heaven with a dun-colored smudge. The sumac bushes and long grasses lashed the ground as though they also wanted to lunge forth into the sweep of sand and dust. The gray tumble weeds went leaping and spinning by like living things. The wind became a voice, calling across incalculable desert wastes. As we approached the Spike-S at twilight we saw the evergreens in the little private ranch graveyard writhing and weaving like giant ghosts of the dead beneath.

But there was smoke in the chimney of the Spike-S and there was a light in the window. And as we rode up the path Mrs. Harless came running from the front door. The fringed points of her wrap snapped in the gale and her breath caught in the wind as she said:

"Glad to see you. Bud and Frank are here, but Dick hasn't showed up." She had been alone at the ranch with her young brother "Dutch" and a friend, Miss Ida Hurst. John Harless was then in jail on a charge of changing brands.

We had a supper which I remember yet. We talked and laughed and joked; Frank sat down at the organ, and we all sang. At times the wind became so heavy that we'd keep still for a minute, wondering if something wasn't going to give way.

As such a gust died down we heard a noise at the door. We listened, and the sound repeated itself. Some one was knocking timidly. We put our Winchesters within reach, and Mrs. Harless opened the door.

A neighbor named Kelley stepped in, his hat pulled down over his face. He stood digging at one eye with a broken thumb nail; then he saw the rifles and started. In stammering words he explained to Mrs. Harless. He had got lost—plumb lost. It was so dark you couldn't see your hand before your face, till he sighted the light. No, he wouldn't take a cheer. Now he'd found his way, he'd better be going. Wasn't it reedic'lous for him to get lost? It was, shore.

134

THE END OF THE TRAIL

As soon as we took him in we had dropped back into careless attitudes. Frank went on fingering the melodeon; the rest of us hummed a song in an undertone; but no one paid Mr. Kelley much outward attention. Inwardly I was thinking. That sounded a little like a fish story. Still, Mrs. Harless seemed unsuspecting. Only when he had mounted and gone did she turn to me, saying:

"He lost! That Kelley! As if he didn't know this country as well as I know my kitchen!" I jumped to the door. He was gone, and the sound of the hoofs in the distance showed that he was riding like the wind.

It looked terribly suspicious; we all agreed to that, though we joked over it, and Frank drew a laugh by imitating Kelley's manner. But an outlaw can't afford to begin worrying. We put it out of mind and went on with our music.

I was wakened that night by the hush and the still insidious cold which followed the death of the storm. It was less night than a black trance of earth and air. I recalled the incident of Kelley, and, now that I thought it over alone, it looked a little more important. Slumber overcame me again before I determined what to do, and the next thing Mrs. Harless was calling us to breakfast.

I dressed. I found Mrs. Harless in the kitchen

135

wishing that Dutch, her brother, would come back from the well, down by the barn, with the bucket of water. "I could have gone to Snake River and back by this time," she said. Whatever apprehension I felt the night before had gone with the darkness. It was a bright morning of a Southwestern winter, with a clean tracing of frost on the trees. I remember joking with Mrs. Harless about the absent Dutch. It was no joke to Mrs. Harless and Miss Hurst, with their morning's work waiting for that water. Finally Mrs. Harless threw a shawl over her head and went to find Dutch. Meantime the rest of the boys came down, and we began breakfast.

Suddenly Mrs. Harless burst through the door. Her hair was falling down her face in wisps. She clutched the melodeon for support until she got her breath to shoot out the one word:

"Surrounded!" Then she gasped a few particulars. They were in the barn—they were everywhere to the north of us. They had said that she and Miss Hurst might go down to the graveyard before they opened fire.

"How many of them?" I asked.

"Thirty," she said. Then her arms flew up over her head, and her fists clenched. "Thirty or forty against four—you poor boys—what is to become of you?"

THE END OF THE TRAIL

Frank and Bill had left their Winchesters up-
stairs. They stole away to get them. Bud, I remember, was still crunching a piece of bacon between his teeth.

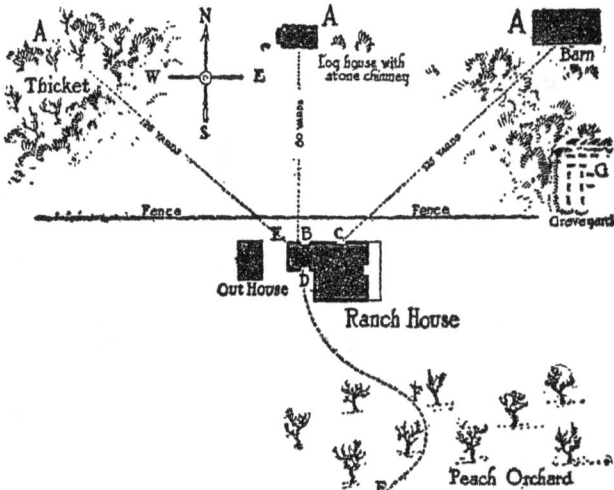

A—Firing line of the marshals; B—Window from which the Jennings boys fought; C—Window from which Bud and Bill
fought; D—Door from which the bandits escaped to the peach
orchard; E—Corner from which Al Jennings shot Marshal Ledbetter; F—Line of retreat; G—Refuge of the women.

"Ain't this hell?" he said. "No chance to feed!"
The women ran for it. We held a brief council of
war. Evidently the attacking forces were all to the
north, the only cover. In that direction, and to the
right, stood the big red barn, where Mrs. Harless

had met the marshals. Directly opposite stood a log house with a stone chimney. To our left was that same thicket which had been our old stronghold at the Spike-S. (See diagram.) All these positions, as we soon found, were occupied by the enemy.

I decided that Frank and I should hold the kitchen, while Bud and Bill fought from the front room. We had no alternative but to fight. Our horses were with the enemy in the barn. If I had stopped to think, I should have realized that the moment had come which I had always expected—the moment of expiration when I should die with my back to the wall. But in such times one doesn't think. He feels and acts.

I crept to the kitchen window, and poked up my head to reconnoiter. Bang! The window smashed in my face, a piece of broken glass laying my cheek open.

Rip! came a volley along the whole line. The insult of that slap in the face raised all my temper. I threw up my Winchester and fired at the log house, where an arm and hat had been visible an instant before. I saw the plaster fly. Then the fusillade opened in earnest, from all three positions on their line. The bullets sang everywhere about us. I remember hearing a tin pan give a "cling" as though a great rain drop had struck it. An instant later the melodeon boomed out a deep note.

"D flat!" said Frank. "She's playing 'Home, Sweet Home!'" And all this time we were fighting methodically—firing to draw a volley—leaping back —jumping forward and firing again to get the enemy before he sought cover. I kept hearing bullets plump into the wood above my head. The posse in the barn was wasting ammunition on the upper story. The woodwork began splintering about our feet. Bud Ledbetter and Paydon Talbot, in the log house, had opened on the edge of the floor, under the impression that we were lying down.

I had fired and backed away from the window, so that I could see into the front room, when Bill got his. I saw him jump grotesquely into the air and come down doubled up. I pumped my Winchester, jumped forward, fired, and looked again. He was up and fighting, but I saw that his boot top had turned red.

In that instant I happened to glance down. I saw a trail of blood on the floor; a lazy stream was running from my left knee.

"Here, too!" they say I responded. I never knew when I got it, and through the rest of the fight I remembered it only at intervals.

As I fired and backed away again there came a

heavy metallic clank, and a piece flew from the stove.

"That was a 45-90," said Frank, pumping the lever of his gun.

"She wasn't—she was a 30-120 steel jacket," I said. Between shots we debated the matter, ridiculing each other in monosyllables, advancing data to prove our points.

Small débris littered the floor—splinters of wood, fragments of glass, cartridge shells, broken dishes. When I glanced into the front room I could see crisscross trails where Bill had bled and he and Bud had trampled in it.

And then I got mine again. I had fired, standing sidewise, and started to leap away, when a bullet clipped me across both knees with such power that my legs knocked together and I staggered to the back wall. Slight as it was, I felt this wound more than the other. It filled me with a desperate, choking anger. Sixteen years later I revisited the Spike-S for the first time. As I stood by the same old window, that sense of illogical but overwhelming rage, at being shot down like a caged rat, swept across me again. That spirit seemed to infect us all. We fought blindly, desperately, without husbanding our ammunition. As I came out of this mood and recovered my reason, I saw that the fire had grown hotter. They had located us, and stopped aiming at the second story. Every shot seemed to plump into the woodwork man-high. Piece after piece jumped from the stove; fragments of broken crockery slapped our faces.

Frank saw the inevitable first.

"Gee!" I heard him gasp. "We've got to get out of this—we haven't a chance!"

"Try it lying down!" I yelled. We dropped, just as a bullet ran the whole length of the floor, tearing up splinters.

"We'll be killed like rats!" repeated Frank. It was no time for hesitation, I decided at once.

"You and Bill go to the orchard!" I said. "Fog 'em from there, and Bud and I will come." They started; I went to my station at the window and fired to draw the attention of the marshals. When I jumped back to the door, Frank and Bill were streaking across the yard, and the bullets were tearing dust around them like hail. I couldn't turn my eyes away—I looked each moment to see Frank go down. Once he stumbled, and I thought he was gone, but he came up again unscratched, dropped to his knee, followed by Bill, and began pumping lead into the barn at the left of their firing line. The log house wasn't within his line of fire. The shooting from the barn died down.

"Come on, Al!" yelled Frank.

141

BEATING BACK

Bud and I made our break. It occurred to me that we'd better finish off the barn before we took to the open. We rushed to the front corner of the house. As we whipped up our Winchesters a hat appeared above the rock foundation of the barn. Bud and I shot together; the hat jumped into the air.

"Got his head!" I said. At once the fire from the barn stopped. We had shot Deputy Marshal Lewis through the hair—not the head—and the nesters in his force had taken to a corn crib.

A big gun opened from the grove at the other end of the line. Those fellows were in a position to rake our backs as we made toward the peach orchard, and a man who forgets such things in the heat of battle gets killed. I ran to the southwest corner and pumped a few shots at them. My movement stopped all shooting in that quarter—they thought we were charging them, and ran away. Now, I figured, was the time to finish the battle. Both flanks were silenced; there remained only the forces of the log house at the center of the line. I dodged to the northwest corner of the house. As I reached firing position a head and arm shot out from behind the chimney of the log house. I fired and he fired, almost as one motion. I felt a slap in the face —his bullet had torn a lath from the corner of the house. I saw his gun and arm go up in the air and drop out of sight.

"Another!" I said to myself. This was hanging now, and I didn't care—hadn't time to care. I pumped in another shell as a puff of smoke came from a crack in the log house. I fired at it.

And instantly shooting ceased from that quarter —the enemy was silenced altogether. That log house, it appears, formed the key to their position. In it were only Bud Ledbetter and Paydon Talbot. Those two men had done more execution than all the rest put together. Bill's wound and both my wounds came from that steel-jacketed 30-caliber Winchester which Ledbetter carried, and to this day the marks of that little gun in the Spike-S wall show that he landed most of the effective shots.

My first bullet from the corner had wounded Ledbetter in the shoulder; my second had struck the masonry just in front of Talbot and filled his eyes with plaster. I had put the leaders out of commission at one stroke. How we lived through that fight, I can't see yet. They were firing at less than a hundred and twenty-five yards, and they could shoot, too. Mrs. Harless counted two hundred and eighty holes on the north side of the Spike-S, besides those which went through the windows and left no mark. Frank had twenty bullet holes in his clothes. As for us, though we had silenced the enemy, we had wounded only one man—Bud Ledbetter. How large their force was I shall never know. Bud Ledbetter has said that he had only seven men. He means seven marshals—he doesn't count the nesters. Dutch, and another friend, whom they held captive in the barn, say that they counted twenty-seven.

"They've quit; let's get out," shouted Frank. We broke and ran across open prairie to the south. No one fired until we got nearly out of range, when some nester opened once with a 45-90 Winchester. By now I realized that I was wounded. The blood pumped and chugged in my boot, and every step gave me agony. But I clenched my teeth and pressed on.

We had crossed the divide a mile from the house before we dared stop to examine our wounds and hold a conference. Transportation was our problem. All our stock, all the ranch stock, remained with the enemy in the barn. Frank suggested a bold flank movement—skirt the graveyard, attack them suddenly from the rear, drive them off, and get our horses. We could have done it I verily believe, so thoroughly had we beaten them. However, we'd have had to kill a good many, so, of course, it is better that we didn't try. But I felt that we couldn't risk it with two wounded men—no telling how long we'd last. The best thing, I said, was to make a getaway, for now the whole country would be roused. So we crawled on to Snake Creek, where Bill and I made shift of dressing our wounds, while Bud and Frank guarded our rear.

How Bill walked at all I couldn't see. I could have put my hand into the hole in his leg. My wound was smaller, but eventually more troublesome. That steel-jacketed bullet had lost its core as it came through the boards, and only the jacket had entered my leg. It drove a piece of my corduroy trousers ahead of it; and there the foreign matter stuck for months, making constant trouble.

We went on from there, without horses, without any means of escape but our own feet; and two of us dragged wounded legs. The mountains offered our only hope. To reach them we must pass across a stretch of open prairie, where we would be a fair target if the marshals pursued us. We decided to take the risk. We forded the icy Snake Creek, and reached the foothills. It had turned bitter cold and a storm was coming. Bud and Frank warmed themselves by stamping and beating their arms. Bill and I hadn't the energy for that. Before the day ended, the blood on my wound had frozen. Each step racked me with pain, and mentally I was in that state of depression which follows a battle. Never have I known such misery.

All day we crawled along, and met no one except an Indian woman gathering wood. Just a little daylight remained when we saw some half-wild Indian ponies grazing on the banks of a stream. Frank and Bud went to catch them. While they were gone I heard the sound of a wagon. I thought it meant pursuit. Bill and I dropped to our stomachs, our rifles ready. The wagon came into sight. It carried two Utche Indians. A hundred yards away they stopped and began to gather firewood.

I had thought that I couldn't walk any more, but when I saw that I ran as I used to run on the cinder track. We showed our guns. Without a word the two Indians let us grab the bridles. Even when we told them that we'd pay them for the use of the team they made no comment. But, as Frank and Bill joined us, and we prepared to start, one asked in a halting voice:

"Where you go?"

"Never mind," I said. We dared not leave them behind. For the rest of that journey they were our captives. They sat cross-legged in the wagon bed, their black hair falling in straight bangs over their foreheads, the pendants of tarnished silver in their ears swinging with the motion. For two days I never heard them say a word—they communicated with each other only by gestures.

Then came a period of complete misery, while we dodged through the mountains seeking a way out. Cold rain, sleet, mud, all the caprices of a southern winter, hampered our travel. Our wounds became inflamed; at intervals Bill and I were delirious; at other times the jolting of the wagon made me whimper with pain and weakness. My fever increased. I thought my throat would crack. That was bad enough, but worse luck followed. Bud fell desperately ill from the complaint that had troubled him before we met at the Spike-S. Frank had three invalids and two captives on his hands.

A brief chronology of those seven days runs about as follows: The first night we went south through Okmulgee, making the passage of that little Indian town after everyone had gone to bed. The next day we lay in the brush. That night Frank tried to drive back toward Oklahoma, where we had friends. In the middle of the night I saw that he had lost his way. He was on the Eufala trail, and it was too late for turning back. We four, the three half-delirious invalids and the worn-out driver, held a conference. Over the mountain lived one man who would help us—Benny Price. He was not an outlaw, but a friend, nevertheless. At the foot of the mountain, on the way to Price's, stood a country store where we might get something to eat; we had fasted for forty hours.

It was the worst night I ever saw. We three invalids had to get out and help push the wagon up the frozen, slippery mountain road. At one o'clock in the morning we reached the store.

Luck had failed us again. The store blazed with light. We drew up by the North Fork and consulted. Hunger decided the matter. Frank determined to risk entering the store, while we cripples waited with the wagon and the Indians. Frank was gone a long time. Bud and Bill, now that the jolting had stopped, fell asleep. I nearly dropped off to sleep myself when I thought to look at the Indians. One of them was missing. Instinct told me where he had gone. I seized a gun and broke for the store.

In the meantime Frank had knocked at the door. After some moments of absolute silence it opened. He stepped in to face ten or twelve men, all armed. He recognized the symptoms at once. This was a night meeting of the vigilantes. His only chance lay in a bluff. As carelessly as possible he asked for cheese, crackers, and canned goods. The storekeeper started to fill the order. Everything looked serene, when the door opened, and in popped our

148

Indian. Before Frank could grab him he emitted the first remark he'd made that trip.

"I want to go home!" he said.

Frank yanked him backward out of the door, slipped his 45, and covered the crowd, as I stepped in with my Winchester. I held the rear while Frank kicked the Indian all the way to our wagon. I watched them aboard, and then said to the crowd, sternly and emphatically:

"The first one of you yaps that sticks out his head will get it torn off." I ran to the wagon. Frank laid leather on the horses; we took the banks of the North Fork like an avalanche. Halfway across we stuck. All hands, except poor Bud, piled out. With one man at each wheel and one lashing the horses, we got loose, and crossed into the dense timber. We saw no more of the vigilantes. Before morning we arrived at Ben Price's. Here we turned the Indians loose with their wagon. I reached in my pocket and gave them what I took in the darkness for a ten-dollar bill. Next morning I found that I'd handed over an old Confederate bill which I'd carried for years as a pocket piece. I hated to lose it, and I'm betting that when thoses Utches tried to pass it at the country store they hated just as much to have it!

"When you get back, you keep your mouths shut,"

I said. Indians are Indians—they did, in spite of the way we'd treated them. Both Ledbetter and Mrs. Harless tried to pump them about us. They wouldn't say a word.

At Price's we had our first meal in three days. Sick and fevered as we were, Frank had to warn us or we would have gorged ourselves to death. From Ben Price's we went to his father's—he also was an honest man. Mrs. Price, the elder, did what she could for us. Ragged, dirty, our wounds festering and offensive, we were awful guests for a decent house. Moreover, every hour we stayed put these people in danger; which helps account for what happened next.

Sam Baker came to see us. If you remember, I stayed with him on my way up to the Spike-S, and I suspected him on account of his curiosity about my movements. I suspected him still more when he appeared among us with a lie in his mouth. He had heard about the Spike-S battle, he said. It was a great fight, but we had killed two marshals. Of course we hadn't; we'd merely wounded Bud Ledbetter. We must get clean out of the Territory, "or they'll sure hang you," said Baker. He had a sister just in from Alabama. No one suspected her. We could stay with her until he arranged to send us to Arkansas. There he had many friends.

THE END OF THE TRAIL

Why I listened to him I don't know yet. **Proba-**
bly my fever and weakness killed my better judgment. Frank was hot against it. We could go, he
said finally; he knew better than to trust Baker.
So we parted, and six nights after the Spike-S fight
Bud, Bill, and I, all in desperate need of a doctor,
went by Baker's covered wagon to his sister's. As
the wagon rumbled off, I had the feeling that it was
a hearse. Once, on the way, we considered overpow-
ering the driver, tying him to a tree, and escaping
with the team. I suppose that weakness of will,
brought on by fever and hardship, prevented us.
When we reached the house of Baker's sister, Bud
became so ill that we thought he'd die. Baker wanted
to take him home, and Bud consented; by now he
didn't care what happened to him. And that night
Baker said he was ready. He had put quilts, pil-
lows, and provisions in an old covered wagon. "If
Bud can't drive, I'll provide some one who can,"
said Baker. When at midnight they called me out
of bed to start, I found Frank sitting on the driver's
seat. I was so weak and incurious that I didn't ask
why he'd come. As a matter of fact, Baker had sent
for him, explaining that we needed him badly. If
I'd known that, probably I'd never have started. I
thought Frank had come of his own accord.

As the wagon jolted along I fell into a delirious

half doze. The voice of Baker roused me. He was bidding Frank good-bye.

"Just keep straight along that road," he said. "No one will stop you there. Good luck!"

I dozed off again.

I was wakened by the sudden clamor of many voices. Above them came Frank's voice, yelling:

"Damn you! Shoot if you want to!"

I sat up. A felled tree blocked the road. Across it in the moonlight I saw the barrels of a dozen rifles—pointed at us.

Sam Baker had delivered the goods according to program. The long riders had reached the end of the trail.

CHAPTER VII

IN THE GRIP OF THE LAW

CONCERNING my fourteen months in county jails, after our capture at Rock Creek, I have little memory, after all. Troublesome as it was, the wound which I had received in the battle at the Spike-S helped to soften my change from a wild man, loose in the wilderness, living an out-of-doors, adventurous life, to a flabby prisoner. The hardships which I endured in that week of pursuit had given me a bad turn. For a little time I didn't care whether I lived or died.

Bill, my brother Frank, and I were placed under guard in a hotel at Muskogee. In the last stage of our ride from the Spike-S we had left Bud behind us, sick. Sam Baker, who led us into Bud Ledbetter's trap, betrayed him also; when the officers brought him in, they dumped us all together into a cell at the Muskogee jail. Little Dick—the fifth member of our gang—we never saw again. He arrived late at our rendezvous on the Spike-S. By

153

then both his pals and the marshals had gone. For seven months he was on the dodge all over Indian Territory. At last they cornered him and shot him dead. A time was coming when I considered Little Dick the lucky member of our outfit.

That confinement in one cell just suited me. It left us apart from the other prisoners, and gave us a chance to build our fences. The months went on, and the Territorial authorities had a hard time to get convictions against the Jennings gang. Every day, it seemed, people came to our cell door, under escort of the guards, to look us over. Among them I recognized men who had the goods on me absolutely. But they always shook their heads before they went away.

The jailers and marshals used every dodge known to the police. One such attempt I remember for its absurd finish. The Spanish War broke out three months after they put us in jail. I had been a great reader of history and military tactics; I always wanted a chance at real warfare. Here was the chance—and I couldn't take it! Lieutenant Capron came along, recruiting his company of the Rough Riders. He visited me in jail; we talked over the regiment.

So I was full of war and patriotism when they operated on my leg. The steel jacket from Bud

IN THE GRIP OF THE LAW

Ledbetter's Winchester and the bit of corduroy which had been driven ahead of it remained in my wound. The detectives had heard that a man under ether will sometimes tell everything he knows. As soon as I had lost my senses a half a dozen deputies stepped into the operating room. They brought with them a prison chaplain, who was present out of curiosity, I suppose.

They say that I lay like a log until the ether had nearly gone from me. Then I spoke just one sentence—"We're all Americans under the flag!" From that time on no one could make the chaplain believe that I wasn't innocent. He said that a man with such sentiments in his heart couldn't possibly be a criminal.

The first charge they lodged against me involved a minor affair. A year or so before I had robbed the safe in the post-office at Foyil. This was only an experimental job. A burglar called "Yankee" had brought into camp a "set screw" used for twisting the lock from a safe. In robbing a train I had always used dynamite on the safe, which was cumbersome and dangerous. This looked like a better plan, and I robbed the Foyil post-office just to see how it worked. The lock came off easily, and we took seven hundred dollars just to pay expenses. The test didn't prove anything. This was an obsolete safe; and, as Louis, my burglar friend, says, you need only a parlor match to open one of those old-fashioned boxes.

When they placed me on trial my lawyers had prepared a careful alibi—and an honest one, too. The people who swore that I was elsewhere on the day of the Foyil robbery were simply mistaken. However, I got myself free of that charge by outwitting my own lawyers. The postmaster identified me in jail just before the trial. I was wearing a moustache and goatee. He went on the stand and testified that he had seen me in his store, wearing a moustache and goatee, on the afternoon before the robbery. His memory played a trick on him. Just before I went to the store I was wearing a beard. At the hotel I met a traveling salesman who had the first safety razor I ever saw. He offered to let me try it. I accepted, and appeared at the store with a face as clean as a baby's. When he made the slip in identification I saw a chance. I went on the stand and astounded my lawyers by admitting that I was at the store on the afternoon of the robbery. Then I had the salesman called to testify as to my shaving. This discredited the main witness for the government, and the jury acquitted me. I was guilty, of course.

Next they tried me for shooting Marshal Bud

IN THE GRIP OF THE LAW

Ledbetter in the battle at the Spike-S—assault with intent to kill. There I stood no chance. Yet they worked on me some wild and woolly law. Ledbetter had no right to open fire unless he caught me in the act of robbery, or announced that he was an officer with a warrant. His only announcement that morning was a bullet through the ranch-house window. In this opinion I am contradicted by the Supreme Court of Oklahoma and sustained by the Supreme Court of the United States. The jury found me guilty; the judge sentenced me to twenty-one years at Fort Leavenworth Penitentiary. That night some one called his attention to a little mistake— the maximum penalty was five years. He was thinking of the law in another State where he used to practice. He hastily reconvened court, revoked the former sentence, and handed me the five years.*

I am speaking now from the legal point of view, not the human one. And, from a legal point of view, the next step was the most arbitrary of all. The authorities wished to get rid of me, because I had made a great deal of work for the law in Indian Territory. More than that, the marshals and deputies

* Bud Ledbetter has lately denied that he was wounded in the Battle of the Spike-S. I can only reply that testimony was introduced at my trial to prove that I did shoot him in the shoulder; and, on the strength of that testimony, I was convicted.

157

wanted the price on my head. There were no rewards for the Foyil robbery or the "assault" at the
Spike-S ranch—no rewards for anything on which I
could be convicted in the jurisdiction of Muskogee.
Without warning, without process of law, the deputies took us all out of the Muskogee jail and spirited
us away to Ardmore. Not until a woman with a
child in her arms looked into my cell door did I
know the reason. She was the keeper of the section
house between Chickasha and Minco. Hers was the
child to whom I gave the bananas after the Rock
Island train robbery.

So they tried me, separately from the other
three, on a charge of robbing the United States mail
with force of arms, thereby endangering life. For
that offense, under the old Federal law, there is only
one penalty—life imprisonment. I was rather glad
that they had picked out this job. I have told before how I rode all night and impressed a false date
on the minds of District Attorney Pittman and
Sheriff Motley, in order to prepare an alibi. I confided this alibi to Judge Cruse, my attorney. Convinced of my innocence, he prepared a magnificent
defense. District Attorney Pittman and Sheriff
Motley, after the manner of witnesses, strengthened
their testimony when the prosecution impugned it.
I had a dozen acquaintances among the passengers

on that Rock Island train, most of whom knew that
the little man in the bear-skin mask was Al Jennings.
None of them came forward to identify me. The
only strong testimony for the prosecution was
that of an express messenger. Nor had I robbed
the mail—only the express safe. However, a registered letter was missed when the smoke cleared
away, and the government presumed that I had
taken it.

The prosecuting attorney, I understand, hoped
only for a disagreement, but here the authorities
capped the climax of illegal law. They wanted to
get clean rid of me, collect their rewards, and proceed with the next bandit. So, while the jury stood
ten to two for acquittal, the judge sent to them a
marshal with a special message. If they would find
me guilty, he would give me the lightest sentence
under the law. Believing that this meant a year and
a day, they returned a verdict of guilty. They even
smiled at me reassuringly as they left the courtroom.
But I was a lawyer, and I understood. There was
only one possible sentence—life. Which the judge
promptly gave me.

I am not complaining, understand. I committed
that robbery—and many more. As the law stands
I deserved about all I got. Neither am I talking
wild. Ten jurymen have sworn to this transaction;

159

their affidavits are on file with the Department of Justice. I'm relating these circumstances of my conviction only because they explain what happened later—why I am sitting now at a desk in a comfortable hotel room, expecting to go to the theater to-night and to attend court at Enid to-morrow, instead of standing at a machine in a dark, foul prison factory, expecting nothing, so long as life remains, but darkness, silence, routine, brutality, and dull torment of soul.

While the jury was deliberating and when—though I didn't know it—the authorities despaired of convicting me, father called me to my cell door. He seemed in special distress of mind.

"Joe," he said (Joe was his old pet name for me), "I must say something to you which I thought I'd never have to say in all my life. If you and Frank will tell the whole story, implicating everyone who's been associated with you, they'll let you walk out free."

I loved and honored my father more than any other man in the world, and my answer came hard.

"Father," I said, "I'd rather be taken to prison and carried out by the ants in pieces."

Father's face changed. He looked almost happy as he said:

IN THE GRIP OF THE LAW

"God bless you, my boy—you're my son, after all. It was my duty—but I'm glad you won't betray a friend. Joe, stand it, boy, though this is the bitterest day of my life."

So I rose in court for my sentence. I've heard about that moment when the actual words are spoken, and his fix gets on a man's imagination for the first time—how it goes through him like a knife. It had no such effect on me. With half my brain I'd been expecting the worst. With the other half I was still doing lawyer tricks—figuring on errors, new trials, pardons, commutations. Even when they started me for the Ohio State Penitentiary at Columbus, where the Government used to send part of its Federal prisoners, my imagination worked only by fits and starts. Now and then when I'd get a flash from the car window of Indian Territory— the prettiest country God ever made—the thought would strike me that I'd never again see those little green hills and chestnut groves and clear streams. Now and then, when I'd see a pretty, pleasant-looking woman, I'd remember with a jerk of my heart that I could never talk to a woman again, and the world would go black before my eyes. These were only spasms. Most of the way I talked and joked with my guards—and I wasn't acting, either.

CHAPTER VIII

CONVICT 31539

IN a daze I made the passage from the Columbus station to the building of the great stone walls. In a daze I saw two uniformed men step forward and begin searching my clothes. The indignity seemed to wake me. I turned and said a word to the guard at my right. He made no answer, only went on exploring my pockets. I spoke to the guard at my left; he did not even seem to hear me. When they had finished one of them said a single word:

"Come!"

I stepped forward between them to the big door which separates the warden's office from the main prison. Another silent guard unlocked it. If he had been letting water through a sluice box, he would have noticed it more than he noticed me. We stepped through; the gate closed behind me with a peculiar, reverberating clang.

And there my imagination woke at last. I can

feel yet the shock which ran through my whole body, the tightening of my scalp, the stiffening of my backbone. That gate had closed on me forever and ever. While life remained I should not pass that threshold again. The thing which they would carry out, after twenty, thirty, forty years, would not be Al Jennings, but only his shell. Commutations, pardons, processes of law—I forgot them all.

The silent, automatic guard guided me down a dark corridor, with a blank, whitewashed wall to the left and tier upon tier of uniform, miserably small cells to the right. There came to me a sickening odor—the prison smell, the smell of decaying souls. Another silent, automatic guard opened a little door. We were facing a low building with two barred windows. These windows were a nightmare of pale, drawn faces; and there came to me a chattering, broken with screams. One man, as we walked on, thrust his arms between the bars. His hands were not clenched, as you would have expected; they hung limp. I looked at the guard, but I held back my question. However, after a minute he began talking as though to the air.

"Nut house," he said in a low monotone. "After they're in here a few years men· go crazy, and we ·have to confine them there." That comment, as I learned later, was a special mercy, and against the rules.

Before that shock passed we had entered a long room with rows of tables which looked like rough writing desks.

"Sit down!" said the guard. Another automaton appeared from the doorway. He was carrying a pie pan full of molasses, a square piece of reasonably white bread, and a can of water. I glanced at this food; then I folded my arms and sat looking straight ahead. Several minutes passed.

"Go on and eat," said the guard finally, and still in that monotone which seemed to fray every nerve I had, "I can't stay here all day."

"I don't want anything," I said.

"Come!" said he.

We moved across the deserted prison campus, through another steel door. Now I was facing three crude barber's chairs, made of common boards. The guard motioned; I sat down. The barber stepped forward as though some one had pulled a lever and started him going. In silence he shaved my face and head. It was the silence which was killing me. I felt that I must have some human response, I didn't care what, or I should burst inside and die.

As we started back I remembered that I had left my hat. I turned and faced a man in a gray suit—

a trusty, as I learned afterward. He was wearing my hat, and he stood holding out to me a little brown slip of a thing which looked not unlike a clown's cap. Full to overflowing, I ran over.

"Give me my hat!" I demanded.

"You've got no damn use for it!" he said.

I exploded into action. With one hand I grabbed the hat, and with the other his hair. It brought the human response. The barbers—all convicts— laughed. But my guard never cracked a smile. He laid his hand on my shoulder, and said:

"You're going to have a hard time here—too much temper. Come on!"

Next we were in the state shop. Men all alike in appearance and costume sat making and mending clothes. Two of them rose as we entered. As silently and automatically as the rest, they stripped me and dressed me in an ill-fitting gray suit, with a blue stripe, like that of a cadet uniform, down the trouser seam. I am only five feet four in height, and those clothes were large enough for a broad-shouldered six-footer. I had to roll up the sleeves and the trousers legs to use my hands and feet. They took away a good pair of shoes, and gave me brogans with copper rivets in the sides. These were number sevens—and my size was four. Only by shuffling as I walked could I keep my feet in them.

The cap, on the other hand, was a size too small. I didn't know until afterward what this meant. Cowboy fashion, I was particular about my clothes. I had arrived too well dressed, and they hung these clothes on me to humiliate me. They succeeded most admirably.

We went to the bath house, where about a pint of water was sprinkled over me—the usual prison bath except when they send a man to the cellar for punishment. Then he gets too much. Next it was the transfer office. A clerk at a little window bade me look up while he read in a monotone the book of rules. I didn't hear a word until he ended briefly:

"Number 31539." That was my number. I had lost my name.

We passed on to the Idle House, where men are held temporarily until assigned to a cell and a company. There the guard who had been with me since I entered turned without a word and left me. At the end of the room was a raised platform, where another guard sat in a kind of high-chair.

"Sit down!" he said. After which he paid me no attention. Here was I, a new arrival—I expected at least some curiosity. Were they treating me like a log of wood to humiliate me, I wondered?

After a few minutes of absolute quiet, I began to

look around. The room was dingy and cobwebbed. It seemed as though the windows had never been washed. In the shadows I made out three or four companions sitting on the pine benches at my right. My eyes became glued, with the fascination of disgust, to one of them. He had a long nose like the beak of a bird, and a deep-set eye of an uncertain greenish yellow. His hair had grown out; on his face was a stubble of beard which reminded one of a wheat field newly mown. He was chewing tobacco, and the amber fluid was running from the corners of his mouth.

He held in his fingers something which I saw in time was a feather. He was stripping it into little pieces. He would tear off a filament, blow it into the air, and keep on blowing until it got beyond range of his breath. All the time he would follow its course with his fixed, dead, incurious eyes. And I wondered how long it would be until I, too, should lose my grip and go to stripping feathers.

Then a little monotonous buzzing caught my attention. I looked and saw that a blue-bottle fly had caught in a cobweb at the window. He was trying to release himself. For a space like a century he buzzed and fought. I felt that I must release him. I turned to the guard. He had fallen asleep in his chair, his head on his breast. All day I watched that fly struggling for his liberty, and I thought that he had a better chance than I.

There was a dank odor in the air—a mustiness, very sickening to the senses. I get that smell sometimes from old cellars, and it brings back to me that day when I sank into the very depths. The half-wit in the corner—the impersonal, sleepy guard—the trapped fly—the odor—they did their work in my soul. Never until then had I thought of suicide. But if I had possessed the instrument, I should have killed myself that afternoon.

That was the bottom of the curve. I was to learn later that a prison is, after all, a little world, with its own peculiar ambitions, intrigues, worries, hopes, and pleasures. But then I thought of it as a thing which makes machines out of men. And that is a hell—to turn a living, growing thing into a machine.

The whistle blew; the guard started awake, formed us into line, and marched us outside. A company of convicts came up, halted, took us in, and went on to the dining-room. There a waiter slammed down the same ration of molasses, bread, and water. Still I couldn't eat, although I tried. A negro sat at my right. By a gesture, he indicated that he wanted my food. I nodded. He picked the flies out of the molasses, and my rations vanished like a flash. Then a guard said:

"Come!"

He led me to a cell in the third tier of the A and B block, locked me in, and ordered me to put two fingers of one hand through the bars until he returned for the night's count. I fumbled in the darkness to survey my surroundings. I felt a little swinging iron bed, drawn up by chains against the wall, a shelf with a Bible, a tin pail fastened to the door by a hook. I did not understand its purpose until a convict came down the range and filled it with water.

"Don't I get a light?" I asked. He made no response, but turned and went on. Presently I heard a voice down the ranges, and recognized the call of a newsboy. Though I didn't know it then, certain convicts earned a little money of their own for overtime, and they were allowed to spend it for papers. As he came nearer I heard him call the name:

"Al Jennings!" I wondered, and I crowded close to the cell door. He came into sight presently—a convict with a bundle of papers under his left arm. I saw him glance deliberately up and down the range before he stepped into the alcove in front of my grating and began to talk in a low voice.

"I've sold all my papers, except this one, on account of you," he said.

"I have no money," said I.

169

"That's all right. This is on me," he replied. And he passed it between the bars. I told him that I needed a light. He replied that there was a gas jet, which I might use until nine o'clock, and he handed me a match.

"But don't tell anybody I talked to you," he said, "or I'll lose this job. They've got you in a bum cell, but a fellow like you will soon be getting the gravy of this institution." I lit the gas and looked over the paper—the *Columbus Press-Post*. The front page opened with three columns about me and my arrival at the prison! All the time when the impersonality of the place had been eating into my soul, I had been a sensation. I didn't know as yet the prison language, which expresses whole paragraphs by the turn of an eyelash.

I slept little that night. I've been asked since if I felt any remorse, and I'm forced to answer that I didn't. I was not yet broken. But I did go down to the very depths of despair.

I dropped off in time. A reverberating gong awoke me. I didn't realize where I was until I saw the bucket hanging on the grated window. And as I struggled out of sleep I found that the sickening sense of despair had left me; I felt that I was going somehow to get out of that prison. When I fell into line for breakfast I began to read the prison language. Here and there men would shift their eyes toward me and shift them instantly back to attention. I knew by instinct that they were looking at the fellow of whom they'd been reading in the papers. Some of them have told me since that they didn't believe it was I—in that make-up. I went back to the Idle House. The half-wit had gone to the "feather foundry," where they worked the weak-minded men not yet bad enough for the "nut house." The fly had escaped from the spider web. Yes, decidedly, things were better; this world held some hope and interest.

As I waited, a well-dressed man came through the door. The guard rose and saluted.

"I want 31539," he said.

"Number 31539, stand up!" said the guard.

I sat there—I hadn't thought of my number since they hung it on me. The stranger looked over our line. As no one rose, he added:

"A man named Jennings."

I stood up in a hurry. The gentleman looked at me as though I were really a human being. "I have an order from the deputy for you," he said. "My name is Laney, and I'm superintendent of transfers. We've had some good letters, speaking highly of you. When I learned you'd arrived, I asked the warden for you." So we talked freely and pleasantly as we walked across to the deputy's office, a brick building in the middle of the prison campus beside the chapel. Just before entering the door, Mr. Laney said:

"Be guarded in your conduct before the deputy. He is a pretty good fellow, but rough, and he is the boss around here. Even I have to take orders from him."

A tall, broad-faced, big-eyed man with huge shoulders sat in a swivel chair. He turned as we entered, and looked me over. It was Deputy Bradford Dawson, the strong man and the character of that prison. In a deep but quiet and drawling voice he asked:

"Your name is Jennings?"

"Yes, sir," I said.

"You're a lawyer, ain't you?"

"No, sir. I used to be."

"Well," said the deputy, almost purring, his voice grew so quiet, "you won't get much practice in here. The warden has turned you over to Mr. Laney. I wouldn't have done that—don't believe in it. I think a fellow ought to get used to this place before he's handed any favors. You'll have one of the nicest places in this institution—a clerk. You've got a long time to stay in here—if your health is good. Still, seven or eight years on the average lets

172

out a man who has a life term. They get pardoned
somehow. But not always. Behave yourself. Obey
the rules." He stopped. I started to turn away,
when he added, "And don't trust anybody. This is
a prison. It's full of the worst men in the world.
That's all."

As we walked away, Mr. Laney was laughing.
"He spoke to you more kindly than I ever heard
him," he said.

So I was jumped at once into the first class and
made a transfer clerk. The transfer office stood,
'then, at the end of the G and H block. Built up four
or five steps higher than the main floor, it had two
windows, heavily barred, of course, and a closet
which entered a tower. From the windows you could
look across to liberty—the river, Spring Street, the
steward's office just across the street. Mr. Laney
led me in. A young man in the gray uniform of a
first-class clerk sat working at a set of books.

"He'll teach you your duties," said Mr. Laney.
"He's going out."

He was a life-termer, for all his youth, that fellow
in the gray uniform; he had been in prison almost
continuously since he was fourteen. As he began to
instruct me in my duties, he talked in a monotone
from one corner of his mouth. I took it then for a
little congenital peculiarity. Really, it was a habit

he had formed while in the shops. Conversation was forbidden to all but the first-class convicts. When they want to talk they look past the hearer to a distant object, and speak from the corner of the mouth nearest him. You could watch the other side of their faces all day and never see a movement. He had learned the habit so young that he couldn't break it even in the transfer office, where he had no rule of silence.

At intervals we talked other things besides business. I told him that he was lucky to get out; I didn't dare expect as much. He said:

"Neither did I. Those things come about somehow. But I don't know whether I'll be in any better shape. I got one jolt when I was a boy. After I was released nobody would give me work. There was nothing to do but go back to the graft. I croaked a fellow in a job, and got a life bit. I have no trade, and as soon as I hit the street the bulls will be after me again. I'll be back—here or somewhere else—before long." A few days later I bade him good-bye. I've never heard from him since.

So I settled down as transfer clerk. While I wasn't a trusty yet, I had most of a trusty's privileges. I was free, after supper and on Sunday afternoons, to go to the office instead of my cell. That's

174

a privilege which no one who hasn't been a convict can appreciate. My duties weren't especially hard. Transfer clerk means what the term implies. I kept track of the entries and departures of the shifts from one department or one gang to another. Every night, when the men were locked in their cells, a guard counted them. According to routine, when there were two men in the same cell, he'd make one thrust out one finger of his right hand, and the other two fingers of his right hand, to make sure that there had been no escape. My books and slips must tally with his count, or I had to reckon with the deputy. I ate in a separate dining-room—called "Jericho" in prison slang—with the other first-class clerks. Besides, men in the shops were given, for special services or extra good conduct, weekly tickets to Jericho now and then. We were allowed knives and forks. The food was plain but wholesome. Best of all, we could talk. They gave me new quarters on "Bankers' Row." These were the largest, airiest cells in the place; and here were confined men of means, like cashiers, directors, and the like, who had gone up for embezzlement or juggling funds. Of course, they had money; and, of course, they used it. Hence their special privileges. This prison, as I learned soon afterward, was run on a strict political system, and hadn't escaped graft.

BEATING BACK

The bankers were allowed to decorate their cells and to buy special food.

Now all this time, with the picking and stealing in certain departments, the food of the regular dining-room at the Ohio State Penitentiary grew worse and worse. I hadn't learned enough about prisons to recognize the signs of revolution. I did notice, now and then, certain fluttering disorders in the lines, and a difficulty in enforcing discipline. The convicts were getting ripe for a break. It was not so much the bad food as it was the contrast between the general lot and those luxuries on Bankers' Row. Then we began to whisper the truth round the clerks' table in "Jericho." An explosion impended; the fuse had begun to sizzle. As I, in my plain gray uniform, with my white shirt and collar, passed the crowds of third and fourth class prisoners in their dirty, disgraceful stripes, I understood perfectly their point of view. Too much favoritism had been allowed men with money, like the bankers, or with influence, like me.

The riot broke suddenly. I was crossing the campus to our Jericho dining-room, when from the main dining-room I heard a noise like the roar of a hundred tigers—a strange, inhuman, ghastly combination of bellow and wail. I've since heard stage mobs try to imitate that sound; and I always laugh, it seems so cold and feeble. The real thing sent

176

shivers down every nerve. The door of the office opened, and Deputy Bradford Dawson came running out, as pale as a sheet. A guard came up from the other direction, carrying a gun.

"My God, man," yelled Dawson, "put that thing down!" Unarmed, he ran toward the dining-room, and I ran after him, drawn by curiosity. The fourteen hundred prisoners were on their feet, throwing plates and bowls, smashing tables with their feet, running about aimlessly. As I entered, a guard plunged head first through an open window.

Then followed the finest exhibition I ever saw of character and personality. Dawson shot his big form to the platform at one end of the dining-room, and shouted:

"Men! Men!" His voice wasn't quiet any more; it came out with its full force. The riot went on for a second, as though struggling for its life, and died out. Some of the men stood still, their arms stretched back—frozen in the act of throwing a plate.

"Men," said Dawson, "sit down! I'll right your wrongs! Nobody will be punished for this. Sit down and go on with dinner!" They dropped back into their places as though drawn by strings. The men who had been running about found their seats. In less than a minute everything had stopped.

The fear of a break always hung over the prison

authorities. Once let those 1,700 tough, desperate men move together, and no body of guards could have held them. The safety of a prison depends on keeping the men from concerted action. This time they nearly developed that uniform mob spirit. The authorities took no more chances. Next day a squad went through Bankers' Row, pulling down the pictures and ornaments. We clerks in Jericho lost many of our privileges, and for a little while certain gentlemanly grafters had poor pickings, while the food in the main dining-room became almost palatable.

Some of my acquaintances in the transfer office appealed to me, and some did not. I shall always remember one first-class man whose position gave him the run of my office. From his hatchet-faced appearance I called him in my own mind "the fish-hawk." Externally he was smooth, plausible, and agreeable. He had been looking for the job of transfer clerk, I learned; and he probably resented my quick promotion. The porter round the office, a life-termer charged with murder, was illiterate but dapper in dress and with good manners. These men, in their different ways, caused me great trouble.

First it was the turn of the fish-hawk. In the routine of his job he sometimes had access to the prisoners' effects. When this happened he would

invariably pilfer some little tool or trinket. It made
no difference to him whether he could use the article
or not. He'd show his plunder to me before he hid
it in the transfer office. I didn't like to tell the warden—that would have been "snitching," which is the
blackest sin among convicts. Nevertheless, these
stolen articles put us all in danger; and one day
I told him that if he brought in any more plunder
I'd report to the warden. He took it hard; one
word led to another; and suddenly my red temper
exploded. I jumped at him. I had in my hand a
little, sharp desk-knife. I went straight at his neck
—hesitated, and quit. I had meant to cut his
throat. I think it was his very immobility—for he
was paralyzed with fear—which restrained me.

Trouble like that is severely punished in the
prison. But the fish-hawk showed no disposition
to report me. In fact, he became friendly, obedient
and humble, all of which put me on my guard.

I understood his meekness when 1,500 cigars
which had mysteriously disappeared from the cigar
shop were found by the patrol guard in the tower
of my office. I was summoned to appear before
the deputy. I told him, truthfully, that I knew
nothing of the matter.

"Have you ever smoked any cigars in there?"
he asked.

"Yes, sir," I said.

"Where did you get them?" he asked.

"Given me by the prisoners," I replied. The transfer clerk is in a position to do small favors. In return a cigarmaker would smuggle me out a cigar, now and then, in his shoe. The two ends would be smashed flat from the heel and ball of his foot, and so we called them "fan-tails."

"Don't you know that's a violation of the rules?" he asked.

"Yes, sir."

"You'd better not do that any more. Who put those cigars in the tower?"

"I don't know."

Deputy Bradford Dawson put me through a severe cross-questioning before he told me the news. The porter had "snitched." The fish-hawk had stolen and concealed those cigars, with the idea of laying the theft on me and getting me transferred. He'd confided the plot to the porter. That was his great mistake.

"I've transferred him to the glove shop," said the deputy. "He can stay there for a while. He's been doing favors for ——— (he named a high official), and any man who does that can get what he wants in this penitentiary."

Dawson was severe, applying strictly the barbar-

"I went straight at his neck"

ous rules of the Ohio State Penitentiary. But he was also just—the memory of his justice helped save him during the riot in the dining-room. Nearly every other sub-official was accepting graft in one form or another. Dawson never took a cent—I happen to know because later I had access to the books. He hated pull and personal influence. A few days after that, I was in the guard-room when they brought up a new prisoner—a well-dressed, plausible Italian pickpocket. Dawson had no guard available at the moment, and he asked me to walk with him while he convoyed the prisoner across the yard. The Italian talked a steady stream, explaining his innocence, and advertising his talents. The deputy seemed not to hear him until he said:

"Perhaps you don't understand that I speak nine languages."

"You do, do you?" said the deputy. "Well, you'll only talk one language here, and ——— little of that!"

CHAPTER IX

THE DEPTHS

FROM February to August, 1899, I worked in the transfer office, gradually extending my acquaintance, in the slow, furtive prison way, among both prisoners and guards. As the newsman prophesied, I had "got the gravy" of the institution. My work was fairly heavy and exacting, but not difficult after I mastered the routine; and it kept my mind occupied. I found time for much reading. I wore a gray suit with a collar and tie; nothing except the cadet stripe down the trouser leg would mark me as a prisoner. I ate in Jericho, where the food was pretty good; I had the blessing of conversation at meals. I began to see a little of Warden Coffin, and I think he liked me. As for Deputy Dawson, he showed me certain signs of friendship in his queer, gruff way.

However, no prisoner ever lived contented in his prison. It is against human nature to endure voluntary restraint. To get away is the nightly dream, the daily ambition, of the convict. What greed, position, fame, or love of woman represents to a free man, escape represents to a prisoner. And I had certain special reasons driving me to escape at this period. Bud, Bill and my brother Frank still lay in jail at Ardmore, charged with the Rock Island robbery. Because they were unknown to the people of El Reno, it was harder to convict them than me; yet I knew that the authorities would get them somehow. Only one penalty stood on the statute books against that charge—life.

Under the windows of my office ran the Sciota River. It empties into the Ohio, and the Ohio into the Mississippi. Let me get through those barred windows, and somehow I might drift down the river to Arkansas, from which I could go overland into Indian Territory. Once there—so ran my dream— I would gather the remnants of my outlaw friends for a raid on the Ardmore jail. I would release my comrades, or die fighting, as I had always expected I should die. The plan became an obsession. When I was alone in the transfer office I'd stand with my hands against the bars watching the driftwood on the Sciota. It was going from the Sciota to the Ohio, from the Ohio to the Mississippi—why not a piece of human driftwood? I planned how I would slip from the window, drop to the wall under the guard tower, and make a run for the river, taking the chances that the guard would miss me in his excitement—if he ever saw me. I thought about a change of clothes, and even planned to hide an outfit in the state shop. All that restrained me was a few steel bars.

The routine threw me in with one of the guards. He liked me, I think—I did all I could to make him. During the leisure and freedom of my evenings we would sit in my office, while I told him stories of the long riders and the cow country. Without seeming to plead my own cause, I let him know how I had become an outlaw. At last he began to express sympathy for me, and I grew bold to approach my point. I remarked, casually, that a man in the transfer office might easily escape by sawing those bars. He made no response—simply turned and left me. There I let the matter rest for a time.

When again we talked alone he found me in one of my despondent moods. Something, I've now forgotten what, had happened to impress my situation upon me. He noticed it, and he asked:

"What's troubling you? You don't seem to be feeling well."

Then I gave in, and unbosomed myself. I wasn't acting now; I was sincere. I told him all about Frank—how I had got him into the trouble, how he

184

hated the whole business, how he stood in danger of a life sentence. And I hinted at a plan to release him if I could only escape.

The guard sat silent for a time. Presently we saw some men coming along the hall. He said:

"I will see you again," and walked away without another word.

Nearly a week later he came into my office with his wife and two little girls. His wife brought me a pie. When they were leaving he turned back to me as though on a sudden impulse, and slipped something into my hand.

"I've brought you a little package," he said. "I hope you'll appreciate it."

I put the bundle in my pocket, and never took it out until I was alone in my cell. But I knew, even before I opened it, what it contained.

He had given me five little diamond-edged saws!

With hope again in my world, I set to work. The window bars all through the building were of steel especially composed to resist saws. These diamond-edged briers, however, would cut it—only very slowly. The porter was the only man regularly in the office with me. At certain hours in the morning he was away, moving and transferring beds. Those periods I chose for the work, first assuring myself that there were no guards in the neighborhood and no watchers at the windows across the street. Then, too, I must choose always a time when some external noise killed the scraping of my little saws. Every day, when I had finished, I filled the cuts with a mixture of soap and filings. As I got on with the work I figured that I would be something like two weeks altogether in cutting through two places in two bars, so that I could wiggle through.

All this time my friend the guard, who gave me the saws, had avoided me. One day when I was working on the books he came and stood beside me.

"I've been studying this thing out," he said abruptly, "and I think I've made a mistake. Not in you, Al, for I know you're O. K., but if a rumble should come you couldn't explain this."

"Well," said I, "if a rumble does come, you needn't be afraid. I never betrayed anyone in my life, and I won't you."

He replied: "Al, you don't realize your position. If you're caught they'll put you to the torture." He looked at me a minute, I remember, before he added in a serious voice: "Al, they'll kill you if you don't tell."

I said: "Then I'll beat the prison, won't I?"

"No," he said. "You'll tell. No man alive can undergo that punishment and not squeal."

THE DEPTHS

"There's nothing on earth will make me squeal," said I.

Then he approached it in a new way, and suggested that, if I did confess, he would get ten years for helping a felon to escape. "And then what will become of my wife and babies?" he asked.

"Of course," I answered, "I'd quit rather than see your wife and babies suffer. Old man, don't be afraid of that."

And suddenly he changed.

"Go on!" he said. "I want to see you get out of this. It's a hell. I'm going to quit it as early as I can, but I'm a poor man."

I worked on; and now, I suppose, I grew less cautious. For one day I heard a rustling and looked over my shoulders. There stood the porter. He had sneaked up on rubber-soled shoes.

Thinking like lightning, I saw that my only way was to let him into the game.

"I'm working a hole here," I said.

"I've always wanted to suggest that," he replied. "But I was afraid to. Where did you get the saws?"

"That's none of your business," said I.

"No, it ain't," he said, "but I'd sure like to go along."

"You're in it," said I. He began to keep watch

187

while I worked. And now the bars were hanging by an eighth of an inch of steel. That evening, unless something happened to break our routine, the porter and I would go out.

That day I had to hold myself to my duties—I wanted to shout and run in my excitement. At four o'clock I was coming from the G and H block, when a convict upon the range put his hands to his mouth and said so that I alone could hear:

"There's something doing in the transfer office. I saw the main and second finger go in there a few minutes ago." He meant the warden and deputy.

My blood seemed to congeal like ice; there came over me the sickening feeling which a man has when he's caught in a trap.

But I didn't hesitate; I couldn't. I managed to walk briskly up the corridor to the transfer office. The deputy stood watching the warden, who was scraping the soap away from the window bars. I never knew for certain who gave me away, but immediately afterward the porter became the warden's runner.

They hadn't noticed me enter. It seemed an hour before the deputy looked around.

I stepped forward at once.

"Warden," I said, "are you trying to find where I cut those bars?"

188

THE DEPTHS

"You admit it then?" said Warden Coffin.

"Yes, sir," said I. "There are the saws."

The warden's face grew black with anger. I'm not exaggerating when I say that.

"Deputy, take him to the cellar," he said. And so, in silence, I walked to the deputy's office. I knew what to expect. I understood by that time the blacker side of the Ohio Penitentiary.

"Sit down," said the deputy. "You have played hell. A man with a life sentence—never did a lick of work—put in one of the best offices——— What did you do it for?"

"I wanted to get away—I wanted to help release the other boys before they got what I've got," I said. And I told him all about that. I was determined to be frank, except on one point.

The deputy settled back, looked me over, and began in his quiet voice:

"I'm awful sorry for you. I kind of took a liking to you. One thing: you've never lied to me. Now I'm going to advise you to tell me where you got those saws. If you'll do that, I won't punish you."

"Deputy, I can't tell," I said.

He flared up.

"I will make you tell," he said. And I rather forgot myself.

"You'll be the first man who ever did that," said I.

BEATING BACK

"Wells," said the deputy to his assistant, "take him over to the cellar. I'm going to find where those saws came from. This thing has got to stop."

Wells, the assistant, talked to me as we went along. He was sorry for me. How did I come to do it? They'd make me tell who gave me the saws.

"I won't do that," said I.

"Then God help you," said he. He took away my coat and shoes, and clapped me into a solitary cell. It was cold, damp, and pitch-dark. Feeling around, I discovered a pair of chains with handcuffs at the end, hanging high on the wall; a water pail hitched to the door, and a board, raised a little at one end, on the floor. That last was my bed. There I stayed, without food or company, until nine o'clock next morning.

Then they took me into the cellar for trial. I found there two or three convicts suspected of complicity in my escape. One of them I recognized. A burglar, doing a life term as a habitual criminal, he was also a fine mechanic and a privileged character in the shops. Once, long before, I had carelessly told him—half in joke—that, if ever I got a chance to escape, I would let him in. When the chance really did come I had forgotten all about him.

Regret piled itself on the rest of my misery when

he came forward and "confessed" that he had given me the saws. This was exaggerated convict chivalry. Believing that he would have benefited by my attempt, he stood by his pal!

I heard all this from outside the little office in the cellar—he was talking loud so that I would hear. It didn't convince the deputy for a moment.

"You're lying," he said. "But put him in the fourth class and set him to work." The burglar passed me as they led him away, and he gave me a look which meant: "Follow my lead."

Then they took me before the deputy.

"How do you like your new home?" he asked.

"Not very well, sir," said I.

"I didn't think you would. Captain, how many men have died in solitary?"

"A good many," said the captain. He spoke the truth, too; and I knew it.

"Jennings," said the deputy, "make a clean breast of this. A fellow has told us he gave you the saws, but he's lying." I answered:

"Deputy, that's an awfully good boy. He did that only to save me. I've never lied to you, and I won't now."

"Well," said the deputy, "I haven't hurt him much. I've put him in the stripes where he'll lose his tobacco and march in the lockstep for a while,

to show him he ain't running this prison. Let's get
down to business. Are you going to tell me who
gave you those saws?"

"No, sir."

"All right," said the deputy. "Take him out and
give him fifty-five."

"Fifty-five" meant fifty-five lashes. They fasten
you across a trough by steel handcuffs and anklets,
and whip you full strength with a hickory-wood paddle soaked in oil. The first blow of the paddle raises
a blue blister. The second breaks the blister, and
the blood comes. I have seen the scab still on men's
back months after they were punished; and the scars
never disappear.

I forgot that I was in prison. I forgot that men
who resisted in that cellar often died of the water
torture. I forgot everything except the humiliation.

"Deputy," I said, "if you strip me like a slave
and beat me in that manner, some day I'll kill you,
if it's the last act of my life." Then my rage
choked me, so I couldn't talk any more; I was shaking all over.

Judging by his look, I didn't disturb him. As
softly as though he were speaking to his girl, he said:

"Jennings, I order men whipped only to make
them obey the rules. I believe it would only make

you worse. But, by ——, you're going to obey. Take him to solitary indefinitely."

So I went back to solitary, and there I stayed for more than a month.

You have looked into a kaleidoscope, I suppose, and seen the colors combine and recombine as you turn the tube. But you couldn't describe any one of those patterns. There are too many of them, and they move too fast. No more could I describe to you the shifting, changing, miserable emotions of that month. There were too many of them; they came too fast. Further, my memory, when I look back, is all confused. I can't say just when it was that I found myself unable to concentrate on any single line of thought, and began beating my head against the wall with the crazy idea that the action would whip my brain back to reason. Through it all ran one fear: that I should lose my grip and betray the guard. Every day, when they opened the slot to push in a can of water and a piece of bread, a voice used to ask me if "I was ready to talk." I would never answer, for fear my tongue would run away, once I started. Sometimes in this period the temptation came over me. I could end it all by a word—why not? I had to fix my mind not on the guard, but his wife and children. I thought of them deprived of their support, their husband and father thrown into prison with the rest of us, and tormented by his old associates—I knew what they'd do to him. I arranged and rearranged mental photographs of his wife doing washing, his children picked up starving in the streets.

A time arrived when that temptation ceased to assail me. And the daily voice at the bars also ceased. Only the one episode of the day, when the slit opened to admit bread and water, showed that I was not forgotten by man and God.

There followed another misery which wasn't mental. Before I went to solitary my digestion had been going bad. The monotonous diet of bread and water finished it. Try as I would, I couldn't retain this food. And I realized that I was starving to death. This starvation brought with it phenomena of which I had read—and always disbelieved as novelist's inventions. I had periods of light-headed, almost happy, delusions. Then I was sitting before banquets, before good meals which I had eaten in the past. I would come out of these visions into the gnawing misery of hunger. Acute physical pain, and finally dumb weakness, overcame all my mental misery. And finally consciousness faded. Some men die twice. That was my first death; the other can never again appeal to me with its former dread.

THE DEPTHS

The prison doctor—I recognized his voice—was saying:

"It just has to be done if you don't want him to die." That is the first thing I remember. Then I seemed to fade out again until they had me in a hospital bed with a cloth over my eyes. Some one gave me a little thin gruel, which I managed finally to retain; bye and bye I grew conscious of my surroundings. They had me in a ward, with one Louis, an old professional post-office burglar, for my nurse. No woman could have been more attentive and tender than he. As day followed day, and I seemed to get no better, Louis took me into his confidence.

"They want to get rid of you," said Louis. "I don't believe the croakers (his word for doctors) are doing anything for you. I believe they'd give you the black bottle if I didn't watch out." Prisoners have an old belief that when a man gets overtroublesome the authorities put him into the hospital and give him a narcotic which finishes him. That's what they mean by "the black bottle." There's more than superstition in this idea. The outside world can never understand how calloused prison authorities become, how many deaths of dangerous or obnoxious convicts are caused by their neglect or absolute intention. However, in my case they were simply giving the wrong treatment. I had been an out-of-doors, meat-fed man. My digestion had refused to assimilate any more cereals—and they were trying to nurse me back on gruel. What I needed was the solid food which my appetite craved. I told Louis that, and he understood.

"You're right," said Louis. "You've got to have it, or you'll go out of here in a wooden overcoat. But I'll fix it."

He did—in his own way. Every night Louis sneaked past a sleeping guard, picked the padlock on a pantry, and brought me a bit of substantial food—sometimes only a bowl of cream, sometimes a piece of cold meat. I believe he saved my life. He took a fearful risk. Had he been caught, he would have dropped from first class to fourth, which is like dropping from liberty to prison.

I lay in the hospital for two weeks before they took the bandage from my eyes. At that, I found my sight, which had always been perfect, permanently impaired. It was a week more until I could get about. Still shaky on my legs, I was ordered into the fourth or lowest class of convicts, and assigned to work on the bolt contract. No more recreation, not even chapel, no more tobacco, no more letters home—nothing except sleep and work, work and sleep! I marched to and from the shop in lockstep. I ate bread and molasses between two negroes. And I had to keep absolute silence or risk another session in the cellar.

But for a time they stopped questioning me about the saws. Nevertheless, everyone knew who did it. The guard had been my best friend among the officials. From the time when I began to hack my way out he avoided me. That was a mistake in tactics. He endured ostracism and petty persecution. Finally he resigned and went to farming.

So here I was, at the very bottom of the prison. This was to be the lowest point of my existence; from then on, it would be a climb upward. But, of course, I didn't know it then. When I tottered to the bolt shop for my assignment to hard labor, I felt as I had felt that first day in the Idle House.

CHAPTER X

THE DAWN OF HOPE

PRISONERS at the Ohio Penitentiary were divided into four classes, graded downward according to their privileges. After my attempt to escape, my month in solitary, and my three weeks in hospital, I was placed, as I have said, in the fourth class, which included rebels, incorrigibles, and men undergoing heavy punishment. The ordinary convict, upon entering the penitentiary, took his place in the second class. From there, if his conduct was good, he might work upward to the first class. The fourth-class men also rose in time, if they showed a repentant spirit and weren't caught disobeying the rules. The only practical difference lay in the dress. We wore black and white canvas stripes, with a blue stripe down the back of the jacket; the third-grade men gray suits with black stripes. We looked at a distance like Bengal tigers, and they like African zebras. We divided our time, without variation, between the workshop, the dining-room, and our cells. Alone among the prisoners, we walked in lockstep. On Sunday chapel broke the monotony for the first and second-class men. We were not allowed even that. Sunday dinner was supposed to be a special affair. We each received a plate of beans blue with soda, a ration of fat pork—often rancid—and a piece of "punk" or heavy prison bread. When we had finished we dug a hole in the remains of our bread, filled it with beans, and carried the whole mess to our cells for supper. The rest of the day we lived in solitude. We could send out no letters. We had no visitors or newspapers.

The fare at "nigger table"—the prison name for our dining-room—scarcely suited the needs of a man just recovering from starvation. Under it I continued thin and weak. Others more strongly constituted seemed to thrive. I had next to me for several weeks a prisoner named Barker—let us call him —who, at Sunday dinner, would grab up my untasted beans and bread and tuck them into the breast of his shirt. If the guard looked away for a moment, he would raid the common supply. Often, in marching behind him, I've had to step sidewise to keep from slipping on the beans which rattled from his clothes.

Of Barker it used to be said that he never obeyed a rule. Once, during my term in the transfer office, I saw him standing on a box in the middle of the campus. He wore a sandwich sign which read:

"I am the meanest man in the Ohio Penitentiary. I have been whipped every day since I was committed." The guards paraded the lines past him, so that the other men could witness his disgrace. Then the warden approached him and said:

"You have been held up in the sight of your comrades as one who has disgraced them."

"Warden," said Barker, "it's the first time I'd had a chance to see all the boys since I came in here." Even his criminal record was unusual. He had been convicted three times for stealing the same horse.

As I worked along in the fourth class, watching everything convict-fashion, getting my gossip by hints, gestures, brief conversations from the corner of a mouth, I learned for certainty a few things about punishment which I'd previously known only by rumor. While the whippings scarred men for life, they never killed anyone to my knowledge; but men died of "the water."

In this form of torture the guards took the culprit to the cellar and stripped him. One or two guards in mackintoshes would hold him from behind while another turned on his breast and arms a stream from a big hose at sixty pounds pressure. It stung like a million needles. Then they'd turn it on his face. He'd hold his mouth shut as long as he could, but in time he had to gasp. Then the stream would go "swish!" into his mouth, filling his lungs and stomach. It always bowled him over. He'd lie on the floor until the doctors revived him, after which it was usually a term in solitary. One little rebellious negro who worked next to me in the bolt shop got "the water" twice in succession. When he came back from the second dose he looked weak and shaky. And suddenly he spoke to me against orders.

"Boss, I'se mighty sick!" he said, and immediately the blood gushed from his mouth. They took him to the hospital, and there he died. This is the only case to which I can witness personally, but I know of others on information which I cannot doubt.

I found, also, the uses of that high-hanging pair of handcuffs which I noticed in my dark cell. By them the guards "strung up" especially vicious prisoners. The man was suspended until his toes just touched, and sometimes he endured this position for forty-eight hours. When let down he always collapsed.

From time to time, exposés of such conditions in American prisons reach the press. They always come from convict sources, and the wardens and guards always deny them.* The average, respectable citizen hears the word of a convict against the word of duly appointed officials—and you know whom he believes. There's a little whitewashing—the local color of a penitentiary is whitewash—and things proceed as ever. I am speaking now of conditions during my prison terms. I've taken very little interest in the Ohio State Penitentiary since 1901.

My work lay in the contract department of the bolt shop. That was illegal. According to law, Federal prisoners, in which class I belonged, could not be worked on contract. But in the general graft system of Ohio the authorities overlooked that. The contractors paid thirty cents a day for the services of each convict, and made what they could. The very hell of the institution was the foundry, where men labored ten or twelve hours a day at steel work. It killed a good many, and wrecked the health of others. Constantly men turned ladles of hot metal over their own feet in order to get into the hospital and rest up.

* For example: When this part of my story appeared in a periodical, certain ex-officials of the Ohio Penitentiary rushed into print and called me, point-blank, a liar. Perhaps, also, some of them feared an exposé in the succeeding chapters. In answer, I can only reaffirm the truth of this narrative both in substance and, so far as human memory goes, in detail.— A. J. J.

THE DAWN OF HOPE

I am aware that the United States Steel Corpora-
tion works its men, on certain processes, twelve hours
a day, and that the workers live through it. But
the two conditions are very different. The free la-
borer is fitted by constitution for the work, or he'd
never stay by it. He can take a day off now and
then. In his leisure he can get open air and recreation. He can buy the food which suits him. Finally,
and most important of all, is the mental attitude.
He doesn't have to do it.

My size and weakness saved me from the foundry.
The bolt shop was then, I understand, the largest
factory of its kind in America. For six months I
worked there eleven hours a day at various jobs.
First, I separated faulty wagon-tire nuts from the
perfect ones. The product came hot from the boiling water employed to cut the grease, and my fingers got very sore. Then they put me on the header
machine. A guard who liked me transferred me to
the shipping room as a bookkeeper. It was against
the rules for a fourth-class man to do clerical work.
The deputy discovered this irregularity and put me
back. I ended my term in the bolt shop as opera-
tive of an automatic nut machine. This was the
finest piece of mechanism I had ever seen. I came to
have for it a queer personal affection.

The men on "piece price"—an institution devised

to beat the statutes—received a certain allowance from all work above a certain assigned task. Some made as much as eighty cents a day—though this was uncommon. The convict must deposit these earnings at the warden's office against his release, but he was allowed, as I recall it, a dollar a month, which he could spend for tobacco, leathern pies from the restaurant, or newspapers. But we contract men had no wage allowance of any kind.

One day as I was driving my machine a well-dressed man stepped up beside me and watched the nuts hammering out into the box. I recognized him; he had an interest in the contract.

"What is the capacity of this machine?" he asked.

"Fourteen pounds an hour, sir," I replied. I quote this and the following figures from memory. I may have them wrong.

"How many pounds an hour do you turn out?" he proceeded.

"Sometimes only eleven, sometimes as much as thirteen," I replied.

"If you'll speed this machine up without breaking it, I'll give you a quarter of a cent a pound for every pound you make over ten," he said. That meant perhaps ten cents a day—only a little, but it gave me an object in life. No free man understands what that means to a fourth-class convict.

THE DAWN OF HOPE

The nut machine was a delicate thing, and must be sped up cautiously. Twisting a screw a sixtieth part of an inch too far might smash all the tools on the head block. I nursed it like a baby, and ran it almost to capacity. By the end of the month I had earned—if I remember right—something more than two dollars. On pay day I presented myself in line for the money. The clerk stared at me—he couldn't find my name on the list.

I complained to the general manager of our shop. He looked sorry for me as he said:

"I don't want to hear any more about that! He did it to prove that you could speed up the machine. It's an old trick!"

I worked on languidly now, my one object in life gone. So I looked up on one depressed day, and there stood the sub-contractor who had worked this trick on me. I saw him suddenly—before I had time to get myself under control. We eyed each other for a moment. And I spoke first—against the rules.

"Where's that money you promised me?" I asked.

"You're entitled to nothing," he said. "You've proved that you can run your machine to capacity. Now do it, or I'll send you to the cellar and have you punished."

I heard a movement at my back, and knew that the guard was closing in on me. He started too late. I grabbed my hammer and struck to kill. The contractor dodged, and ran down the steps, the hammer after him. The guard grabbed me, and an uproar followed.

"You'll go to the cellar!" he said, and in an undertone: "I hate to do it, but too many saw this!" I turned sick. I knew what I'd suffered in the cellar before.

I was surprised when I reported for trial next morning to find myself charged simply with talking without permission. The guard, however, had made a full verbal report to the deputy. Things were sometimes done that way, in order to keep the offense off the records. A full investigation would have brought out the contractor's little trick.

Deputy Dawson looked at me a long time, in his cool, determined way, before he said:

"You have an awful temper. Maybe you're not to blame this time. That man had no business there." I remember that he sputtered for a moment before he added: "I wish I were boss here! I'd cut those damned contracts out of this place. They make most of my trouble with the prisoners."

So I returned, this time, without punishment or reprimand. When Deputy Dawson had a free hand he could be depended upon to deal out justice. I'd have trusted him much sooner than the average police magistrate. But he, like the prisoner, was confronted by the system which controlled Ohio politics.

That trick of the contractor appeals to me now as the most despicable thing I ever knew. And I was not the only victim of this device for increasing profits. A few weeks later the fire bell rang in the night. The guards took their places along the cellar tier in order to get us out if the fire should reach our block; and they told us that the shops were burning. The fire, as we learned later, started in the bolt shop. Perhaps I was the only man, besides the incendiary, who understood its origin. Even then the evidence is circumstantial. A life-termer, who had been "speeded up" in some such manner as I, had asked me in passing snatches, a few days before, if I knew how long it would take an inch of candle to burn.

While they were rebuilding the bolt works, six or seven hundred of us loafed in the Idle House. In a month they had the new buildings roofed over, and we returned to our jobs. Nearly six months had passed since I had first put on the fourth-grade stripes. My health was failing fast, owing to my trouble with prison food, and the silent routine had begun eating into me.

Besides the hope of escape, the only interest of a

fourth-class man is the attempt to break that killing, deadening routine. For example, our prison
consumed twice as many drugs as the prisoners ever
took. A fourth-class prisoner would put in an order for quinine or pills just to make the clerk come
to his door in the evening for a chat or a spat. When
the visitor had gone he'd throw away the drugs. I
could write a chapter on the malingering by which
men imitated the symptoms of tuberculosis or
chronic digestive troubles, in order to get pardons.
There was just as much malingering to get a day
in the hospital, with leisure and special food. Every
morning the doctors thrust thermometers into the
mouths of the "sick line." Unless one could show
a temperature, he usually returned to work. To
produce this effect the men would put cayenne pepper under their tongues—an agonizing process,
which, however, usually brought results. In this
connection, I once broke routine myself by a practical joke.

A little negro worked next to me in the shops.
One morning he got a chance to say from the corner
of his mouth:

"Boss, how does those fellows git sent to hospital?
I'd pow'ful like to rest up an' eat some good grub."

"Jack, I'll tell you," I said. "To-morrow morning report yourself sick. Then steal a piece of ice

THE DAWN OF HOPE

from the water cooler, and, just before the croaker
takes your temperature, put it under your tongue."
Next morning I reported myself sick and followed
the negro to see the fun.

The doctor took the thermometer from the negro's mouth, and looked it over carelessly until he
caught the figures. Then his eyes popped out of
his head.

"Jiminy crickets, nigger!" he exclaimed, "you're
dead!"

At that the negro's mouth flew open with surprise,
and out came the piece of ice. Doctors, convicts,
and guards joined in the laugh.

"Get into bed," said the boss doctor. "You've
sprung a new one on me, and you deserve a reward!"

The time had long passed when, according to custom—there was no rule in the matter—I should
have been promoted out of fourth class; and still I
wore stripes and worked in the bolt shop. By this
and various other signs I realized that from one of
the pet convicts I had become a star sinner, with a
reputation for trying to escape. Had they only
known it, my main, driving motive for escape was
gone. Frank, Bud, and Bill had been sent to the
penitentiary at Fort Leavenworth under circumstances which, when I heard them, made me almost

happy with gratitude and admiration. The authorities had a hard time getting enough evidence to convict them of complicity in the Chickasha robbery. Finally an under official made them an offer which they accepted. If they would plead guilty to a minor offense and take five years, the authorities would see that my sentence was commuted from life to five years. Had they stood pat, they might have gone clear; they cheerfully took a sentence to release me. The authorities acted in bad faith again. Once Frank, Bud, and Bill were safely landed at Fort Leavenworth, they made not the slightest move for my release.

A lucky circumstance brought my promotion from fourth class. Before my attempt at escape I had played the tuba in the prison band. When I went into stripes, with no privileges, the band stopped for want of a tuba player. Some special entertainment was coming in prison chapel, and the guards who arranged the program wanted a band. Moreover, a real bandmaster, a thorough German musician, had just entered the prison. So there came a sudden order transferring me from the bolt contract to the state shop, and from fourth grade to second. That night the guards took me over to the school room, and we had band practice. I was sitting there enjoying myself mightily with my new liberty and my instrument, when Warden Coffin entered the room. He cheered our rehearsal and seemed in high spirits to know that the band was playing again, until he got sight of my face. He stopped like a pointer dog on a quail.

"Who brought you out?" he asked. I didn't know, and I so informed him. The guard in charge explained that I was the only tuba player in the prison. Again, as it turned out, I owed gratitude to the gruff but just deputy. He had seen other men, no worse than I, promoted from fourth class over my head, and he had taken the first chance to raise me. I understand that the warden and deputy had high words that night; but it was done, and couldn't be undone without trouble.

Now, Ohio had elected a governor, which meant a change in administrative offices, and a new warden— Darby. The news went through the prison, followed by suppressed excitement. The transfer of office was to be made, and the new warden to take charge, during chapel services of a Sunday. Not a heart in the institution but beat a little quicker as the time approached. In this man lay all our individual hopes of easy berths, and perhaps of release.

Yet, as it happened, I was perhaps the only man among us who did not see the new warden enter chapel that morning. The band had prepared a special overture, and I played a tuba solo. I had groomed that solo to the last hair. Also, I felt like playing that morning. I put my whole heart into the music, and, when I finished, the men called me back three times to repeat. Applause during chapel was one thing which the guards could never stop. The boys used even to applaud the chaplain's sermons. So I grew a little drunk with the cheering, as all dramatic stars do, and forgot to watch the vacant chair on the platform. As I turned to my seat I faced it. No longer was it vacant. A big, pleasant-faced man sat there, clapping vigorously. I acknowledged his applause by a little inclination of my head.

Prisoners grow very observant. They are always scrutinizing faces for the little, unconsidered turn of expression. Especially do they watch their superiors for any signs of mercy or severity or personal attention. All during the sermon I had a corner of my eye on the two wardens as they sat covertly whispering. I saw that they were in earnest conversation, and presently the new warden, Mr. Darby, turned and looked straight at me. The thermometer of my expectations went down forty degrees; for I knew that the retiring warden was loading him up with information. If I had been called upon to repeat my solo, it would have gone flat. Then I saw

the new warden settle back with a strange, determined look which I didn't undertsand. They went on
talking, and the old warden seemed to be excited.
His face took on a heightened color; he even forgot
the place and the eyes on him, and made gestures.
I left the platform in doubt, which did not last long.
After chapel service the other musicians remained
in the hall, while I was locked up—a special mark
of disfavor. So plain was the sign that other convicts, passing my grating that afternoon, asked me
from the corner of the mouth what in blazes I'd done
this time. Let me say, before I dismiss him, that
Warden Coffin had a pretty good heart. He felt,
though, that I had betrayed him when I took ad-
vantage of my special privileges to attempt an escape, and for such a performance he had little admiration.

On Monday morning I went back to the bolt shop
with the feeling that another hope had died. That
afternoon I was working mechanically when a warden's messenger, distinguished by a red stripe on his
trousers, handed my guard an order. The guard
turned to me.

"You are wanted out front by order of the warden," he said.

Now if, at this moment, the President of the
United States, say, should send for me, I'd think at

once of something pleasant—I'd go to him expecting
good luck. But when a prisoner is summoned by the
authorities he thinks of nothing but bad luck. That
is one great difference between a free man and a
prisoner. In prison all the lines run downward. As
I left my machine I wondered what I had been discovered doing. I had smoked two or three cigars
surreptitiously. I had talked against orders. Yet
these offenses would take me to the cellar, not the
warden's office. Then I got a shock like a flood wave,
which left me, in my underfed, weak condition, as
limp as a rag. I remembered that a summons to the
warden's office generally meant bad news from home.
A prisoner has nothing but his imagination to work
on. Mine ran so vividly that I was staggering when
I reached the guard room.

That big, broad-shouldered, kindly faced man who
was the new warden met me at the door.

"Sit down," he said, and his voice was kind.

In my dirty, oil-soaked working suit I sank into
a chair. Never in my life have I been in a more uncertain state of mind.

"I had a very good account of you from Warden
Coffin yesterday," he said. Then it wasn't death in
the family!

"I'm surprised," I said. "Warden Coffin hasn't
reason to say anything good of me, for I violated his

confidence by trying to escape," I went on, I remember, and explained just why I had sawed the bars.

"I was a little surprised myself," said the new warden, "at the kind words he used. He said you were the stubbornest son-of-a-gun in the institution." We both laughed, then we fell to talking freely.

"When I came into this place I made up my mind that no one would prejudice me against a soul in here. After all, we're just men," said Warden Darby. He went on frankly to tell of his first impressions. The things he had seen in the "nut house" and the foundries had pretty well sickened him. He led me to give my own impressions and to suggest remedies. He seemed impressed by two of my ideas—first, that most of the prison mutinies, murders, and disturbances came from inconsiderate treatment in little things, and, second, that it was a crime to work light and weak men on heavy contracts. All this time a place in the back of my head was at work, wondering what this man would do for me, and hope grew. Suddenly he broached that subject, and spoke about as follows:

"I know about your history. I've had it from both sides. You have been handled roughly, and again you've been treated pretty humanly. You're in delicate health. You can't live long on the bolt

215

contract. I'm going to give you a chance, for I believe you are all right."

You can imagine how happy I felt for a moment. But he hadn't finished talking. He went on:

"I know that a guard gave you the saws by which you tried to escape. A man who does that isn't fit for a place in this institution. He was prompted by kindness, and for that I'll be merciful. He could get ten years, but, if you'll tell me who he was, I'll send him home without further punishment, and I won't mention your name."

The world went black again, and never in my life was I so tempted as in that moment. By now everyone knew who gave me the saws. He had made the mistake of keeping away from me. If he had maintained his friendly attitude no one would have suspected him so much; this made certainty of suspicion. He'd lose his job eventually; I wouldn't hurt him very much if I did tell. I wondered, too, how long I could live on the bolt contract and on the food at the common dining-room. I had to get up all my resolution to answer:

"Warden, I expected something better from you than that. I've never betrayed a trust, whatever else I've done. I can't now."

Warden Darby turned abruptly to a guard.

"Take him back to the bolt contract," he said.

THE DAWN OF HOPE

If I had possessed the weapon, I should have killed myself on the spot. I remembered that there was material like knives and crushing machines in the bolt works. I went back with the firm, fixed intention of ending my life sentence then and there. But as I crossed the yard a whistle blew. The men came out of the shops, and a guard shoved me into line. We marched to the dining-room, where we sopped up molasses with chunks of bread—no knives, no tools of any kind. After that it was my bare cell; and, when I'd thought all night and got a little sleep, I was willing to take another chance with life.

But before I'd settled down to my machine, the warden's runner came in with another order: "Send 31539 to the state shop." The state shop was the place where they changed a man's clothes when he went from one grade to the other. I didn't begin to understand until I saw them coming with a shirt and tie. I ventured to ask the superintendent what had happened:

"An order from the warden to dress you in first-class uniform is all I know," he said. Then a patrol guard led me to the chaplain's office, and explained. I was promoted to the first class and a position as chaplain's clerk.

I suspected then what I knew afterward—Warden

BEATING BACK

Darby had been merely testing me. He knew that a man who stood by his word had manhood in him, even though he were "the stubbornest son-of-a-gun" in the Ohio State Penitentiary. When I refused to betray the guard I paved the way for my liberty. We never know our luck when we see it, I suppose.

CHAPTER XI

PLANNING MY COMEBACK

I LAUGH now when I think that I got into trouble on my very first day with the chaplain. I had been appointed over his head; naturally he preferred to pick his own men from among his sincere or insincere converts. The first morning he held prayers in the office. I was then a skeptic of skeptics, though I've changed my views concerning religion since. Therefore, I refused to kneel. He reported me. I went to the cellar. The deputy, after hearing both sides, ruled that no man could be punished for his religious convictions.

Part of my duty was to interrogate incoming prisoners concerning their private life, and to enter the answers on the proper blanks. Then and there I had a light on prison statistics. One of the questions ran: "To what do you attribute your downfall?" In nine cases out of ten the experienced prisoner answered "drink." Men who never tasted liquor, because they didn't like it, returned that answer just the same. To begin with, it was a good, easy, conventional reason, which stopped further questioning; and then it gave the burglar, the murderer, and the counterfeiter an excuse to work up sympathy. Men who had served many terms used to smile as they said it, and I grew so tired of putting down this insincere answer that I used to write "natural depravity" or "common thief," which was just as near the truth.

In time they transferred me to the post-office. There I served under the Hon. Tom Brannan, postmaster of the institution—a state appointee, not a convict. He was one of the most sincere Christians I had ever known. My fellow assistant was Billy Raidler, a train robber, doing a ten-year sentence from Oklahoma. The marshals shot him, crippling him for life, when they captured him. We had with us also a murderer doing a life term. There are conversions in prison, and again there are other conversions. Some convicts sincerely embrace religion; others do it for policy. I won't say in which class he belonged, but, since Mr. Brannan was religious, a little religion didn't hurt the chances of an assistant. This man made a great parade of hymn singing and prayer, so that Billy and I would throw weights at him. Then Mr. Brannan would interfere, saying that, while the boy might shoot a few craps now and

then, it was a great thing to be on the Lord's side.
When Billy and I started swearing in the office, Mr.
Brannan would only whistle and say: "Boys, this is
awful." We respected his feelings so much that we
cured ourselves of the habit.

The post-office was one of the interesting departments—you can't appreciate how interesting and
how touching unless you yourself have lived within
stone walls, eating your heart out for a word from
home. My duty, besides helping address letters on
writing day, was to deliver mail on the ranges. By
the rules, the letters which came into the prison post-
office were opened by the postmaster or his clerks
and spread out in great stacks on the desk for reading and inspection. Sometimes they contained money
ranging in value from ten cents to ten dollars. That
was always appropriated and deposited to the prisoner's account. More often forbidden things were
said in the text, owing to the writer's ignorance of
prison rules—such as abuse of officials, plans for escape, and information of measures on foot for release. This last class of news is supposed to come
only through the warden. The penalty for these
offenses fell not on the writer, but on the convict,
who, upon being reported, lost his writing permit.
When such a matter came to his attention Uncle
Tom Brannan would undergo a struggle between

Christian duty and Christian mercy. He always made the same decision. He would put the letter in his pocket, find occasion to have a quiet talk with the prisoner about it, and officially overlook the incident. Sometimes we'd find little bits of fancy work, like embroidered handkerchiefs, done by the prisoner's women folks. To confiscate these articles—which we must do according to the rules—gave my heart the greatest wrench of all.

Sometimes letters would go astray. Then the prisoner would write to the warden, accusing Mr. Brannan and his clerks of every crime from larceny to highway robbery. The investigation always proved that we had exercised the strictest honesty. I used to think that no man, unless he was devoid of every principle, would think of holding out a penny or a line of writing under such circumstances. However, it had happened. One of my predecessors put away several hundred dollars by appropriating the loose money whenever it was not mentioned in the text. Billy Raidler learned this, and for the first time in his life, he told me, he had to fight temptation to turn state's evidence. The exposé came from other sources, and this man went back to work on the contracts.

I have returned from my nightly rounds with the tears starting in my eyes. They were so pathetically eager, and so often disappointed! Almost universally the friends and relatives of a new man fail to write during the first month, which is the hardest of all to bear. I recognized these new men by the serial numbers on their doors. They would creep to the bars and whisper—for they are generally timid when they first go in—"Ain't there a letter for me?" I knew there was none, but I'd stop and run through my pack to satisfy them.

Though prisoners were supposed to have no money, except the little tobaco allowance for overtime, the old and experienced among them knew ways of keeping cash about their cells for emergencies. And I hadn't served in the post-office long before they began offering me bribes to get out extra letters. The first-grade men could write letters on two Sundays a month; the second-grade on one. That made Sunday and Monday busy days for us. I would deliver the paper, pen, and ink, without envelopes, to each privileged man. Then I'd help out the illiterate. On Monday morning we collected these unsealed letters, stacked them in the post-office for reading, and finally addressed, stamped, and sealed them. Now, some men with many friends wanted to write more than one or two letters a month; and others wanted to send out information which wouldn't stand inspection. They would poke

223

a silver coin or sometimes a bill at me; I would profess not to see the motion. On the other hand, I did help certain friends or certain others who had an especially appealing reason. Every prison, I suppose, has this transmission of contraband mail. It is called, vulgarly, the "sewer route." Before I had been in the post-office long my brother Frank, in the Fort Leavenworth Penitentiary, himself connected with the sewer route. Using some old associations as an entering wedge, he became friendly with a guard. This man went home for a visit every fortnight. I sent my letters for Frank to this guard at his home address. He would pass them to Frank when a good opportunity came. He also smuggled out Frank's letters to me. From my position in the post-office I had little trouble in preventing the inspection of my incoming or outgoing mail.

During my term an escape was arranged by the "sewer route." We had among us an old professional burglar whom I'll call Charlie. He belonged to a famous gang which, as soon as he went up for a long term, began planning his escape. The subsequent plot involved a guard, who passed the letters in and out. It was arranged to have Charlie called as a witness in another case. He went under guard, of course. On his return trip the train was packed with his confederates. Just as the train stopped, one man threw red pepper into the guard's eyes, and pulled a gun. The rest of the gang grabbed the nearest passengers by the shoulders, yelling: "Sit down! You'll be shot! Don't take chances!" Charlie and his confederates got away without pursuit, and friends in Columbus hid him until he could be smuggled into Canada. I was to see Charlie again years later, under curious circumstances.

Though, as I have said, I took no bribes, Billy and I did have a form of graft which we considered perfectly legitimate at the time. The office allowed one two-cent stamp to each prisoner on each writing day. Some of the men had no friends outside, and some had fallen into a state of bitter despair, in which they hated the world. The stamps which they didn't use belonged to us by custom. Sometimes Billy and I each made as much as four dollars a week by this method. It served to buy a few little comforts and luxuries, such as contraband beefsteaks from the commissary department. It served, too, another purpose. Often, when a patrol guard entered the post-office to mail a letter, he would throw down the money for the stamps. Billy and I would shove it back at him, and stamp his letter from our private stock. When next that guard saw us with contraband goods he would turn his head and look the other way. Only two or three couldn't be corrupted by this small bribe—notably one laced-backed Puritan whom the men hated for his severity. Billy Raidler, on account of his disability, was a privileged character in the Ohio Penitentiary. One day he said to this guard:

"What makes you so mean?"

The guard's face turned purple. Then he said:

"I am just as strict with my own children at home."

"Then God pity your children," said Billy.

Perhaps because of the reaction from the bolt shop and the dark cell, those post-office days were the happiest I knew in prison. We slept in the office. On Sundays, when our writing-day business was over, we had the freedom of the offices and the yard; we were even allowed to play checkers or dominoes and pitch quoits. We could also gamble at penny ante—surreptitiously. This was an offense punishable almost by electrocution. That we sometimes took the chance shows what men will do just to beat a prohibition. We had found a little nook over the chapel study. There, of Sunday nights, we could be pretty safe from discovery, and that became the Monte Carlo of the first-class clerks. The stakes were high, considering circumstances. To lose twenty-five cents might mean the

226

loss of tobacco for a week. When a jack pot mounted as high as forty cents there were some anxious faces.

That institution was running full blast even back in the days when I worked as transfer clerk, and once it got us all into a tight fix.

One cold, sleety Sunday night, Ikey, a clerk in the construction office, helped me carry Billy Raidler up to our nook over the chapel study—for Billy couldn't walk alone. The party included seven or eight men, all holding important jobs. I was dealing, when one of my old intuitions, which so often saved me on the plains, made me look up at the transom over the door.

There was the deputy!

We had sprinkled ashes on the steps, so that the crunching would warn us of an approach, and we kept the dominoes ready to sweep into the place of the cards. But the deputy had done the unexpected by coming through the chapel.

The look on my face was sufficient warning to the crowd. I got up as nonchalantly as I could, and opened the door.

The deputy looked us over pretty thoroughly, and his first words reassured me.

"Who brought little Billy Raidler out this cold, dark night?" he asked.

"I was one of them, deputy," I said.

"Boys, don't you know better than to play poker?" he asked unexpectedly. You cannot understand in ten thousand years how ticklish that moment was. His words were falling soft and low, but I didn't know whether to take fright or encouragement from his tone.

"Jennings," the deputy went on, "you got the money. That was what you were sent here for, wasn't it? I'll take it now." I handed it over. He dumped it—three or four dollars—into his coat pocket, nearly breaking our hearts.

"Now," he said, still as softly, "some of you take Billy back to the post-office." Then he burst like a storm cloud: "Get to the places where you sleep, and, if I ever catch you again, you won't sit down for six weeks!" His face looked as it used to look in the cellar, and we disbanded in a hurry.

I think that Deputy Dawson had another reason than mercy for letting us go without punishment. These men were the brains of that prison. Some of them, as secretaries, were doing the real work for political incompetents. Had they all been reduced to the stripes, the prison routine would have gone to pieces.

"I reckon none of you fellows will mention this," said the deputy as we passed him. We didn't. And next week he turned over the money to our separate accounts.

I had been in the post-office, to the best of my memory, some four or five months, when Warden Darby gave me a not-unexpected promotion. The warden's confidential clerk, who had served under Coffin and knew more about the prison than any other man, was pardoned—and I got his place. So I became the star convict among seventeen hundred; none, except the warden and deputy, had more personal power, of the kind which counts in prison, than I. Before I took office Mr. Darby and I had a little talk. "I'm going to make you a trusty," he said. "But I want your word to me, as man to man, that you will never escape."

"Not while you're in office, warden," I said. "But, if you ever go out, the promise is off."

"I suppose that will take care of itself," said Warden Darby. "All right. It goes. When I leave this prison is no affair of mine." On those terms I settled down in his office outside the great stone wall. And I soon learned nearly as much as the warden himself knew about the workings, great and small, of the Ohio Penitentiary.

The job of warden under a machine administration is like the job of police commissioner in a big, well-districted city. No matter how good his intentions, he will be beaten by the system. Coffin, under whose régime I nearly died in solitary, had himself been known, in his early days, as the "prison-reform warden." Darby, with his big, kind heart, at once abolished or mitigated all the punishments. When he took office he found a steel cage in the cellar for the "prison demons," men supposed to be incorrigible fighters against discipline. Now I know from experience that no sane man is wholly incorrigible. There's a road to every heart.

Worst of the demons was a man whom I will call Fred. Through convict sources I learned his story. Naturally morose, he had in a fit of anger killed a man who foreclosed a mortgage on his little house and tract of farm land. He came to the prison in a fury of resentment. The guards started to take the temper out of him. They knocked him down on every occasion. It only made him worse. He underwent whipping, stringing up, and solitary confinement. This put him into such a state of mind that he wouldn't come out of his cell; so the guards fastened hooks on long poles and jerked him out as an elephant trainer jerks his elephant. At last they dumped him into the "demon cage," and there from a big, powerful man he wasted to a shadow. While I was still in the chaplain's office I told Warden Darby about all this, and ventured the opinion that Fred was really a good fellow. Warden Darby had a talk with him. He had to coax Fred from his cage to a cell as they used to coax the tigers when we moved the circus. He accomplished it at last. Then he said to Fred squarely: "If you behave you'll have the same treatment as any other man. I have abolished those punishments."

Fred accepted the terms, and became a model prisoner. By the same process Mr. Darby tamed the rest of the prison demons, and the steel cage became a curiosity.

Darby went on, giving the prisoners more just privileges. He permitted them to wear the shirts, underwear, and hose which their friends sent them. He broke away from the old prison idea that the guards alone should be heard in cellar trials. One Sunday morning he announced in chapel that he had instituted a change in the system of reporting prisoners. Formerly the guards had proceeded on the theory that he who made the most reports was making the best record, and so prisoners continually went to the cellar on trivial or false charges. Now, Warden Darby said, he intended to hear the prisoner's side of every report; and, if the prisoner convinced him, he would discharge the guard. Immediately the reports fell away from one hundred and fifty a day to twelve or fifteen. This one reform bettered and purified the whole atmosphere of the prison. Under his inspection the dining-room had better service and better food.

Yet the system beat him. He was only a cog in the Ohio political machine, dependent upon it for his own position, and liable to removal if he defied his bosses. Although in theory he had the power of removal and appointment over every minor official, in practice he must accept about what the machine sent him. And, finally, he couldn't beat the contract system whereby certain gentlemen were given, at the rate of thirty cents a day a man, the privilege to get all they could out of the convicts. The contractors complained that they couldn't make men work at the old pace without punishments, and before I left some of the barbarities of the cellar had been restored. That contract system is the curse of American prisons, the greatest barrier to reform.

Warden Darby reached finally the obnoxious position of a figurehead, while the contractors, as of old, ran the prison; and this led to his resignation. If he could have defied the contractors and used his own humane ideas, he would have made the Ohio State Penitentiary a model institution. I hope that the public will believe me in this, as it refuses to believe most ex-convicts. No man ever occupied a better position to know all about a prison than I when I was the warden's secretary.

Now, in all these later months my friends on the outside had been pulling every string to get me a pardon or a commutation. My brother John had given the matter all of his time and most of his fortune. The irregularity of my conviction formed our best argument. John secured affidavits from ten jurymen as to the little transaction which influenced their verdict. Others helped him, notably our old family friend, Judge A. A. Ewing. Yet I was informed that the Department of Justice at Washington seemed firm in my case, and I cherished little hope.

One morning, as I sat at work in the warden's office, a big, portly man entered, and stood looking me over in a negligent, impersonal way.

"Where's the warden?" he asked.

"He'll be back in a few minutes—sit down, Senator," I replied.

He laughed, and I noticed what his pictures could never show—how much personality and likeable human quality he had behind that powerful face.

"How do you know I am a senator?" he asked.

"From seeing your picture in the *Enquirer*," I replied.

"—— —— the *Enquirer*," said Senator Mark

Hanna. "I never see the dirty sheet. I'm looking for a prisoner named Jennings."

"I'm Jennings," said I.

"A shrimp like you?" replied Senator Hanna. "Oh, no! You can't possibly be a dangerous desperado from Indian Territory."

The warden joined us at about this point in the conversation. He and the senator were old political and personal friends. When they had finished their reunion, the senator said:

"That little man tells me that his name is Jennings."

"Yes," said the Warden. "He's my confidential clerk. He's here in my office because he wouldn't betray a friend." And the warden said some kind things to my face.

"But I'm still surprised," said the senator, "that a man so insignificantly small has kicked up such a racket in that wild and woolly West." Then he went on to say that my friends in Oklahoma, notably Judge Ewing, had called his attention to my case.

"What I want to know," continued the Senator, "is whether you were guilty of the charge against you."

"No, sir," said I.

He looked a little disappointed. He thought,

234

of course, that I was about to pose as a persecuted man.

"Not of the charge on which I was convicted," said I. "I'm here for robbing the United States mail. I didn't. I held up a train, blew the express safe, and frisked the passengers. That mail didn't interest me."

The senator laughed.

"You're a lawyer, all right," he said.

"It's more than a fine distinction," I replied. "You get about ten years for robbing the express, and life for robbing the mails." Then the talk drifted westward, and I began to tell him stories of the old long rider days. He'd never heard such incidents first hand. Apparently they interested him. I was talking for my life now, and I didn't fail to let him know how and why I became a bandit. I felt that I had his sympathies, so he didn't surprise me when he turned to the warden, saying:

"This young man made a mistake. The financial world won't stand for his kind of financiering, and yet it isn't so crude as that which they practice in the effete East. Are you up for a pardon?" he added, turning to me.

I told him what my friends and my brother had done for me.

He jumped to his feet.

"It won't amount to anything," he said, "so long as Griggs is attorney-general. It won't get past him. Billy McKinley is the kindest man in the world, but he has to take such things through his subordinates. I'm going to get the hide of that man Griggs! Some day you write to me in Washington, and don't be disappointed if I don't get action at once. I'm a very busy man." He looked at me rather sharply before he went on: "I want to help you to get out of here and succeed in some legitimate business."

"As for that, Senator," I said, understanding what he implied, "I suppose I regret my past more than anyone else."

"You'll make no mistake, Senator," put in the warden.

So the matter rested, and for the first time I had a definite, concrete hope.

But I didn't write to Senator Hanna. I knew that I express myself best by word of mouth, and I knew—pardon me for saying it—that I have personality. I understood by common report that Mark Hanna, when in Ohio, came often to the penitentiary for political conferences. Impatient though I was, I determined to play the long game, and wait. I talked this over with the warden, and he was of the same opinion.

PLANNING MY COMEBACK

It was perhaps six months before Mark Hanna returned to the prison, and gave me a chance to talk over my pardon. As I remember it, he himself introduced the subject. I told him that I preferred a commutation to five years. Besides the life sentence for train robbing which I was then serving, five years at Fort Leavenworth for shooting Bud Ledbetter hung over me. I took it for granted that these two sentences ran concurrently. By the time I'd served five years on my life term I'd be clear of them both, and I preferred to stay in my present berth rather than take chances with a new institution.

After that I saw Mark Hanna quite frequently. "The Warwick of America" stood then at the height of his power; he held national politics in the palm of his hand. However, Ohio politics gave him some temporary trouble, which led to many conferences in the warden's office. They used to talk things over freely in my presence. I sat on my stool, pretending to work, and listened with all my ears. I still consider those communications confidential, but I suppose that few living men know more about the side of the Hanna-Foraker feud than I. Characteristically Mark Hanna never failed to notice my presence; occasionally he would throw a word or two my way. To the others I was like the cat.

One night they were debating on a problem which puzzled them a good deal. Suddenly I saw a perfect solution. I turned impulsively on my stool, broke into the conversation, and gave them my opinion. The rest appeared astonished, even a little bored. But Mark Hanna said:

"The little fellow's right!" From that time he used now and then to ask my advice.

I had never liked machine politics. As a free man and a county official, I had fought "the system"; to it I attributed the miseries of our prison. But a man goes far to get his liberty. Moreover, political scheming gave my mind something to do, and, still further, I liked Mark Hanna personally. I disliked his trade, but I loved the man. He was human above any other big person I ever knew.

We had in prison a convict whom I'll call Davidson. He belonged to an opposing political faction which Hanna had crushed. The Hanna men found irregularities in Davidson's conduct of public affairs, and he got five years. When I grew to know him he discussed his case with me. As many Ohio people suspected, he was the scapegoat of his gang; the more guilty men escaped. Davidson had a pretty, quiet little daughter about thirteen years old, who came in, scared half to death, every visiting day. And once, when she applied to me for a permit, Hanna stood in the office.

"Who's that?" he asked.

"Davidson's daughter," I replied.

He followed her with his eyes.

"It's a shame to have her coming here," he said.

I was always pleading the cause of convicts who hadn't received a square deal, and I took this opportunity to speak for Davidson.

Senator Hanna seemed scarcely to hear me. He was looking off toward the door. And he said something about a pardon.

"That would be a generous thing to do," I said. "He's been a political enemy."

"For that," said the senator, "he could go hang! It's the little girl there." He choked, and I saw that his eyes had filled with tears. Suddenly he started for the telephone, saying, "Hold her when she comes back." He called up the governor's office. In as natural and matter-of-fact a way as though he were buying a collar he ordered a pardon for Davidson. "Send it over here at once," he added.

When the little girl returned to the gate, her eyes bleared from crying, Mark Hanna engaged her in conversation. He had her laughing when a runner entered and handed him an envelope.

"Here's something for you, my dear," he said
after he had opened it, "a pardon for your father."
It was a minute before she understood, but when I
left them she had thrown her arms about his neck,
and they were both crying.

We had so many like Davidson in our prison!
Some were only half-guilty scapegoats; some,
guilty perhaps of other offenses, had been convicted
on trumped-up evidence in order to make police
reputations; and a few, I am convinced, had never
seriously transgressed the law. Now I occupied a
queer and ticklish position in the warden's office. I
would not and dared not betray the men; yet neither
would I betray Warden Darby, who had done so
much for me. My only policy was to keep a tight
mouth, and play square with both sides. I knew
of plots to escape, and, though I gave them no help,
I kept silent. On the other hand, if I had learned
of a plot which involved the safety or honor of Mr.
Darby, I should have felt obliged to "snitch." In
time, I think, both officials and prisoners came to
understand my game.

One day I had started across the yard on some
business, when the captain of the guards ran after
me and handed me a telegram. The silence of a telegram is disquieting to most of us, I think; and this

was the first I had received in prison. I stood for a moment looking at it before I got nerve to tear it open.

"President McKinley has commuted your sentence to five years, with all allowances for good conduct," it read.

I wanted to shout the news aloud; I wanted every man in the Ohio Penitentiary to know my good fortune. I saw the West again and the glorious Indian Territory. Then I was almost mastered by another emotion. Skeptic of skeptics though I was, I had for the first time in my life an overwhelming impulse to fall on my knees and thank God. I am glad now to give testimony to that.

What I did the rest of the day I can't exactly remember. I do know that every guard and every privileged prisoner shook my hand and congratulated me. This, from certain men who had no hope themselves, brought the tears to my eyes.

I have said nothing about the change in me, which sent me out of prison determined to make good and justify the faith of Senator Hanna, Warden Darby, President McKinley, and my loyal family. That change is hard to describe. It came gradually. Perhaps the turning point was that morning when I left the bolt works and went to the state shop for a first-class uniform. But I didn't know it then.

Before that I had continued in rebellion against society. The fourteen months in county jails, the horrible first impressions of prison life, the month in solitary, the dreary routine of the bolt shop, had failed to tame me. In fact, they only intensified my rebellion. I was going the way of Fred, the prison demon; only where he took it out in violence I should have used craft. Had some miracle released me then, I should probably have gathered my nerve and tried to take revenge on the human race. All the time I knew in my heart I couldn't beat society; that was the valuable lesson of those horrible days. But the thought only maddened me, and drove me to further rebellion.

On top of that came my first experience with Warden Darby. He treated me like a fellow man. He gave me credit for the good, as well as the bad, that was in me. The feeling that I must lie down to society was in process of evolution, and, after Mr. Darby lifted me from the depths, I found that I could do it with self-respect.

Perhaps I can put the situation in another way. Victor Hugo has said: "I feel two natures struggling within me." I worked that out for myself before I ever heard from Hugo. Only I believe that in me those two natures are more widely separated than in most men. I kept the better nature dominant until the killing of my brother Ed. From then on the worse nature ruled my actions. Now, with my new hope, I found the worse nature going down and the better coming up. It didn't happen all at once. I had my bad days, when I felt the yearning to break loose and run amuck. But I managed to control these impulses, and, as time went on, they became weaker and less frequent.

When I told Senator Hanna that I intended to make good after I got out I spoke sincerely. I had gone so far then. But it wasn't until after my commutation that I thought out the details. Probably I owe my final plan, and my eventual complete reform, to the Ohio Penitentiary Club and to a friend whom I made there.

A club in prison—literally that! It was the queerest institution I ever knew. The boys had laid the foundation before I returned to first class, but it had its great days during my term in the warden's office.

Certain convicts in responsible positions, like me, the post-office clerks, the commissary clerk, and so on, had privileges even above the other first-class men. Sunday afternoon was an off time. The others must stay in their cells after chapel; but we, on the theory that our work demanded it, had the run of the institution. The guards winked at any of our infractions which didn't bump into the letter of the law. They had to; we knew all about the workings of the Ohio Penitentiary. I believe it was a burglar, gone out before I rejoined the first class, who sprang the idea of Sunday dinners. The boys worked like beavers on his plan. They got some of the expert burglars and counterfeiters—all fine mechanics—to cut a cupboard in the loft above the construction office. Over this they fitted a secret panel. These same mechanics made a gas stove, and connected it with the prison mains. It stood on a shelf, which swung out and back into the wall, like a shelf of drawings. Piece by piece, the boys picked up from the kitchen, pantries, and dining-rooms a complete set of dishes, knives, forks, spoons, and pots.

Every Sunday at the regular meeting the president appointed a dinner committee. It was their duty to find what supplies were needed for next Sunday and to collect them. The committee prowled through the prison all the week, using every trick and device. Frankly, they often stole the stuff. Morals are the rules of the game, and the prison game is decidedly peculiar. I for one didn't regard this quite as larceny. More often, we wheedled the guards. For example, we knew a friendly guard in the commissary office, a big, generous fellow, who had his pinching streaks. The committeeman would ask him for a ham, say.

"What do you fellows suppose I'm running this institution for?" he'd yell. "A ham! Do you think you're the whole cheese over there? You'll have to get an order."

"Oh, come now—a little ham—what does it mean to you?"

"Well, take your damn ham and get out!"

No one liked to antagonize us—we knew too much, and we handled too many little privileges for guards and convicts alike. Yet often, as the week went on, we'd still find ourselves short of some little thing, like salad oil or cloves or garlic. The whole committee would start out as though this was their one object in life; and their adventures brought many a laugh next Sunday. No one can know how much this little interest did to lighten our lives. When news went about that we'd secured a roast, a turkey, or some other special delicacy for next Sunday our mouths watered for two days ahead.

He whom I'm going to call Bart—my best friend —beat everyone else as a forager. He was a gentleman, not only by birth, but actually. Even in his prison clothes this big, wise, silent man never lost his appearance of quiet dignity. Bart, from his position and talents, could get more provisions in a day than all the rest in a week. He had made slits in the lining of his coat, and there he carried his plunder. I can see him yet, walking through the gate, looking neither to right nor left, his coat bulging with a Mother Hubbard effect. As he passed the patrol guard, he would cast one quiet glance, and the guard would look in the opposite direction. Had the gate closed on him suddenly, his coat would have resembled the wreck of a grocery wagon. Once he even brought in six bottles of wine.

Bart and a defaulting French cashier, whom I'll call Jean, acted as cooks. They knew nothing of cooking when they began, but Bart had talents for anything, and Jean was a Frenchman. They worked it all out from books. Bart cooked by instinct, and Jean by weight and measure. Bart would measure out a pinch of this or that, and Jean would say "Let's weigh it." Bart would reply by dumping it in, saying: "It's in the soup now." Jean liked things high-seasoned, French fashion; he and Bart quarreled pleasantly all the time. "There's no taste to it," Jean would say. "All right," Bart would answer, "wait until our guests object." No one ever did object except an old, Southern bank president, who, even in prison, kept up his ante-bel-

246

lum manners. He was a curious convict—I believe he
never realized he was in prison. The president used
to assign, turn about, the duty of setting the table
and washing the dishes—but never to the old bank
president. He'd have smashed club property if anyone had suggested this common labor. He treated
us as his employees, and the guards as his servants.
He criticized the cooking on principle. He'd taste
the soup and say to Bart:

"This is not quite right, sir."

Then that sedate wag, Bart, would throw a glance
at Jean, wink, and reply:

"Sorry. We forgot to weigh it."

Happiness goes by contrasts. It hurts me still
to think of the penitentiary. To rake up that passage in my life has given me a terrible case of blues.
But I remember with real pleasure those Sunday
afternoons when, after we'd finished with Bart's
cooking, we'd light our fantail cigars and settle
down to smoke and talk.

Bart's term was nearly over. We never asked
each other personal questions in the Ohio Penitentiary; that would have been a most serious breach
of etiquette. So I had to wait for years before I
learned his story; and I didn't get it all from him,
either. Not to mince matters, he had no business
among us. It was characteristic of his real gentil-

ity that he took an unfair deal like a man, and never opened his mouth.

My own term approached its final year. And so, on leisure evenings in my office, we used to discuss our future. Now and again, when I told him stories of the trail, the old sense of adventure would come over me, and inwardly I'd wonder if I shouldn't take to the road again. I never expressed this to Bart, but he understood; and he'd check me with just the right word for the situation.

We knew by now what society does to ex-convicts. I'd been behind bars long enough to see many a man leave and return. Usually it was the same pattern story which the boy life-termer in the transfer office told me during my first week. A man would go out, reformed as he thought. But the police would keep after him. Some job in his own line would occur in his vicinity. The police would take him in. Even if he wasn't falsely convicted of that crime, he would come out of detention nauseated with the injustice of things, and go back to his old ways. "What's the use?" they said to me again and again.

Others changed their names and tried again in new vicinities. Then would come exposure. If they didn't lose their positions at once, they were watched so closely that it irritated them to madness.

PLANNING MY COMEBACK

A slip, like a Saturday night debauch, which might be forgiven another man, is not forgiven an ex-convict. And always, for the man who got up in the world, there was blackmail to pay—certain weasels make their living by discovering criminal records. I used to think, cynically, that every sentence to the penitentiary is a life sentence.

Bart and I discussed these things, and I came to my resolution.

"Bart," I said one night, "there's only one legitimate calling for me, and that's law. I've ability and training for no other—except maybe cowpunching, and the range is gone. I'm too light for hard labor, I have no mechanical talent, and as a business man I was always a poor fool. I propose to take the bull by the horns. I'm going back to Oklahoma, where my criminal record is known, and grow up with the country. I'm going to tell every new acquaintance exactly who and what I have been. I'll manage somehow for a year. Then I can get my citizenship restored and hang out my shingle. It's such a hard game that my remarks must sound to you like a joke, but it's my way." To plot my future on these lines became an obsession. I told Bart finally that he'd better follow the same plan.

"I can't, Al," he said. "Perhaps it's the only

BEATING BACK

method, but I'm reserved where you're forward, and
besides I'm too sensitive."

Bart had mapped out his own line of work. As
soon as he left prison he went at it with a single
mind. He fought blindly, savagely, with all the
great spirit that was in him. And he made a great
success, so that the best of our nation both loved
and honored him. The heartache he endured I
know as the world did not. That, and that alone,
I believe, caused his premature death. Had he
taken my advice, stood the humiliation, mastered it,
he might be alive to-day.

So I worked along, always a bit excited within,
until I could count off on my monthly calendar the
days to my freedom. My heart jumped a little at
times when I thought of men, probably less guilty
than I, whom I was leaving behind. I had no illusions about my own case. I was going out of prison
not through my merits before the law, but through a
combination of luck, appearance, a personality
which made friends, and devotion from a loyal family. The same qualities had won me an easy berth—
if any prison berth is easy. Those others had
neither luck, personality, nor friends, and they
were still there, eating out their hearts. Society
has set up an institution where all shall be equal

250

in degradation—and it has failed even in that.

After ten years I haven't yet formulated all my ideas on prison reform. Some time, when I am older and less busy, I shall sit down, I think, and try to figure out the problem for myself. Certainly the contract system is all wrong. I believe nothing more firmly than that. Further, I disagree with most scientific prison reformers on the subject of heredity in crime. An old, habitual burglar swore falsely that he had given me a set of saws, in order that he might bear in my place the torments of the cellar. Louis, another burglar, risked all his prison privileges when I lay sick in the hospital, to get me proper food. There were loyalty, generosity, and self-sacrifice, beyond anything I ever knew outside.

The trouble with most habitual offenders against property is their early environment. The pickpocket from the New York East Side might have been a different man if he had been educated in different surroundings. Once such boys start wrong, the police seldom permit them to continue right. So it becomes a mental habit. Indeed, in any breeding ground of criminals, it is the exceptionally gifted boy, with nerve, initiative, and superior keenness, who is most likely to go wrong. For such there is no reformation in a penitentiary. Take my case.

I learned to steal in prison—I had robbed before, but never stolen. Moreover, to ox-like men of poor early surroundings a penitentiary is often no great punishment. Many of these, after the first shock, are like the hog who eats the acorns—he grunts and he goes on. To sensitive, high-strung men, accustomed to comfortable surroundings, it is supreme torment of soul and body.

On the other hand, a tendency toward crimes of violence may be called hereditary—in a sense. Certain men like me are born with a bad temper. When I got angry, nothing in the world could stop me. Society? I am society! That was my old attitude when my temper overbalanced me. Such men come into circumstances where the temper gets beyond all control, and they kill or take to the trail. These men, I think, the prison generally reforms. They learn the awful penalty of ungoverned passion, and the knowledge helps them to keep their tempers. Yet, as I have said before, strict prison discipline would never have cured me. It was discipline and kindness together.

Even then I wasn't entirely cured, as I shall show later. They had checked the main symptoms, but the disease almost broke out in another form before I myself found the proper medicine.

CHAPTER XII

THE SETBACK

A S I reached the last fortnight of my term in the Ohio State Penitentiary, I used to tear off the leaves of our office calendar with a jerk. My imagination ran free, as I created and recreated my new world. At my release I should receive a ticket back to Oklahoma and five dollars in money; on that foundation I must begin to build a whole life. I could not get my citizenship restored for a year; after that I would plunge into the law. I should encounter sneers, coldness, ostracism; I had no illusions about that. But in my state of mind I gloried in those obstacles. I would conquer them all; because of them my victory would be the more notable.

Mark Hanna had said to me: "Come to Cleveland when you're free, and I'll see about placing you." Warden Darby had offered to lend me as much money as I should need to get my start. But when I'm broke I become the most independent rascal on earth; and I brushed aside both those chances. I had other offers which I declined in a spirit of amusement. Two or three old professional burglars approached me and whispered that I would make a great "outside man" for a house-breaking job. They could give me introductions, they said, to pals on the outside who would make me rich.

Finally, a week before my term was up, along came a letter from my brother John, inclosing four twenty-dollar bills. At that time this seemed like a fortune. It gave me heart to face my impossible task.

So the next calamity fell on me like a stroke of lightning. On the third day before my release date I was in the post office talking to Billy Raidler, when the warden called me aside. I caught a peculiar sadness in his face—a look which I did not interpret until he began to speak.

"I'm sorry, Al," he said, "to tell you what I must, but I think I'd better mention it this morning. A marshal is waiting for you in my office. You must leave for Fort Leavenworth prison in an hour to serve that other sentence."

I'd been a hopeful fool. Lawyer though I was, I had taken it for granted that my two sentences ran concurrently. Here I faced five more years in one of the toughest American prisons. I shan't try to tell how I felt.

As soon as I controlled my crying and got my brain clear again, I realized that I was going against an especially hard situation. Convicts at Fort Leavenworth had murdered some guards and attempted a wholesale escape. My brother Frank, himself serving a five-year term in that prison, believed that certain bad conditions led up to this break. He sent his facts through the "sewer route." I got them to our territorial delegate, who secured a congressional investigation. Of course, Fort Leavenworth was whitewashed, but the inquiry brought out my services in the affair. I knew that every official in Fort Leavenworth yearned for a chance at me.

Warden Darby parted from me with tears in his eyes. "If you'll promise me not to escape on the road," he said, "I'll make them take you away like any other traveler." I promised, though it came hard. Why, I kept thinking, hadn't Warden Darby given me an advance tip and let me escape? In such times the mind gets warped.

Mr. Darby repeated my promise to United States Marshal Fagin, who had come for me and added: "You can rely on him, marshal. I want you to treat him as you would your own son."

BEATING BACK

And so, on an hour's notice, without time to bid my friends good-bye, I started for my second prison in a state bordering on suicidal mania. Marshal Fagin kept his word. No one would have known me for a prisoner.* We stopped that afternoon in Cincinnati, where Fagin went to his office for a smoke and a talk. A big, bluff fellow entered the room, and Fagin introduced him as George B. Cox, the Boss. We talked a little. He had heard of me. "Why did you take to train-robbing?" I remember him asking. "There's easier ways of making money!"

Every hour I had a chance for escape; but only once did the temptation hit me hard. That was when we changed cars at St. Louis. The station was crowded; constantly people came between me and the marshal, who, relying on my promise, paid no special attention to me. I could have fallen behind and slipped away. And I all but did it, before my promise to Mr. Darby came into my mind. The rest of the way I stuck close to the marshal for fear of myself.

I was not surprised, upon my arrival at Fort

---

* He, too, however, has proclaimed me a liar in print, saying that he did handcuff me. As it happens, I never wore a pair of handcuffs in my life. I came to Columbus in leg-irons. Such a contradiction is trivial, but the press of Ohio has made much of Fagin's statement.—A. J. J.

THE SETBACK

Leavenworth, to notice that the prison band did not turn out. Marshal Fagin handed me over to the guard; I went through the same mechanical process as on my first day at Columbus. By now I was an expert prisoner; I moved like a trained dog. Only one excitement lightened my despair. Perhaps, if the prison authorities were merciful or forgetful, I might see my brother Frank—the one human being to whom I had been closest all my life. As they registered me, dressed me, assigned me to a sewing machine in the tailoring department, I kept glancing left and right for a glimpse of him. When they started me for a cell, my heart bounded with the hope that he might be my cell mate. It nearly stopped when I found that I must sleep alone.

I found the Fort Leavenworth prison far more strictly run than the Ohio Penitentiary. For two days I went on learning to patch overalls in a slipshod fashion, while I watched and waited. Nothing happened; Frank might have been released for all I could see. On the third morning my patience broke, and I took the bull by the horns. I got permission to send a note to the warden, asking for an interview. To my surprise, he granted the request.

When I entered his office he was writing. He knew that I was there, I think; but he kept me waiting at attention, with folded arms, until he had finished.

Finally he turned round. His eyes were half closed, and his fingers clutching. It carried me back to my circus days, when I used to watch the tigers working up to leap against the bars.

"What do you want?" he asked.

"Warden," I said, "I want to see my brother Frank."

He looked at me a long time before he replied: "You've just got here, and already you're asking favors."

Then I stifled my feeling of pride, and pleaded with him. I told him how much Frank and I had meant to each other. I explained that we had been separated for four years. I promised that, if he would grant this favor, I would never ask another, and would live up conscientiously to the rules.

"The prisoners will be turned out on the Fourth of July. Perhaps you will have a chance then," he said. He dismissed me with a wave of his hand.

The Fourth of July was nearly a month away, and as I settled down again to my machine the iron sank a little deeper into my soul. Though I didn't realize it then, my conduct of this interview proved how much the prison had done to tame me. Had I met such treatment when I first entered the Ohio Penitentiary I should have lost my temper and sprung at the warden's throat, come what might.

THE SETBACK

That evening, at the bugle call for company formation, I fell in with the rest of the tailors preparatory to marching to supper. I had found the rules much more strict over all the prisoners at Fort Leavenworth than even among the working prisoners at Columbus. A depression sat on the men. You read it in their downcast looks and their strict obedience to the rules. Everywhere you saw the workings of the "snitch" system, by which men received promotion and small favors for informing on their fellow convicts. The guards appeared very reticent and watchful. I had a feeling that they feared the warden more than the prisoners.

We halted outside, and I stood, my eyes fixed, thinking, as I had been thinking all day, of my pressing problem. The big gates before me suddenly opened, and a body of perhaps three hundred convicts, dressed in old blue overalls and wide straw hats, marched toward us, eight abreast. This was the construction gang, engaged in building the new prison. My eyes traveled toward them, but I watched them without much hope or curiosity.

Suddenly I had a shock which ran over every nerve in my body. There was Frank!

Even in his disgraceful uniform I recognized his swinging, athletic gait. The prison hadn't bowed his fine, erect shoulders. He alone of all the company was glancing to right and left, inspecting the lines drawn up on the sidewalk. He had approached within forty yards when our eyes met. I forgot my surroundings; I saw nothing in the world but my brother.

"Hello, there, Frank!" I called; and I should have done it even if I knew that my voice would cave in the whole prison.

The prisoner behind me gave my back a poke. In the low, suppressed convict tone he said:

"My God! Don't do that! They'll send you to the hole!" Why I wasn't hauled out and reported at once I don't know yet.

But I didn't think of it then. My mind was on Frank. And there followed the prettiest maneuver I ever saw. Swiftly and suddenly Frank dropped back and exchanged places with the corresponding man in the next rank behind him. A second more— and he did it again. No man in the line seemed to be paying any attention to either of us; yet, whenever Frank fell back, the other man slipped into place as though he had been drilled in that very action for a year. The maneuver was kept up, silently, systematically, and so deftly that no one who wasn't watching Frank, and Frank alone, would have noticed even a flutter in the lines. Frank had dropped back four or five ranks before I saw just

THE SETBACK

what they were doing. The construction gang remembered exactly where their line always halted, and
they were taking a chance with "the hole" in order
to bring Frank and me together. Sure enough,
when they halted, my brother stood within three
feet of me.

"How are you, old Sox!" said Frank.

I choked when I tried to speak—he had changed
so much. He was thin and lined and sunburned. His
fine, strong hands were rough and blistered. I
should have liked, at that moment, to be at the head
of a regiment armed with Krag-Jorgensens loaded
to the muzzle with brickbats. I should have swept
the Fort Leavenworth Penitentiary off the face of
this earth.

I got my tongue in time, and, while we waited in
line, we talked from the corners of our mouths—
only commonplaces. Our hearts were too full for
anything else. But Frank did give me some earnest
advice.

"They've got it in for you," he said. "There are
some mean men here. Be awful careful, and trust
no one." Just then came the order to march, and
for a month I saw no more of him than a distant
glimpse.

The Fourth of July arrived at last. Working
silently at my machine, afraid even to whisper for

261

fear of spoiling my chance, I counted off the days.
After dinner of the Fourth they turned us out into
the yard, bidding us stand in line that we might listen to an oration on Liberty, see the flag of Freedom
wave, and hear the band play the Star Spangled
Banner. The guards permitted a little moving
about, and so I found Bud and Bill. After our reunion we began a quiet search for Frank. I couldn't
see him anywhere. Just then the band marched by
to the platform, tooting full strength. There was
Frank, playing the cornet, and playing it poorly—
I could hear him drag a note behind the others. He
had a look on his face which I'd seen a few times
before when he was in desperate straits. He passed
on, and I glanced about me, wondering what it all
meant. Bud was standing beside me.

"You see, don't you?" he said. "It's one of their
tricks. They've put him in the band to-day so that
you won't meet."

I believe that never in my life did the desire to
kill come over me so strongly as in that moment.
But I was learning my lesson. I put it down, though
Bud says that my face looked like death. When I
had mastered myself I crawled and dodged, stage by
stage, down the line toward the warden. He stood
talking to the chaplain. Trying to keep down my
hatred and grief, I said:

THE SETBACK

"Warden, you told me I might see Frank to-day."

He appeared not to hear me. I repeated my words. Still he ignored me. I pushed round, stood face to face with him, and repeated them again. I felt by now as though all the blood had left my body. Never in my life had I held myself under such restraint.

He couldn't ignore me this time. In a kind of a purring whisper, he said:

"Your brother has been put in the band. I have tried to favor him to-day." And he walked away. The irony of that was awful.

Alone in my cell, the rest of that day, I seemed to forget the lessons of self-control I had learned at Columbus.

The days now became a monotonous grind. I bore them better than I had such times in the bolt shop at Columbus. I was growing deadened and inured.

When I entered Fort Leavenworth, father and John employed Sebree & Price, of Kansas City, to apply for a writ of habeas corpus, setting forth that my Fort Leavenworth sentence should have run concurrently with my life term in the Ohio Penitentiary. The two sentences had been imposed in different jurisdictions. This raised a new point of law. Judge Amos Thayer took up the matter in

263

Chambers, and reserved decision. I waited and waited, but the decision didn't come. And I had lived through too much prison life by now, to stake my reason on any one hope.

As I expected, strict confinement and factory work told on my health, as it had at Columbus. My tissues began to waste, my digestion to go bad. Moreover, this was a prison of the Middle Ages. Instead of confirming me in my intention to reform, the strict, almost savage, régime drove me backward, brought up again the worse man in me. Were it not that I remember little flashes of mercy from Deputy Warden Lemon, I should feel like cursing that place forever.

One morning, two or three months later, I was called down to the deputy's office. As usual, I didn't know whether I was going to be hanged or turned loose.

"I've had to be very careful about you and Frank," said the deputy; "I've done more for Frank than almost any man here. He had his chance, and got into trouble. He's too toplofty for this place— he won't humble himself enough. Certain persons here hate him and"—at this point he smiled—"they don't care much for you. But I'm going to do something for you boys, because I like you and have the greatest admiration for your dear old father.

THE SETBACK

I've fixed it to bunk you together in the lower cell block."

I was going to see Frank—to live with him! Only an order of release could have made me feel happier.

That night Frank and I sat up for hours in the dark, whispering like two girls. We were hysterically cheerful, I remember; we had to stifle our laughs and giggles by stuffing blankets into our mouths.

We had all the greater need for care, because a stationary guard post stood just outside our door. The regular guard was an old Austrian who had served twenty years in the United States army. He knew nothing except obedience. Whenever at any time thereafter Frank and I forgot ourselves and laughed aloud, he'd rush at the grating, shake it, and command us to shut up. Of course, we resented him, as human nature always resents restraint; and finally I invented a system to annoy him. All Sunday afternoon we spent locked in our cells, our guard just outside. Without saying a word, I'd go to the bars, fix my gaze on the Austrian, and shut one eye. In no time he'd begin to fidget like a man with a fly on his nose. He'd sit down and try and look away, but he couldn't. That one fixed eye would draw his head round like a magnet. Then

Frank would roll on his bunk, shaking with suppressed laughter.

The guard could contain himself only so long. He'd always end by rushing to the bars, growling:

"What the hell are you looking at me for?"

"I beg your pardon, Guard; I didn't even know you were there," I'd answer.

"You did!" he'd reply. "Your eye was on me all the time."

"Excuse me, but I'm careful what I do with my eyes," I'd say.

I didn't really understand how much I was tormenting him, until one evening Deputy Lemon came to our cell door.

"What are you doing to that guard?" he asked. "He's always been contented, but now he wants a transfer on account of you fellows."

I told him. Mr. Lemon laughed uproariously.

"But please stop it," he said. "He's one of my dependable men, and you'll have him doing the Dutch act."

We had all kinds of regrets, as well as all kinds of jokes, Frank and I. Our conversation ran from the heights to the depths. My determination to make good, which had nearly died out during my first month at Fort Leavenworth, revived in me—especially since I found Frank thinking along similar lines. If you remember, he never liked the long-rider game as I did. He had followed it because of circumstances and his loyalty to me. So he had no such distance to travel as I in order to reach reformation.

However, his presence, and our chatter of old days, brought a new, special horror into prison life. Ever since I can remember, my active, restless brain has kept going by night as well as day. In my youth I talked and walked in my sleep, and I still dream with the greatest vividness. Now, I began nightly to dream of freedom. I was out "in society," talking with pretty, attractive women. Frank and I were rowing down the Ohio, boys again. I was on the range with Jim Stanton, I was joking and laughing around the courtroom door at El Reno. Then a heavy gong would ring. I'd awake to the musty, dreary chill of morning in prison. I must hurry into my clothes and stand at the cell door with two fingers through the bars, while the guard counted us. I must march out into the deathly-still corridors and join a line of gray, pallid men, all silent, all deep in their early-morning depression. I must hurry down a breakfast of eternal bread, molasses, and near-coffee; before the light was clear, I must be huddled over my machine. I used to wish that there was a medicine to stop dreams.

I grew weaker and weaker. When our machines stopped, awaiting a new job, we were supposed to sit erect, our arms folded. But sometimes, in spite of the rules, I would lean forward, my head in my hands.

On the morning which I shall always remember I sat thus, in a black state of melancholy. Suddenly one of my old intuitions made me feel a pair of eyes boring into my back. I jerked upright to position. It was the deputy! From the corner of my eye I saw the other prisoners working fast, their noses down to their machines. No hawk ever struck more terror to a brood of chickens. And he, the judge and jury of the prison, had caught me breaking a rule!

"Get your cap and come," he said. I knew instinctively that every prisoner was pitying me. They thought, and I thought, that this meant the hole.

Outside, he turned to me.

"Are you prepared for a little of the worst news you ever heard in your life?" he asked.

It was a sickening blow. I thought of Father, John, Mary, even Frank. Had he done anything? He hated one guard—had he——

"I have stood many hard blows." I remember beginning, before I lost control and shouted:

268

THE SETBACK

"Quick!"

"You are going to be released," he said. For a second, I hated him with all the fury in my nature. I didn't believe him. I thought he was playing with me, as a cat plays with a mouse. But he put out his hand.

"My boy, I'm glad of it for your sake and your dear old father's," he said. "The judge has decided the habeas corpus proceedings in your favor." His method of breaking the news was only awkward tact, and perfectly well meant.*

It didn't overwhelm me with the same rush of happiness as my original commutation at Columbus. You feel such emotion only once in a lifetime. But I did have an impulse to run through the prison, shouting the news, until another thought turned me sick. I must leave Frank there! Sentenced long after I went in, he had received less good-conduct allowance; he had still more than a year to serve. No word of mine can express how I felt. He, too, was in bad health. At that moment I would have given up all my prospects—I owned nothing else— to exchange places with him.

When they had put me back into the decent suit which I wore from Columbus, and taken me to the

* The citation in this case is 118 *Federal Reporter,* page 479, *in re* Jennings. It is a governing decision.

deputy's office, I found that I must wait an hour for the official notification to arrive.

"May I talk with Frank?" I asked, when I learned this. It was a rainy morning, as it happened; and the construction gang with which Frank worked had been locked in their cells.

"I've been told not to let you see your brother," replied the deputy.

He didn't have to say who'd told him.

"But," he continued, in a low, off-hand tone, "haven't you left something in your cell that you need?"

"Yes!" I replied quickly.

"Then the guard will take you down," he said.

Frank was asleep. I woke him up by shaking the bars. But when I tried to speak I failed absolutely and miserably to say a word. His eyes fixed themselves on my citizen's clothes—and he knew.

"I'm sorry, Frank," I managed to say. "I'd rather stay with you." He was about as tongue-tied as I, but from another cause. Reaching two fingers through the bars, he said:

"Old Sox, let it be straight from now on! You'll meet the damnedest temptations of your life. You've got an awful fight in front of you. Remember Dad and Mary and John, and let's get back where we belong."

THE SETBACK

"I'm for that, Frank," I said. And that was all I could say, for the guard pulled me along. I've looked into the faces of dead comrades, and into open graves, but I've never known such a moment as that.

CHAPTER XIII

BETWEEN TWO NATURES

WHEN the gates of the Fort Leavenworth Penitentiary clanged behind me, and I stood in the open air, I didn't know what to do. I felt like a man alone in the middle of the Sahara desert. A voice at my side called me to attention. There stood a guard whom I had disliked above any other man of his rank in Fort Leavenworth.

"I'm going down to the depot with you," he said. Even at the gate of the penitentiary they don't leave you quite free—the guards see you aboard the train. The presence of this man furnished a splendid counter-irritant; and my first positive act, upon leaving prison for good, showed that the worse man in me was still alive.

We sat on the platform, waiting for the train. I had asked, in my bewilderment, for a ticket to Chicago—the surprise gave me no time to formulate my plans. I had the ticket and five dollars in my pocket, and all my possessions in a newspaper bundle under my arm. The guard began to annoy me by his presence. I was free. Why should I drag the prison with me? The train whistled in the distance. I turned to him.

"I shan't detain you any longer," I said in the most superior manner I knew. The sarcasm didn't reach him.

"I'm going to see you on that train," he replied.

I walked toward him. He was armed and I wasn't, but that made no difference to me then.

"You cur," I said, "get out of here or I'll strangle you." He retreated four or five paces, went to his revolver, turned and walked away.

So, instead of leaving prison, as I had expected, with a fine enthusiasm for reform, I left it torn with emotion, sodden with anger, hating the world. My experience at Fort Leavenworth had dulled my resolution, formed at Columbus, to face things fairly and beat the game—dulled it but not destroyed it. I still intended to go back into the law and make good. On the train I had time to formulate my immediate plans. My father, now seventy-five years old and ill of a mortal chronic disease, lived in Slater, Mo. I would drop off at Kansas City, "scalp" the remainder of my ticket, and visit him. After that I would go to Lawton, Oklahoma, where John was in

practice. This was a new town, and it promised
well. Of immediate funds I could count only my
five dollars and the "draw-back" on my ticket; for,
when I entered Fort Leavenworth, I had returned
John's eighty dollars.

I had several acquaintances in Kansas City, but
only one whom I cared to see just then—an old
Quantrill guerilla who kept a saloon near the Junction. Hungry for companionship, a little afraid
of the world, I went to him. I opened my campaign
by telling him that I had just been released from
prison. He didn't appear cordial; with scarcely a
word to me, he went to the telephone and did some
talking in a low voice. Thinking that he had perhaps called up the police, I started to go. But he
stopped me and held me in conversation, until four
men came running down the steps—two burglars
and two pickpockets who had served with me at
Columbus. They wrung my hand, they danced round
me Indian fashion. When we had finished our jubi-
lee, we sat down and gossiped like women at a sewing circle.

The older and more expert of the two burglars
wanted to know what I had in prospect.

"Nothing," I said, truly.

Immediately he proposed that I throw in with
him and make a trip to the Southwest.

BETWEEN TWO NATURES

"I've got one or two good clean-ups staked out," he said. "Then we'll go on to the Coast." I only laughed. I asked them if they were on the dodge, or planning some job in Kansas City. That question was a necessary precaution. I couldn't afford, on my first day out, to be taken up by the police. They assured me that they were only "resting" in Kansas City; they had reported at police headquarters. Before we went to dinner, I remember, they asked me again if I didn't want a hand in a job. Then I told them plainly that I intended to go square if I starved. At that they shook hands and said it was the best thing to do.

"If you've got the nerve," said one of them. He had the nerve to face guns and policemen and prisons; but he appreciated that for an ex-convict to live on the square takes the finest nerve of all.

After dinner, they proposed a visit to a certain "gun joint," and for the love of companionship I went with them. The place was full of crooks. Presently a city detective entered, shaking hands and making himself agreeable. He approached our crowd. Three of my companions treated him cordially enough, but one of the burglars refused to shake hands.

When the detective had gone, the proprietor of the place turned to the burglar and said:

275

"Larry, you acted like a Rube."

"I don't care," replied Larry. "You can go on fooling with those damn rats if you want to. I know you've got him squared, but none of my money goes to him. The only thing he'll get from me is some hot lead."

"Cut out that talk in this joint," said the proprietor.

"Come on, boys—all these places belong to coppers," said Larry. My companions told me, as a matter of fact, that a city detective held a half interest in that very saloon.

I trailed round with them all the evening, drinking only an occasional glass of beer, while one or two of the others grew pretty mellow. As we parted, Larry said:

"Al, we'd like to slip something to you, but we're all on shorts just now. Anyhow, if you'll go to the place at the Junction in the morning, you'll find a century note waiting for you." I thanked him; but, when I got up next morning, I determined to keep away from the place at the Junction. I wanted no such money, and yet I feared the temptation of a whole hundred dollars.

I "scalped" the rest of my ticket and went on to see my father. We kept the emotional out of our visit, though sometimes it almost choked us. He

never reproached me; and he seemed happy to know
that I intended to resume my law practice. He had
seen strange things in his long life; nothing, I
think, appealed to him as impossible. So he never
seemed to realize, as I did, the fight which I was
facing.

As I left him, he asked me if I needed money. I
told him that I had resources for some time to come.
As a matter of fact, when I scoured my pockets on
the station platform at Kansas City, I counted, as
I remember, about two dollars. While I stood wondering how to proceed next I was hailed by an old
friend—a railroad man running between Kansas
City and Oklahoma. He fell on my neck. When I
explained my fix he said that he was going out on
the next through train. If I'd get past the ticket-
gate, he'd see that the conductor let me ride to
Oklahoma. Perhaps the proposition wasn't quite
honest, but as I entered the station through the
yards and sneaked past the porter into the observation car I didn't once think of that aspect of the
situation.

When the train started, I searched for my friend.
He was nowhere in sight. Finally, I inquired for
him of a brakeman, who informed me that my friend,
at the last moment, had received emergency orders
to go out on another run. There I was, a fortnight

out of jail, and already in the position of a law-breaker.

I sat down in the observation car, and waited with my heart in my mouth for the conductor. When he came along, I searched ostentatiously for my ticket.

"I must have left it in my overcoat," I said. And I started forward, as though to get it. I hadn't any overcoat—any luggage at all except a little grip. The conductor called my bluff by following me. I saw that the game was up; and in the vestibule I turned on him.

"Conductor," I said, "I haven't any ticket. A railroad friend on this run was to see me through, but I guess he didn't come aboard. If you have to take any action, put me off at a station, but don't arrest me. You see, I'm an ex-convict, going home from prison. My name's Al Jennings."

I thought he was going to hit me; and I struck a position of self-defense. But he was only trying to put his arm round my neck.

"Are you Al Jennings?" he said. "Well, well! I'm a chum of Dan Dacy, the conductor you robbed at Chickasha—you remember, I guess! Keep your mouth shut and you won't need a ticket! You're my guest." He even gave me a berth in the sleeper.

Now, for the first time I began to feel free. Partly,

BETWEEN TWO NATURES

I suppose, it was the unexpected kindness of the conductor, and partly the approach to Indian Territory. I watched the prairies blend into chestnut
woods, and the hills grow big in the distance. I
stood on the platform and drank the air in big
mouthfuls.

During my trip from the penitentiary to Kansas
City, during my fortnight at Slater, I had kept
apart from people, refusing all overtures. Now, I
expanded and began talking with my fellow passengers. One party I liked, especially—an old doctor
from somewhere in the Middle West, his wife, and
their niece, a pretty, sensible, and attractive young
woman of twenty-five or so. I found myself presently sitting alone in the observation car with the
niece. No one can imagine how pleasant it seemed
to talk freely and on equal terms with a charming
woman. So gradually did we become friendly that
I forgot my resolution to let everyone know my
exact status. She, herself, recalled it to me, as it
happened. Like many people from further East, she
knew of the Territory mainly by its train robberies.
She began asking about bandits. With a queer,
uneasy feeling that I wasn't playing fair, I told her
stories of the trail—I even put some of my own
adventures into the third person.

Fate helped me to do the square thing. I was

sitting with her on one side of the observation car, absorbed in conversation, when I happened to glance across the aisle. There sat a Territorial official who certainly recognized me; and he was talking with her aunt and uncle! I read his expression, as convicts do. He was waiting for the first opportunity to tell them who this little, red-headed stranger really was!

"Let's go out on the platform," I said to the girl. With her, at least, I must anticipate him.

There I told her that the adventures I had been relating were mostly my adventures, and that I had just come from the penitentiary.

"How delightful!" she said. "Please tell me some more!"

Her people, as I perceived when we rejoined them, failed to see it in the same light. But she was an independent American girl, and their disapproval made little difference. We two had a pleasant time all the way. I never saw her again; but I hear from her occasionally. She's married and almost as happy as she deserves to be. She can't know, even though I've told her, how much heart she gave me to begin my fight.

It's easy to remember in detail a passage in your life which is full of action, fight, and big emotion. It's different with the dull places between. My memories of the first month or so at Lawton are dim and confused. I went to lodge in a room over my brother John's law office. I found a few belongings, like a Winchester rifle which I shouldn't need any more; and these I pawned or sold to keep myself going. Everyone appeared glad to see me—especially such old acquaintances as had settled in Lawton. The newspapers all over Oklahoma made a great story of my arrival. Most of them embellished the tale with accounts of crimes which I never committed. These articles burned me up with rage and chagrin. I wanted no more fame or infamy as an outlaw—I wanted to put such a past utterly behind me.

The main question—getting work—was another matter. I must wait at least a year before presenting at Washington a petition for restoration of citizenship. Until that time, I could not hang out my own shingle. I had hoped that some attorney at Lawton might employ me to draw briefs and prepare cases. But the place was small, new, and over-lawyered. All the practicing attorneys, including my brother John, had time to prepare their own cases. John would have employed me, nevertheless; but my pride wouldn't let me take anything more from him.

I thought, then, of business. I had no training in commercial lines, but I had learned clerical rou-

tine, after a slip-shod fashion, in the Ohio Penitentiary. Through friends, I sent out feelers toward
several firms which might need help. The answers
were always courteous refusals. Everyone wanted to
shake my hand and wish me well; no one would risk
the keys of his safe with an ex-convict.

Oklahoma City was large and more settled. Perhaps the lawyers over there might need clerks. I
made the journey in order to approach two or three
firms whose members I knew. These men welcomed
me cordially, asked me to have a drink, and promised to consider the proposition. I never heard from
any of them again.

During this trip I had my first adventure with
the police. Going down, I met a friend from El
Reno. On the night seven years before, when I
visited that town to kill Temple Houston, I had left
an extra revolver with that man and he had carried
it ever since. Now, he took his first opportunity to
restore it. I slipped this weapon carelessly into my
pocket, thinking to pawn it in Lawton.

When I had finished my business with the lawyers,
I determined to visit Purcell, near by, to see if I
could collect an old debt. As I stood before the
semicircular ticket office at the station, I saw a
man in plain clothes looking intently at me through
the window opposite. I recognized his trade as

282

though he had flashed a badge. He was a detective.
Nine policemen out of ten cannot disguise themselves from an experienced lawbreaker. By the
same token, I, less than a month out of jail, still
had the prison brand on me. To this day, I
myself am always picking ex-convicts from a
crowd.

And there I was, with a loaded 45-caliber revolver in my pistol pocket!

As nonchalantly as I could, I asked the price of
a ticket and turned away. When I went through
the door, I managed to swing my head over my
shoulder with a careless, natural motion. He was
following. I strolled down one street, and then another. Still he hung on. I came to a Chinese chop-
suey restaurant. Making a quick decision, I turned
into this place, hurried through it, brushed aside a
Chinese cook who tried to stop me, and emerged
from the back door.

The detective had anticipated me. He was waiting at the entrance of the alley.

"Come along to headquarters," he said.

"Well, just keep your hands off," I replied. I
knew that above all things I must prevent a search.
When they found that revolver, they'd either hold
me as a suspicious character or put me through for
carrying concealed weapons. Small as the offense

was, the newspapers would howl it from end to end of the Territory. It stood to ruin me.

"You'd better not take me in," I went on. "I'm a personal friend of the chief." This happened to be true.

"That's what they all say," replied the detective.

"He'll take it out on you," I said.

"Sure," he answered. "Come along now!"

I had one more chance—if the chief were in. When they started to arraign me, I asked the desk sergeant: "Where's the Chief?"

"He's gone home," the sergeant had the grace to reply. "Come on now—name and occupation!"

"See here, Sergeant," I said, making a last bluff, "I've told your fly cop that I'm a friend of the chief, and he won't believe me. Now let me tell you that, if you put me in a cell, you'll run against it—hard. I'll give you no further warning—understand?"

He hesitated, and I knew that I had won. Policemen are always afraid that they'll arrest someone with a pull, and lose their jobs.

"If you're such a friend of the chief, you can call him up on the telephone there," said the sergeant.

Ten minutes later, the chief and I were shaking hands. I had escaped both booking and search. I tell this trivial story to show how careful a convict must be. Oklahoma City, at the time, regarded the law against concealed weapons as a dead letter. Probably half the respectable citizens carried a revolver now and then. But that slight offense came near ruining me.

Back in Lawton again, I found myself approaching the end of my resources. I could have lived on John, but my old spirit of independence reasserted itself. I had pawned the last valuable article I owned when I received a business proposition. A wholesale whiskey firm offered me a salesmanship in Indian Territory.

I didn't like the whiskey business then, and I don't now. Yet there is a kinder side to the liquor traffic. Any man of experience knows that a bartender will cash a doubtful check for a stranger when banks and hotels will not. And the whiskey men, alone among the merchants of Oklahoma, took chances with me.

In a sense, my new business was illegal. Indian Territory had a strict law making the sale of liquor a crime. I recalled this to my prospective employers. They responded by pointing out that the law did not hold the salesman guilty; it was they, or the resident retailer, who violated the law. I listened to this sophistry, for I was growing desperate with poverty; and I accepted the position at a salary of twenty-five dollars a week, traveling expenses, and a commission above certain average sales.

I never made the commission; for as a whiskey salesman I was a miserable failure. I found plenty of society in the Territory, but it was mainly among people with whom I had hoped never to mix again. They wouldn't let me forget the past. They introduced me round the towns; and everywhere I felt that people were coming to see me as a kind of free show. The newspapers kept making a story of me. When they ran out of facts, they printed the unmitigated lies which grow up, I suppose, about any well-known criminal. I kept trying to find some employment which I considered more legitimate. But here, as at Lawton, the people who wrung my hands and listened to my stories had "no opening at present." Unconsciously, I was slipping backward. But still I dreamed of the day when, with my citizenship restored, I could follow my own business in my own way.

Most of the money I made for salary went toward helping Frank. Then, too, I broke my year as salesman by three trips. First, I traveled to Fort Leavenworth and saw—never mind how—that Frank was made a trusty. I felt it necessary to do that, for his health had nearly broken under the strict régime. Then my father died in Missouri. When the doc-

tors gave him up, I went to him and stayed to the
end. I used all my influence to get Frank pardoned
a few months before his time, so that Father might
see him again. I couldn't compass that.

And, finally, I got track of the cattleman who,
after the store robbery at the Border, had gone to
Mexico with nearly ten thousand dollars of mine and
Frank's. It was old, tainted money—yes. But I
had paid my debt to the law; and these funds could
help me immeasurably in making my start. That I
never thought of restoring this money to the
storekeeper proves that I wasn't yet right with the
world.

So I invested all my savings in a collection trip to
Mexico. It was money wasted. When he heard that
I was in the vicinity, the cattleman ran away. I
came back broke, and resumed the whiskey business
with even less heart than before.

All this time, what with my associations, I underwent a continual, dropping temptation to play for
easy money. Sometimes the offers were dramatic,
and sometimes insidious. For example, I found myself near Lenora, where Billy Raidler, after his term
expired, had gone to keep a little store. Between
his old wound and eight or nine years of prison,
Billy was in bad shape. Feeling that I might never
see him again, I went to him for a short visit. One

day his wife brought the news that three men wanted to see us in the back yard. We found an old long-rider who had belonged to a different gang from mine, and two dangerous looking strangers.

"Boys," said the old long-rider, "we heard that Al was here. We've been keeping track of the bank in Teloga. It ain't any too well guarded. Suppose you fellows throw in with us?"

We told them that we'd gone square, and couldn't think of such a thing.

"Besides," I said, by way of dissuading them, "there's nothing much in robbing a country bank around here. They keep as little cash on hand as possible. I don't believe you'd get more than two thousand dollars."

"Well," said the old long-rider, "two thousand dollars beats old nothing. Can't you boys just be lookout for us, without taking a hand yourself?"

I saw that they were determined; and I also saw that it wouldn't do.

"See here, fellows," I said, "whether we take a hand or no, this stands to get Billy and me in bad. Suppose a bank or a train is robbed while we're in this region together? The marshals will grab us, first thing. Likely as not, they'll railroad us through. You can't make anyone believe we didn't take a hand."

BETWEEN TWO NATURES

"Oh, if that's the case," said the long-rider, "we'll quit. Come on, boys. Let's be riding."

When they were gone, Billy and I went to the saloon across the street to play a little pitch. The proprietor gumshoed up to us, and said:

"Who were those fellows that just rode out of Billy's yard?"

"Old friends," said I.

"What are you boys up to now?" he asked—thereby proving my contention.

On my return to Lawton, Hek Thomas, a famous old deputy United States marshal and then chief of police, called on me, saying that he wanted me to meet a man from the East. We went across the street, and Thomas introduced me to his friend—under an assumed name, as I found later. I suspected him from the first. He had that "bull look" which every ex-convict knows. Moreover, as we got to talking, he asked me too many questions about my past. When, finally, he inquired whether any of my old companions were alive and active, I felt certain of his profession. However, I played innocent, and parried his questions with a few jokes.

Suddenly he asked:

"Who was the little dark-haired American that talked with you in Monterey, Mexico, last month?" The question was sprung quickly in order to surprise a reply—which it nearly did. However, I answered:

"I met several old cow-puncher friends in Monterey. I can't recall exactly the man you have in mind."

The detective turned to Marshal Thomas.

"Hek," he said, "we'd better come clean with Jennings here. He's foxy." Then to me. "My name's Captain Dodge. I'm chief detective for the Wells-Fargo Express Company. I've followed your trail in the old days—you've caused us a great deal of trouble. What's going to be your attitude now?"

"Captain," I answered, "that's a strange line of talk. If I intended doing anything, you may be sure I wouldn't tip it to you in advance."

"I know that," said Captain Dodge, "but I want to make an agreement with you. My men and I have been at your elbow ever since you left prison. We have a regular diary of your movements in our files." He went on, relating incident after incident, until he proved his point. "And here's something which maybe you don't know," he went on. "When you were last at Holdenville, four armed men came into town and behaved as though they intended to hold up a train. The police got a tip, and scared them away.

"There's where I did you a good turn," continued

Captain Dodge. "The chief was going to arrest you on suspicion, but I persuaded him not to do it, because I knew that you had no connection with that bunch."

"I'm glad that I had someone to testify for me," I replied. "You must know what an arrest on suspicion means to an ex-convict who is going straight."

"Now for my proposition," said Captain Dodge. "If you ever go on the road again, I want you to leave Wells-Fargo alone. In that case, I'll be your friend; and so will the company. I don't care what you do to other companies; I'll guarantee that they shan't have the benefit of our information."

"Captain, I've cut that game out," I replied, "not because I'm afraid of you or any other detective agency, but because I'm trying to prove myself worthy of men who have believed in me."

"Well, you may not be afraid of us," said Captain Dodge, "but please remember that we have been able to keep a diary for you as well as you could have kept it yourself. Anyhow, our agreement goes, does it?"

I agreed, and shook hands on it. The idea that I should ever go on the road appealed to me as ridiculous then; but our compact served to drive away the detectives from my heels.

After this, there happened a series of disturbing

events, all driving me toward the same end. Perhaps I had better state the master motive first. I had chosen this time of all others to fall in love. I wanted, and wanted hard, to get married.

I had been avoiding what is conventionally known as "society." I had a few invitations, it is true, but I found that I was wanted only to entertain the morbidly curious. I had determined, also, to give no thought to women. But it seems that in all my struggles an unseen power shaped my destiny. One morning, as I stood before my brother's law office, a beautiful young woman stopped at the fruit stand a few yards away. Impelled by a perfectly decent and yet overwhelming impulse, I stepped up to her and made some trivial inquiry—I've now forgotten what. She answered me with the easy frankness of a Western woman, and let me know by her manner that the conversation was closed. I turned away; but I did not forget her. A few days later, I found that she was the daughter of J. E. Deaton, a commission merchant. In busy times she worked at the store; and so, when business took me there— which it often did—I would talk to her a little. And, in her case, I broke my resolution to lay my whole past before every new acquaintance. I realized that I was deceiving her; but the truth came hard. I didn't get up my nerve to do what I must, until one evening when I walked home with her from the store. Then I deliberately made her stop on the steps of the high school while, in broken sentences, I told her everything. After I finished there was a long silence.

"I have known all the time about you," she said, finally. "Everyone is talking about it. If my assistance will help you, you have it." From that time she was my friend. Her family met me on equal terms. Her mother, a truly Christian woman, made me welcome in a thousand ways.

I wanted to marry Miss Deaton; a dozen times I was on the point of telling her so. But I couldn't ask a young girl to assume such a burden as I; and I was in no position to support a wife.

As though by act of the devil, my last resource fell away from me at this very time. My employer called me from the road to the home office. As tactfully as possible he explained that I "wasn't suited" to the business of selling whiskey. My sales had fallen far below the guarantee. Other firms were getting the Indian Territory business. He'd keep me on a salary until I found something else ·to do; but, meantime, another man would take my route. My pride wouldn't let me accept a salary for charity.

I quit with some confidence, however, because it

seemed then that my period of probation was almost finished. I had been out of prison more than a year now; and I promptly filed at Washington an application, accompanied by the regular certificates of character, to have my citizenship restored. I knew of no reason why it should fail; it seemed to me a mere formality.

In the shortest possible time, the application came back—refused. Why this discrimination I have never known. Perhaps the officials of the Department of Justice were sore because Mark Hanna went over their heads to get my commutation. Perhaps the railroad and express companies used their influence against me. Perhaps I owed it to my conspicuously hard record. At any rate, both position and prospects were gone.

I had scarcely recovered from this blow when another followed. My sister Mary fell dangerously ill. I went to her farm, borrowing the money from John. The doctors had given her up. In this very week Frank's term at Fort Leavenworth expired. I telegraphed to him at the prison, explaining the situation, and asked him to come as soon as the gates opened for him. I intended to meet him with a team at the railroad station, but I mistook the date. So I was sitting on the piazza of Mary's house when I looked across the fields and recognized the swinging, athletic stride which I knew so well. I ran to him.

"How's Mary?" he asked—and his voice choked. As for me, I couldn't speak. I only shook my head. I took his hand, as I used to do when I was a little boy, and we walked in silence back to the house.

Mary didn't die, after all. Her disease required nursing more than medicine. Frank took hold, worked with her night and day, and pulled her through.

With Frank out of prison I felt a queer rebound. The hopelessness of my present situation was pushing me unconsciously toward crime; and my fear of consequences began to weaken. When an old long-rider hunted me up and told me of a flimsy, ill-guarded bank in a new town near Mary's home, I listened, although I pretended to laugh at his proposition. For a day or two I struggled with temptation. The old habit had begun to reassert itself— the habit of taking chances for easy money. The worse man in me tricked the better by whispering that I needn't stick with crime after this one job. Let me get away with it unsuspected, and I'd have the money to marry and start the honest life. Finally, I approached Frank and opened the matter by a series of hints.

"My God, Al, what do you mean?" he said, when

he got my drift. "Don't you understand that we're both of us going on the square?"

I passed it off as a joke. But Frank's words stiffened me like a dash of cold water. I returned to Lawton with a new determination to conquer the world.

Then came the most miserable, degraded period of my free life. I had no money whatever. As I have said, John gave me the use of a room over his office. There I lodged with my nephew, Young John, son of my brother Ed. I ate irregularly. John kept urging me to board at his house. I refused; I couldn't take any more from a brother who'd spent a fortune in my behalf. Sometimes, I would accept from him an invitation to supper. Otherwise, I lived on scraps which Young John brought me from the restaurant where he worked. Young John had just enlisted in the United States Navy, and was filling in time, while he waited for assignment, on the first job he could find. I made efforts to get any kind of work. But, by now, people had rather forgotten me as a melodramatic train robber, and remembered only the ex-convict part of my life. No one, it seemed, would have me.

My one decent associate, outside of my family, was Miss Deaton. And, actually, I didn't know how long I'd have the clothes to appear clean in her presence. Otherwise, I drifted into the only company which I could frequent on equal terms. Small and new as the city was, Lawton had a "gun joint" where crooks resorted. I began to hang round this place. And the inevitable happened.

Two bank burglars came through town.

I met them in the "gun joint." One, whom I'll call Dutch, had been with me in the Ohio Penitentiary. An experienced hand, he was breaking in a young fellow named Tom. And they had staked out a bank burglary at Fort Cobb. But they were off their regular beat, and a crook in a strange neighborhood is like a cat in a strange garret. They wanted an outside man, who knew the territory, to guide them, keep watch during the job, and assist in the getaway. Dutch put his proposition plausibly. The danger was mostly theirs. Even if the police found me in the region, no one would suspect me. I'd been a robber, not a burglar. By now, the bulls had stopped shadowing me.

I let the worse man fool the better again. If I pulled off this job safely, I could get married. True, there was a risk—but nothing venture, nothing have. With hardly a struggle I slipped back into the old life—only one stage lower than I had ever gone before.

We started the next night, in a buckboard. But

first I called on Miss Deaton. I told her that I was going away on a business trip, and hoped, on my return, to have a talk with her about my future. At that, she looked me straight between the eyes, and said:

"See that your business is of the right kind."

"Oh, sure," I replied, carelessly. But I noticed that when I said good-night she remained at the door, watching me.

I proved a poor guide. We missed the road. We drove for two days before we reached a grove in the region of Fort Cobb, and sat down to make the "soup." Burglars and yeggs carry the explosive, for safety, in the shape of dynamite sticks. Just before the job, they boil it. That brings the nitro-glycerine to the surface in the form of a yellow, greasy scum, which they pour carefully into a bottle. In this form it becomes a dangerous compound, whose whims no man thoroughly understands. For safety, they pour a layer of water on top of the mess before they cork it. I was nervous during the operation. Dutch noticed it, and laughed uproariously to see an old train robber and marshal fighter afraid of a little "soup."

At about midnight we walked into Fort Cobb, leaving our horses tied in the grove. I have told before how my first train robbery affected my nerves.

BETWEEN TWO NATURES

This was a great deal worse. An engine down by the station began to blow off steam. I jumped as though at a shot. I rounded a corner and saw a light in a hotel window. It sent me cringing against a wall. And new considerations sprang into my mind—things of which I hadn't thought when I carelessly joined this burglary. Suppose I were caught or even arrested on suspicion—what a repayment to Mark Hanna and Warden Darby and John and the others who had stood by me! They would know that I had absolutely broken my promise; they would think that I had been fooling them all along. And Miss Deaton! People were cutting her already for associating with an ex-convict. She'd be disgraced—she might even be arrested. On that, I stopped completely.

My pals hadn't failed to notice how I felt. And it's a curious thing about a criminal job that, when one man loses his nerve, it affects all the rest.

"What's the matter?" asked Dutch. His voice was shaking.

"I don't like the looks of this town," I said. "A train has just come in. People will be around for quite a while. You didn't tell me that the hotel kept open all night."

In the shadow of a building we talked it over. We had all become ringy.

"Well," said Dutch at last, "we'd better get out."
No man in the world ever felt more relieved than I
at this moment. If Dutch had decided otherwise,
I should probably have gone through with the robbery.

When we got clear of the town, Dutch began to
laugh at me.

"You had cold feet, that's all," he said. "They
generally do, first job out of prison." After we'd
had some sleep, Dutch and Tom held a conference.
They had been watching a little town in the region,
it appeared. The local jeweler carried a pretty good
stock in an "easy" safe. If I'd drop them near the
town, they'd lay out this job, Dutch said. Meanwhile, I had better go back to Lawton with the buckboard. They'd join me in a day or two, and we'd
make a fresh start on the new job. I heard this plan
with inexpressible relief.

All this time Dutch had carried the "soup" in an
inside pocket. As we were parting, he said:

"Of course, you'll have to take the soup back with
you—we can't be pinched with it on us. Keep it
warm against your body—if it freezes, up you go!
Watch it. When it starts to bubble from the bottom, it's getting dangerous, and the only way to
hold it is to pour in a little more water. Don't get
sudden when you pull the cork!"

BETWEEN TWO NATURES

I tucked the bottle into my inside pocket, where it lay like a devil all the way. The further I went the more it got on my nerves. I was half-way home, and driving through a district without inhabitants or water courses, before I thought to take it out and look it over.

It had begun to bubble from the bottom!

Between this, my recent failure, and my bad conscience, I had a terrible case of nerves. I couldn't find any water. There was a light fall of snow on the ground. I thought of melting snow with my hands. Then I grew afraid that, somehow, the warmth might set the stuff off—Dutch hadn't told me anything about the effect of warm water on nitroglycerine. I thought of pouring it on the ground, but I couldn't be sure that the exposure to icy air mightn't freeze it. I thought of throwing it away; but I felt that I couldn't send it so far that the explosion wouldn't kill me. If I left it by the railroad, someone would surely strike it. I lashed the horses, hoping to reach a water-course of some kind. Then it occurred to me that the bumping might set it off and I slowed the team down to an easy trot. It seemed years before we crossed a hill and sighted a brook. There, I broke the ice, and watered my nitroglycerine.

From the miserable confusion of that expedition

I can't pick out the actual moment when I reached
an understanding of myself and my present situation. But I arrived at Lawton a criminal in spirit.
I had fallen; and I felt that the old way was the
only way. I kept only one promise with my better
self. I wouldn't disappoint those who had helped
me. I would take to the road in some remote country, where the news of my fall and end wouldn't
reach them. As for the girl, I must give her up
forever. I had been a fool to think of joining her
life with a life like mine.

That night I called on her. She looked me square
in the eye, as she asked:

"Did your trip succeed?"

"No," I said, "it didn't."

"I'm glad you've come back as you are," she replied.

When I left, I bade her good-night as carelessly as
I could; for, to me, it meant good-bye.

I went to bed with the dynamite in a warm corner
of the room. Young John was out at some party or
other. When he came in and started to undress, he
began throwing his clothes and shoes around, boy-
fashion. I sat up in bed, my hair fairly raising; and
suddenly I lost my nerve.

"For God's sake, keep still!" I cried. "There's
a pint of nitroglycerine in that bottle over there!"

"There, I broke the ice, and watered my nitro-glycerine"

BETWEEN TWO NATURES

Young John stopped as though he had frozen. He said nothing; only as he finished undressing he kept looking at me. He was a sharp boy, and he understood—no honest man keeps nitroglycerine in his room.

Next day, I buried the "soup" in a warm place. I determined not to go with Dutch and Tom on the new job; I would take no more chances near home. Nevertheless, I had crossed the line. All day, I moped about, thinking. I sat late that night on the steps of my brother's office, until my final plan shaped itself in my mind. I would go to Mexico, where I knew three or four long-riders, refugees from the Territory, who had been doing well. There, I would pick up a gang, and play the game through. Of course, the rurales or the natives would kill me in the end. No bandit with any sense expects to finish his days in bed. But it was that or suicide. As for Miss Deaton—that was only another place where I was being seared. I would go to Mexico—and to the devil. The only question was how I should get my fare.

I had my face buried in my hands when Young John came along, and plumped down beside me.

"What's the matter, old boy?" he asked.

"Nothing," I replied, of course.

"I know there is," he answered, "ever since what

303

happened last night." I couldn't get around that. The nitroglycerine in my room had given me away completely.

Little by little, Young John wormed it out of me. By the end of an hour I'd told him everything.

"Hang on a while, Uncle Al," he said. "If you won't take money from Uncle John, you'll sure take it from me. I join my ship next week, and then my pay starts. I'll send you every cent until you get on your feet."

Though this touched me to the very roots of my heart, I shook my head.

"Then, how about the girl?" proceeded Young John.

"If I go," I said, "I'll leave everything behind. She'll never know."

"Old Sox," said Young John, "why don't you marry her?"

"It takes two to make a bargain," I replied. "And how can I ask her when I can't support even myself?"

"Oh, hell!" said Young John, "any girl ought to be glad of the chance!" I'm reporting just what Young John said, understand.

In that very moment, as I remember, one of my sudden turns came over me. It was as though the better nature, almost put out in the struggle, had risen up and dealt the worse one a crushing blow. I saw everything differently. I'd fight it out to the death—and I'd take the decisive step at once. Before I went to sleep that night, I hatched an idea which I wouldn't have dared entertain before, it was so daring. The first thing next morning, I went to Judge Frank E. Gillett, one of the best and kindest men in the world, and an old family friend. I found him alone in his chambers.

"Judge," I said—as nearly as I can remember now—"you know how I'm fixed. I don't have to say that I'm down and out. There's only one legitimate line I can follow—law. And I'm not a citizen. Is there any way for me to practice in your court?"

"No one's going to say who'll practice in my court," replied Judge Gillett. "Come on and say nothing about it until someone objects!" I know that the human understanding of that big and noble man had enabled him to read my mind. He saw that by this straining of the law he was saving a life and a soul.

I dared not draw back now. I went clean through. Calling up Miss Deaton on the telephone, I asked to see her at once. I told her of my trip with the burglars, my conversation with Young John, my new opportunity—everything. Plainly and squarely,

I asked her if she cared, under such circumstances, to throw in—at once—with a poverty-stricken ex-convict.

She did.

I proceeded with that marriage about as I used to hold up a train. Before I left the house, I had made her parents consent. I started at once for city hall. I had asked County Judge Hussey to issue a license and perform the ceremony, before I remembered that I hadn't a cent in my pocket. I told him so, frankly. "But I'll pay you when I get the money," I said.

"My God, boy, is that all you want?" replied Judge Hussey, jumping to his feet. "I'd do ten times that for you. And I know and admire the young lady. This wedding's on me." We started afoot for the bride's house. On the way I implored the judge not to make any long talk; long talks to me from the bench always made me nervous. "Just enough to make it binding, Judge," said I, at which he laughed.

They had gathered the wedding party—Maude's parents, Mr. and Mrs. J. E. Ramsey, their daughter, who was Maud's dearest friend, Young John, and Fred Deaton. I hadn't the nerve to notify my brother John. He would have considered the proposition too ridiculous. So we were married, and sat

down to a wedding feast got together in a hurry.
I remember that I needed it; for I was hungry.

A few days later, two things happened almost at
once. Dutch and Tom returned to Lawton with
news that the job at the jewelry store was ripe; they
wanted me to come along, and bring the "soup." I
dug up the bottle and handed it over; then I broke
the news that I had finished with crime for good.

"That's what they all say!" said Dutch.

Before the two burglars had got out of town a
man in jail, charged with stealing cattle, sent for
me and asked me to defend him. I plunged into that
case as though I were defending Standard Oil before the United States Supreme Court. The job
proved a hard one, but I got him off. He paid me
fifty dollars down on a two hundred and fifty dollar
fee. With that, Maud and I went to boarding.

Now that I had a practice of my own, my pride
permitted me to accept a partnership with John.
We hung out the shingle, "Jennings and Jennings,
Attorneys-at-Law." Every time I entered or left
the office I used to view that sign from all angles.

When I last mentioned Frank he was leaving
Mary's farm to find work. Unlike me, he had the
frame and the patience for common labor. He
drifted about for a time, trying many things—all

honest. First, he worked as carpenter's helper on a new grain elevator. The contractors rushed that job, neglecting every precaution to save the men. Before they finished, eleven mechanics were killed or maimed. Frank has told me since that every time he mounted the scaffolding he expected death. "And yet they send men up for train robbery," he said. He landed, finally, in Oklahoma City. There he met Miss Nellie Bunyan, who was society editor of the Guthrie *Leader*—an able and beautiful young girl. They had known each other only a few weeks when they were married at the home of United States Marshal John Abernathy. With her help, he worked back into the law. He's located in New Mexico, and doing well. My last letter brings the news that Mrs. Frank has been elected president of the Women's Club, and that they think of returning to Oklahoma to get a wider field for his law practice.

Probably no one will be surprised to learn that both Frank and I believe in woman suffrage!

CHAPTER XIV

REHABILITATION

FROM the day when I married and crept back into law by a side door, the old life, with its sense of adventure, its restlessness, its continual uneasiness and its feeling of disgrace, passed forever behind me. I could afford to take no more chances. Now that I had a good and innocent woman to consider, I had to control the promptings and temptations of that worse man in me.

As I went on building up my practice, I began to notice how my powers had increased between the age of thirty-two, when I took to the road, and the age of thirty-nine, when I made my final peace with society. I had grown rusty in law, and had to acquaint myself with the new decisions. I found myself absorbing books as a dry field absorbs rain. It seemed that I had but to glance over a passage in order to remember it. When I rose to speak in court I possessed a confidence, a mastery of words, and a power of emotion which I had never known before. Above all, I found that I had a new knowledge of men, by which I read their thoughts before they spoke.

I realized in time that I owed all this to my five or six years in county jails and penitentiaries. Up to the point where it breaks a man, prison life is a drill for the memory—one has nothing to do but remember. The tragic sense of misery, and the restraint which you must keep over your terrible impulses, tend to develop all the harder powers. And, if you expect to live through it and get any alleviation at all, you must learn such skill in reading faces, gestures, and hidden meanings as no free man ever acquires. The guard is always with you; your happiness and comfort depend on fooling or persuading him. With nothing to occupy you except mere mechanical labor, you watch his face day by day to see what he is thinking. You keep the same scrutiny over all your surroundings. To this day, I am always surprising my friends by deductions which they take for a kind of clairvoyant instinct. For example, I will be sitting with a group of a dozen people having a talk. Someone will look up and say: "Why, where's John gone?" No one but I will know—I can always tell when and how he left the room. Usually I have learned by his expression and gesture what made him leave—and all that with-

out losing any of my absorption in the conversation. I wasn't so before I took to the road; and I
got the habit in prison. That my old crimes and
my punishment raised me from a rough country
practitioner to a real lawyer I haven't the slightest
doubt.

My first client, as I have said, was charged with
cow-stealing. I picked up two or three more briefs
of the same kind before I began the systematic
course of soliciting small law-business which would
he called "ambulance chasing" in a larger city. No
one would as yet trust me with cases involving property; I knew that and I didn't attempt such practice.
On the other hand, the criminal element, as soon as I
began to prove my competence, showed a disposition
to employ me. They regarded me still as one of their
own kind; they could tell me everything without fear
that I would break their confidence. Moreover, I
had a special, technical knowledge of their game; I
could bring out points of which the ordinary lawyer
never dreams. I worked up from small cases to
really important ones, such as a murder famous in
Oklahoma. Before I knew it I had all the criminal
practice I wanted.

The sign, "Jennings and Jennings," was not
weather-beaten before I had my last offer to adopt
the old life. One day, when I returned to the office

311

from court, I found my brother John looking serious and severe.

"Al," he said, "there's been a man here asking for you. He wouldn't give his name, but I shouldn't call him honest from his looks. He's watching the office now—over on the corner."

I peeped through the shutters and recognized my man at once, although he had grown a beard since I saw him last. It was "Charlie," as I have called him, the old bank burglar who escaped from the Ohio Penitentiary with the help of the "sewer route," a party of accomplices, and a can of red pepper. I went racing over to him. Charlie was a portly and dignified-looking person, with polished manners. As he stood there, you'd have thought he owned the street.

"Who's that fellow in your office, Al?" he asked the first thing. "Has a kind of a bull look to me!"

"That's my brother," I replied.

Charlie didn't believe me for some time. It was amusing how he and John read each other at once; if John had been really sure that this was a burglar, he'd have called the police, just to guard me.

"What the blazes are you doing in this country?" I asked. In half the Eastern cities the police had posted Charlie as a fugitive.

REHABILITATION

"Saw from the papers you'd started a law practice down here," said Charlie. "And it struck me
you had a great chance to be an outside man. Say,
that's an easy-looking bank down there—you must
know where they keep the dogs. Fix it for me, and
we'll split." I had a hard time convincing Charlie
that I had gone square, and meant to stay square.
He left me and started back North with the air of
a man who is disappointed in his friend. His offer
worried and amused me; but it presented no temptation whatever—and yet, only a few months before, I
had accepted the very same offer from Dutch and
Tom.

Lawton was a new city, just shaking itself into
form. The courts, like the commercial enterprises,
had been run at first without any great attention to
rules and etiquette—the main object was to get the
business done. But Lawton began to settle down;
and when this happened the ex-convict who had
opened practice before Judge Gillett's court, without the formality of becoming a citizen, attracted
attention from certain conservative lawyers. Further, I had taken away practice from some lesser
lights; and they grew naturally jealous. Three
members of the bar finally made an informal pro-
test to the court. Nothing came of it; and Judge
Gillett never referred to the matter in my presence.

However, the clerk of the court told me afterwards that the judge read them a lecture on Christian charity.

I went along, building up my practice. After a year of our partnership, John moved to Oklahoma City, and I set up offices alone. By the end of three years I shared with one other man the reputation of Lawton's most successful criminal lawyer. I no longer drew all my clients from the criminal classes. Business and professional men, charged with offenses against the law, gave me their briefs. And now I began to hear, through roundabout channels, that I was a "menace to society." That other man, my rival in criminal practice, was "a smart lawyer," a "leading light of the bar"—but he hadn't done time in the penitentiary. So it always goes with the ex-convict.

However, I didn't let this worry me, until the sneers began in court. There was a time when I felt that I stood aloof from the whole bar. I have left the courtroom, after a trial, weak with helpless anger. I am referring not to those exchanges of repartee which any lawyer is a fool to resent, but to subtle and deliberate attempts to hurt my feelings by recalling my past. Against such tactics I could do nothing. I could not even take up the matter outside of the courtroom, because that might

314

REHABILITATION

necessitate a fight—and, above all things, a man of
my reputation must avoid personal encounter.

One day, I finished my argument in a bank-wreck-
ing case, and left court with W. I. Gilbert to get a
glass of beer. "Bill" Gilbert is one of the men whom
I robbed in the Chickasha hold-up. When the firing
began that day he hid his big money and valuables
behind a steam pipe. I tell him that the diamond
ring which he wears belongs to me. When I re-
entered the law he became my friend; we were associated in many trials.

As we stood talking and drinking our beer, an
old lawyer and journalist of Lawton approached us.
I asked him to have a drink. He had already had
too much, it appeared, although nothing about his
manner showed it. He just stood looking me over.

"I don't propose to drink with a damned ex-
convict!" he said.

I felt like sinking through the floor. My pride
told me that I should fight him; but, actually, I
never felt less like fighting in my life. The insult
had taken all the starch out of me; and I knew what
the community would say—"Al Jennings has broken
loose again."

I controlled my face, and passed it off as a joke.
He refused to take it that way. He piled insult upon
insult—asked the whole place to look at the ex-

315

convict who was trying to be a lawyer. Still, I held
my tongue. He made a rush at me. He was a big
man, weighing perhaps 190 pounds, while I was just
a sliver. Nevertheless, I defended myself, without
hitting him, until Gilbert and the bystanders pulled
him off. By this time I had grown really angry;
I was grinding my teeth to suppress my temper.
Several jurors in the case stood about the room.
By way of regaining self-control I forced myself
to talk with them. I had begun to recover balance
when someone yelled:

"Look out, Al!"

I heard a rush behind me, and ducked just in time
to avoid a heavy blow. Then my muscles acted in
spite of my brain. I caught him a short shoulder
punch which sent him on his back. As he rose I
hit him again—how and where I don't know, but I
left him down and out.

I walked back to the courtroom with my face
bleeding from a finger-nail scratch which I had received in the first encounter. The news had pre-
ceded me. During recess, Judge Gillett called me
into his chambers.

"So," he said, "you've had a fight, have you?"

"Yes, Judge," said I, "and it's one that I regret
very much."

"Fights," said the judge, "are to be regretted—

officially. Privately, I'm glad you did it. The incident should teach certain people a lesson." Let me say here that Judge Gillett never let his personal kindness affect his judgment on the bench. If anything, he bent backward. Also, I hold no resentment against my assailant. Sober, he was a gentleman.

I broke loose once again; and that incident I shall regret to my dying day. I had been defending a great many "bootleggers"—our Southwestern slang for illicit whiskey peddlers. I disliked the existing method of enforcing liquor laws, and especially the nefarious spy-system. The feeling between me and the prosecutor had grown pretty bitter. Finally, I took the brief of a notorious bootlegger who had operated openly and, as everyone believed, under official protection. The prosecutors had for chief witness an ex-convict from Texas, whom they used habitually as a spy. I interviewed this man; he admitted that he had often accused innocent people. I made him swear to this on the stand.

The prosecution was forced to turn against its witness. When he rose to address the jury the chief representative of the prosecution was in a white heat of anger. He scored the spy from Texas as a perjurer before he touched on the subject of ex-convicts in general. All of them, he said, were on

317

the same footing; all were a menace to society. Shooting ostensibly at others, he hit me; yet he did it so cleverly that, while everyone knew what he meant, I could not claim protection of the court.

By the time I began my address I had forgotten my determination to ignore such insults. I turned to the jury and laid my record on the table. I told of my criminal past, my prison sentences, my reform. I told of the insults which I had endured from the bar of Oklahoma. I went on to say that I had left behind me in jail a lot of petty thieves with more character and honesty than a number of officials now standing in that very courtroom. I pointed my finger to the objects of my references.

"You know that is true, you white-livered curs," I said.

The judge, who had been sitting as though paralyzed, slammed down his gavel at this point.

"I won't permit such language as that!" he said.

"You'll have to permit it," said I. "This is one time I'm going to be heard, if I go back to the penitentiary for it." Then I went through the court, muckraking man after man—I didn't spare even the jurors. I laid bare old offenses about which everyone in Lawton knew, and no one had dared whisper publicly. A minor court official stepped across as though to stop me.

REHABILITATION

"Stay where you are!" I said. "You're a bribe-taker yourself!" He froze in his tracks as though I'd pulled a gun on him.

After that, neither the court nor the officials tried to stop me. I finished my speech, turned, and left the courtroom.

A half an hour afterward I would have given anything I owned to undo that speech—although all I said was true to the best of my belief. I almost expected to be disbarred, but no one took action. There was pity in this, as well as fear, I suspect.

Let me not convey the impression that every member of the bar jabbed me with my old record. Several of the most eminent, even in the heat of a stiff fight, would handle delicately any reference to ex-convicts. Yet the one thing which hurt me most, during my active days at Lawton, was a constantly recurring episode of court routine. The bar would be sitting quietly, listening to the empaneling of jurors. The judge, as by law required, would ask each juror if he'd ever served a term in the penitentiary. The same thing always happened—two or three lawyers, usually lesser lights, would glance at the court and then at me, and give a smile or a nudge. Probably they thought I didn't see them; but very little in human expression goes past an ex-convict. I remembered these sneers; and when I opposed the culprits in court, I would lash them down the line like runaway slaves.

On the social side of life I was less mortified—perhaps because I gave little opportunity for slights. I have never cared much for so-called "society." Life has been so exciting for me that purely social pleasures seem tame at best. From the first I nailed my colors to the mast, as I had resolved to do when Bart and I discussed my comeback in the Ohio Penitentiary. My old acquaintances knew the worst. Whenever I had more than a passing talk with a new man, I contrived to tell him that I had been an outlaw and a convict. In some cases this has produced an awful shock. But I wanted my new acquaintance to know the worst. It gave him his choice between seeking and avoiding me. Let me say that nine men out of ten to whom I made this frank admission renewed the acquaintance. Of all the disgraces I know, none would sting me more deeply than to have some man say: "That fellow Jennings has imposed on me; I have learned that he is an ex-convict."

I bent backward in my pride. If I was ostracized in Lawton society it was a voluntary ostracism. As time went on, and I worked up in the law, a few people of standing invited Mrs. Jennings and me to their houses. I always found a way to refuse with-

out giving offense. Probably these people sought
me as they would seek anyone else. But at the time,
I attributed the action to curiosity or charity; either
I felt they wanted to thrill their friends by exhibit-
ing a bandit, or they hoped to show me that I wasn't
such an outcast after all. There came, later, a few
such invitations which I could not afford to refuse.
These occasions I never enjoyed. I felt, somehow,
that I was imposing on hospitality; and I took care
not to repeat the experience.

To expose my own prison record has become as
much a habit with me as shaking hands or saying
good-morning. Yet even now I dislike to have anyone else make the first reference. In my early days
of freedom an acquaintance or friend would sometimes introduce me as "Al Jennings, the notorious
train robber." No one ever knew how deeply this
sank into my soul. I felt, at times, that it was a
punishment worse than the Fort Leavenworth Penitentiary. The feeling is illogical, I grant that. But
I have never conquered it.

Yet, very gradually Maud and I become acquainted, in one way or another, with a number of
charming and congenial people who had no social
pretentions. I began to visit their houses. Before
we left Lawton we had a circle not of mere acquaintances, but of real friends.

BEATING BACK

All this time the desire for rehabilitation inspired my actions. Under the curious circumstances, a restoration to citizenship would scarcely have helped my law practice. But I felt about the matter as many noble and advanced women feel about the franchise. They may have no practical use for it, but not to have it constitutes a brand of inferiority. I dreamed of still another advance. When, by election or appointment, I should represent the people of Oklahoma in some official capacity, I should feel that I had completed my rehabilitation.

As things turned out, I came near taking the second step before the first Oklahoma Territory stood on the verge of statehood; the people were electing delegates to a constitutional convention. They had cut our county into two districts. Living a mile and a half from Lawton, on a rural route, I was in the southern district, whereas the city lay in the northern. On one of those sudden impulses by which I have taken most of the turns in my life, I determined to run for delegate to the convention. I had no hope of election; I wasn't even sure if I could legally hold such an office. But the campaign would prove whether an ex-convict could expect anything of the people, and it would help my law practice. I announced myself; no one objected. Court was in session just then, and I had some difficult

"The desire for rehabilitation inspired my action"

cases in hand. So I found time for only two or three speaking appointments. I opened at the town of Chattanooga, where all the candidates were to appear in one meeting. On the way to the hall I passed a saloon. The bartender, whom I'd known during my whiskey-selling days, asked me in to have a drink. To his disgust—he being an old-time Western saloon man—I took a soda.

"I'm going to vote for you," said the bartender, "but some of those candidates have been noratin' around that you're an ex-convict. How about it?" Then and there, a plan which had been growing in my mind took definite form. I had gone down to Chattanooga, as a speaker sometimes will, with several lines of attack in mind. This reference, at the very gates of the town, to my old record, determined what line to adopt.

The rest of the candidates were local politicians; and with professional politicians I had always been unpopular. They sat apart from me as though I were tainted. I found myself scheduled for the last speech; they hoped, I suppose, that the crowd would be going by the time I rose.

In the middle of the meeting someone started a call for Jennings. The rest took it up; and the chairman brought me forward.

I introduced myself by saying that I wanted them

to know me as I was. I had been a train robber. I had done time in two penitentiaries. And I had started to retrieve the past. I hoped that some of the other candidates would be as fair with themselves as I had been with myself.

"For, gentlemen," I said, "I left men in the penitentiary at Columbus who are better equipped by ability and honesty to represent you before the constitutional convention than half the candidates in this string! If these men object to the language I am using, let them take it up now, and not slink through this district assassinating the character of a man who is trying to live down a criminal past!" When I sat down, I had captured the crowd. Out of seventy votes cast from Chattanooga, I got all but three.

I spoke next in Frederick, a town whose citizens held a strong logical objection to me. This was a prohibition center, and I had been a whiskey salesman. Further, the townspeople wanted to divide the county, making Frederick the county seat, and I opposed that plan. No one would rent me a hall. Judge Alexander, a personal friend but against me on the division question, told me that it would do no good to speak in Frederick.

"Judge, I'm going to speak if I have to get up in a wagon on the street," I said.

REHABILITATION

"In that case," replied Judge Alexander, "I'll introduce you. We're against you, but you'll get a fair shake in Frederick." He borrowed a wagon from a farmer, mounted the cart-tail, gathered a crowd, and told them that he wished to present a competent and honest man, though a political opponent.

The news that the outlaw was going to speak emptied the stores and houses; I drew almost the entire town. And I tore in, as I had done at Chattanooga—put my own record before them and proceeded to assail other records. A wealthy and prominent resident had been saying, to my certain knowledge, that no decent man would vote for an ex-convict. I had been acquainted with that man on the range; I knew that if he should receive a year in the penitentiary for every cow he had stolen he would serve two life terms. I said this to the crowd, with names and places. I lost Frederick, in the election, by only fifteen votes.

Now I saw that my campaign was going entirely too well. I didn't want the job. I should probably have been seated without question. So many delegates more powerful than I had records which wouldn't bear investigation that no one would have dared start any muckraking. But such an illegal proceeding might rise up in future to reproach me.

However, I had a close call. In spite of my virtual withdrawal, I lost, as I remember now, by only eight votes. This was a milestone in my progress toward rehabilitation. I learned that the people will stand by an honest man who confesses his sins.

My citizenship came soon afterward. When "Jack" Abernathy made his campaign for appointment as United States marshal for the western district of Oklahoma, I acted as his advisor. He volunteered, out of friendship and gratitude, to put my case before President Roosevelt. We visited Washington. Jack took me into the cabinet room, where many people stood waiting for the President.

"I'm glad to see you," said Mr. Roosevelt, when Jack introduced me. "I've heard a good deal of you. Another time I want to have a talk with you."

I didn't feel like letting the opportunity slip.

"Mr. President," I said, "I've come a long way. I may never have a chance to see you again."

Mr. Roosevelt replied, in his impulsive manner:

"Yes! That's true, and I know what you're after. Your friends say you're all right. John here endorses you, and I can trust him. What I want to know is if you were guilty of the crime for which you were convicted."

"No, sir," I said, "I was charged with robbing the United States mail, but I didn't do that."

REHABILITATION

Mr. Roosevelt's teeth clicked, and he looked ferocious.

"You didn't?" he said. "Weren't you there at all?" He thought—as Mark Hanna had thought eight years before—that I was putting forth the regular talk about injured innocence.

"Yes, I was there," I replied. "I held up the train, robbed the express, and went through the passengers."

"That, sir, is a distinction without a difference," said the President.

"It's the difference between a few years in jail and life," I replied, "and it's the truth."

"That's what I want," said the President, "the truth. Is there anything else?"

"Yes, sir," said I, "a great deal else. But that's the only time I was ever convicted of a robbery. I'm asking you to judge me by what I've done since I reformed."

"I'm going to give you a pardon restoring your citizenship," broke in Mr. Roosevelt abruptly, "because I know you won't violate my confidence, and because I want to help you be a good boy and make a man of yourself." I left Washington with a signed and embossed document which made me a man again.

During our talk with Mr. Roosevelt someone

spoke about Jack Abernathy's method of catching
wolves with his bare hands—Jack used to jump them
and hold down their lower jaws so that they couldn't
bite. The President had told this story, and certain
persons had accused him of being a "nature faker."

"I can prove it by a moving picture," said
Jack.

"I don't believe that can be done," replied the
President, "but I'd like to see it." As soon as we
got back to Oklahoma, Abernathy and I rounded up
an outfit of old cow-punchers, deputy marshals, and
Indians, hired a moving picture operator, borrowed
a camping outfit from the War Department, and
spent six weeks chasing wolves before the camera.
After many failures, we got some good films. We
took them back to Washington, and reported to the
President. He ordered a screen set up on the wall
of the East Room; and there we gave a private exhibition.

"Marvelous!" said the President. "A perfect picture! Can't you show them here to-morrow night?
I'd like to invite some friends." Jack and I figured
that this was going to be a special occasion, so we
hired dress suits. But we were hardly prepared for
what happened. As we stood in the waiting room
talking to Dr. Alexander Lambert, the President
came bounding in.

REHABILITATION

"I'm going to describe these pictures myself!" he said. "Come along and meet my friends!"

We entered the reception room; and it looked like a royal stag party. There were almost the whole Diplomatic Corps, part of the Cabinet, two or three justices of the Supreme Court, Nicholas Longworth, General Young, Andrew Carnegie, the Italian historian, Ferraro, and a few others whom I've forgotten. We smoked a while, and had a round of drinks (I remember, in the light of later events, that the President took only mineral water) before we proceeded to the East Room, stopping on the way to meet Mr. Roosevelt's wife and daughter. The President made a great lecturer. After the guests left, we stayed for a little chat with the Roosevelts and a few intimate friends. I've been sorry ever since that conviction keeps me in another political party from Mr. Roosevelt. I'd like to support a man like that—and not entirely through gratitude, either.

Half of the shrinking from the world, which no ex-convict ever wholly overcomes, passed away from me with my citizenship. I went ahead in the law, working from criminal cases, in which I had made my reputation, to civil suits.

Before I dismiss this part of my life I feel that I must say a little about the law as I have found it.

Eminent lawyers will tell you that they never de-

BEATING BACK

fend clients whom they know to be guilty, or appear
in civil suits for clients whom they know to be wrong.
In the whole world there is not a greater fake than
this. I have known but one lawyer who refused a
case because his client was guilty. He was a clergyman, who studied law late in life. A cattle thief,
jailed in Lawton, asked for an attorney. The jailer,
out of kindness, recommended the ex-clergyman. The
cattle thief stated his case.

"Then you're really guilty?" asked the ex-clergyman.

"Sure!" said the cattle thief, "or why would I be
wanting you?"

"God help you—I can't defend you; I can only
pray for you," said the clergyman.

"I wanted a lawyer, not a preacher," said the
cattle thief. He sent for a regular member of the
Oklahoma bar, who cleared him. The ex-clergyman
was starved out of the law.

Again, there is the matter of suborning perjury
and fixing jurors. No lawyer who cares to look
himself in the face ever actually does such work;
certainly, I never did. But handling perjury which
you suspect to be suborned by your client, appear-
ing before jurors whom you suspect of being over-
friendly to your client—that's another matter. I
believe that every criminal lawyer does these things

in one period or another of his career. Let me take murder as a typical crime. Except in cases where the defense can pick to pieces imperfect circumstantial evidence, how does a guilty man escape? In nine cases out of ten, through the perjured testimony of himself or his friends. The lawyer who handles his case, and who knows him to be guilty, builds the defense on this perjury. In fact, it's an exceptionally conscientious lawyer who doesn't suggest a few trimmings.

I have defended innocent men. I have defended guilty men who deserved no punishment because of considerations which you cannot introduce in court. And I have defended and cleared men whom I never wanted to see again after I left the courtroom.

This is not so immoral as it sounds—at least, not to me. I have viewed the law of the land from both sides of the line. It is an imperfect institution. The men who make a business of enforcing it tend, even if they are honest, to become calloused and oversevere. If they have more ambition or cupidity than honesty, they will go as far to convict a man as the crookedest little shyster to acquit him. "Miscarriages of law"—most people, when you use that term, think of guilty men going free. I know, as few other men do, that the miscarriage frequently runs the other way. The corrupt and careless policeman,

BEATING BACK

being pressed to find the culprit in a troublesome
case, will seize the first likely crook in sight and
railroad him through by inventing or bolstering the
evidence. A prosecutor who cares more for advance-
ment than conscience will take this faulty evidence,
though he understands its real character, patch it
up, and get a conviction. I know three men serving
life terms who are innocent, to my certain knowledge,
of the charge on which they were convicted. They
had committed other and lesser crimes, perhaps—
but not these.

So, with one side, and that the more powerful
one, straining legal ethics, no one can blame the
other side for following suit. The law becomes a
kind of dual game. First, there are facts against
facts—the law as we intended it to be. Then there
are tricks against tricks, one sharp mind outwitting
the other. By adding the scores of the two games,
you get the ultimate result—and justice is done,
after a rough fashion. It would be roughly done
under the best circumstances. For many men who
are guilty under the law still deserve less punishment from my point of view than others who seem
never to have transgressed a law in their lives. In
which would the devil take more delight—a plain
horse thief, or a millionaire manufacturer bloated
with the blood of little children?

REHABILITATION

All this time I had been growing, I suppose, in the regard of the common people of Lawton. And, after my campaign for the constitutional convention, I found myself perpetually mixed with city and county politics. I hate most professional politicians, as I have said before and shall say again; but I began to like the game itself.

Being of Southern birth, I was brought up to believe that no gentleman could be anything but a Democrat. After I began to do my own thinking, Bryan arose. I believed in him; I've seen the country swing to my belief. I was an outlaw when he made his first campaign, and a convict when he made his second; yet, on the road and in our debates at the Ohio Penitentiary Club, I was always talking Bryan. Even before I regained the right to vote I lined up with the Democrats—not from heredity, now, but from conviction.

A little chance meeting led me into the larger politics of the state. We were approaching the primary stage of our second campaign for governor. Lee Cruce, the machine man, and W. H. Murray were after the Democratic nomination. Personally, I favored neither of these men. I should have liked to seen Leslie P. Ross in the field. An Arkansas man originally, he had been chairman of the Democratic Territorial Committee. He had figured as the insurgent in our second Territorial legislature, when, with Senator Ben F. Wilson, he stood between the politicians and graft. Ross, however, hadn't announced himself; and, although many people felt as I did about him, no one asked him to run.

An advertising solicitor named Jepsen appeared at Lawton, and made my acquaintance. One evening we fell to discussing Ross. He held my views. It seemed to us a shame that no one was putting forward a man so well fitted as he to be a candidate.

"Why not start him ourselves?" I asked. He fancied the idea; and we were in before we knew it. Gathering a few prominent Democrats who felt as we did, we drafted a letter to Ross, selected tentative committees in all parts of the state, and announced ourselves to the newspapers.

The movement took. Everywhere people who liked neither of the announced candidates endorsed Ross. We organized a mass meeting at Lawton, and persuaded Ross to address us. Up to this time the politicians regarded the Ross movement as a joke. But after our meeting it gathered momentum like a snowball. We grew so dangerous that Governor Haskell was rushed to Lawton, where he made a speech tearing the hide off Ross. He held his meeting in the afternoon. That very night we got up a

rally. While the speaking went on inside, I read a
telegram to the big overflow crowd. By arrange-
ment, some of our supporters began to yell, "speech."
Others took it up, and I delivered an address wherein
I recited facts about the Oklahoma political machine
which burned in like a branding-iron on a nester
calf. When I sat down the Ross boom was launched.
Because there was no time to pick and choose I became, by logic of circumstances, secretary to the
Ross campaign. However, we were too late in beginning, while our opponents had been building fences
for years. Moreover, as I shall show later, the election laws of Oklahoma are admirably framed for the
uses of election trickery. The machine men ran
things in that election as they have done since. And
Ross lost.

When the campaign was finished the governor sent
for me, quite without preliminary announcement. It
appeared that he was eager to conciliate the Ross
forces; with that end in view, I suppose, he offered
me a state position. He was expecting the resignation of the state enforcement attorney, that official
who prosecutes the violations of our liquor laws.
When the resignation occurred, he said, I might have
the place. It carried a salary of only $5,000 a year.
I was making much more than that in the law. But,
having no social ambitions, I could live on the salary.

BEATING BACK

And it was the complete rehabilitation of which I had dreamed so long. I accepted at once.

In preparation I closed my practice at Lawton, gave up the little house and home acre in the suburbs, and moved to Oklahoma City, the capital.

I acted too impulsively, as I often do. The incumbent did not resign, after all. However, I had been wanting a chance to practice in the capital. So I formed the firm of Jennings & Ross, hired offices in the State Bank building, and set out to acquire a new and wider practice.

It was almost like starting the fight again. My penitentiary record, which I had lived down and half-forgotten at Lawton, stared me in the face at every turn. The bar of the capital appeared solid against me. They were solid, in fact, against almost every newcomer. I never saw a place where law practice went so much by favor, so little by merit.

A year's residence in Oklahoma City gave me a chance to study the business of our state government first hand, and to confirm what I had hitherto suspected about the politicians who ruled us. In one way of speaking Oklahoma is the newest state of all. Those admitted later have a much longer territorial history. We came together as strangers during the few years after 1889. In such circumstances the bluffs and the crooks are quickest to put themselves forward for public office. The state is still paying for its early mistakes in men. As I look at it, there are two stages in public graft. In the first, officials pick and steal from the emoluments of their office; in the second they tie up with the corporations. We still lived in the first stage, though I saw signs here and there that we were passing on to the second. However, the political machines in both parties were fully organized; and, as usual, they worked together, between elections, to keep the graft.

With most Oklahomans I believe that our state is naturally about the richest of all. I take pride with the rest that Oklahoma City, founded less than twenty-five years ago, has grown faster than any other city in the Union. But those very resources, that very growth, constituted a danger and a cause for immediate action. If we did not check the politicians, I felt, the people would awake some day, as California did, to find their resources sewed up by the corporations.

Gradually my mind settled upon one important office—county attorney at Oklahoma City. By our legal system that official represents the people in criminal as well as in civil cases. It is within his power to prosecute every malfeasance in state office. I thought of his chance to clean up Oklahoma, and

I wished that I had it. But I did not as yet make the wish personal.

As I started for my office, one morning in 1912, "Bill" Alexander, the boss of the Democratic machine, came along in his automobile and picked me up. An election was coming; we began discussing the Democratic candidates for the primaries. Some remark of his, I've now forgotten what, stung me a little; and out of my irritation came a sudden determination.

"Bill," I said, "I believe I'll announce for county attorney."

He wheeled half round in his seat and almost ran his machine into the curb.

"You're a fool!" he said. "You can't be elected!"

"If you think I'm asking your permission to run," I said, "you're a mile off the track."

"You couldn't be elected," he repeated. "You have been in Oklahoma City only a little more than a year."

"That makes no difference," said I. "Let a man go after the system here in Oklahoma and the people would listen if the checks were still on his baggage. I'm eligible under the law."

"Well," said Bill Alexander, "if you're crazy enough to think you can be elected, cut your wolf loose."

REHABILITATION

By the time I left the automobile, I had passed through one of my sudden changes. I dropped everything and sat down to write my announcement. My previous experience in the campaign for the constitutional convention had taught me my own weakness and strength; and I didn't fail to anticipate criticism from the other side. Here is the document, as I sent it next day to the newspapers:

In announcing myself for County Attorney of Oklahoma City, I beg to say that it is not without mature and serious thought that I have done so. I have thought over all that is objectionable. I have raked through the gray, dead ashes of the past. I have taken a retrospective glance into the dark recesses of the days that are gone, and I am willing that God's sunlight should be turned full upon every act of my past life.

I have never betrayed a trust or violated a confidence, and I would not deny the truth of my past for any office within the gift of the people. But I would rather have my record in its blackest hue than be pointed out as a public "grafter," "official crook" or "embezzler," who has violated his oath and prostituted the trust imposed in him by the people.

I am offering myself for what I am worth to-day and may prove to be worth in the future.

If the people are willing to confide to my care the office of county attorney, I pledge my word and honor that I will send the men who have embezzled their money and violated their oaths of office to the penitentiary. I will strike at violators of the law, be they high or low, without fear or favor, and I will save the taxpayers of Oklahoma County thousands of dollars by avoiding useless prosecutions.

I colored my language high, I suppose; but that was how I felt, and it was the language for the situation. I took this document to the newspaper offices, and sent in with it the twenty-five dollars which, I understood from my experience in country politics, must always accompany a candidate's announcement. Next day I received from Mr. Foster, editor of the *News,* our insurgent daily newspaper, a letter returning my check. "If it's news it gets printed in our paper, and money can't keep it out," he wrote. "If it isn't news money won't get it in. I'll print your announcement, and, if you feel grateful, you may buy me a cigar when we meet again."

Yet the *News* did something which, for the moment, made me sick. It printed with the announcement a three-column story, giving my record, with all the lurid details and the accumulated legends. I resented that, and I told Foster so.

"You don't expect the people to leave your record alone, do you?" he asked. "If you keep still your opponents will do the talking. Besides, it's news."

I opened my campaign for nomination at Hurrah, a small town on the Rock Island Railroad. I had advertised in advance; the people were waiting for me. As I walked from the station to the hotel I saw only one friendly countenance. The citizens stood glowering at me suspiciously from under their hat-brims. They'd turn down their faces as I approached, and whisper busily when I'd passed. The shrinking, ex-convict feeling came up in me. At the hotel my one friend in Hurrah introduced me to a few residents. They shook hands listlessly, and backed away. I stood until the time came for my speaking—it was to be a street-corner address—talking with an old one-eyed negro, who wanted to know why the Democrats had "franchised" him.

When I mounted the wagon and Jim Jacobs, my campaign manager, introduced me, the crowd remained stolid and silent. No one applauded as I rose. The faces before me were seamed with toil and burned with the sun. The hands showed warts and knots from long labor. And the sight of these plain people gave me encouragement for a plain, honest talk.

I began by saying that I had announced for county attorney because I believed the people needed some one who would really fulfill the duties of the office. "I've been a robber," I said, "but I give you my word of honor, which I have never violated, either as a robber or a man, that, if you elect me, I'll send

the embezzlers to the penitentiary. Many men whom
you have hitherto trusted have been playing with
you. They asked your votes in the name of the Re-
publican or Democratic parties. They were neither
Democrats nor Republicans, but common thieves."
To prove it I read a certain affidavit.

Then I swung into my own record, as I had done
years before in the campaign for the constitutional
convention. I had spoken an hour and twenty minutes before I finished confessing my old sins before
my fellow-citizens.

I closed by reciting the Scriptural story of Christ
and the Magdalen, and leaving the inference to my
audience.

Halfway through I began to see light in the faces
before me. When I read the affidavits a burst of
applause interrupted me. As I touched on my record the old, one-eyed negro began shouting "Glory!"
"Amen!" "Daniel at the judgment!" as though it
were a camp-meeting. At the end there was a storm
of applause. Don't think me conceited if I say that
this was an effective speech. It wasn't Al Jennings
who spoke. It was the experience of Al Jennings.
My years on the dodge, my battles, my days in the
prisoner's dock, my month in the dark cell, my awful
soul-wrench at Fort Leavenworth, my downfall after
I left prison, my struggle back—these had raised me

from a speaker to an orator. Once I could only convince people; now I could move them.

In the subsequent primaries only three Hurrah men voted against me.

I spoke in two or three other small towns before I tried out Oklahoma City. Feeling still uncertain how the people of the metropolis would receive me, I asked Dr. E. T. Bynum, a man of cultivation and wide experience, to go with me to Wheatland and criticize. There I addressed from a wagon fifty or sixty people. When I had finished Bynum spoke enthusiastically.

"But I'm wanting criticism," I said.

"I can give you none which wouldn't spoil your work," he replied. "Talk in the city as you have here and you'll get them!"

So Dr. Bynum and Judge R. A. Rogers arranged a speaking date for me in the capital, advertising it with newspaper space and handbills. They had some trouble in finding the proper man to introduce me. Finally I myself asked Hon. Claude Weaver, a candidate for Congress. He accepted at once.

"Remember," I warned him, "you are a candidate, and it will make you enemies."

"Men who'd be my enemies on that account aren't fit to be my supporters," he replied.

We drew a full house, though people came mostly

out of curiosity. They wanted to hear how the ex-bandit would get around his old record. But, before I finished, two or three machine men, who had previously treated my campaign as a joke, rushed out of the hall and assembled a conference. For my frank statement of my past and my open denunciation of certain state officials took the crowd in the city as it had in the villages.

Several men were already endorsed and in the field. The machine, I understood, decided to put up others, to find, through a kind of preliminary campaign, which seemed strongest, and to concentrate on him. I announced publicly that, with one or two exceptions, all my opponents were puppets of the machine. A few days later they withdrew in a body, leaving the field to me and Zwick. All, except Judge A. N. Munden, who was not a machine man, endorsed Zwick.

Now the fight began in earnest. I rushed like a whirlwind through the county, speaking at halls, schoolhouses, cross-roads, and street corners. I became the feature of the primary campaign. The other candidates took to following me around. At first I seemed to draw better in the country than in Oklahoma City, and so I concentrated on the capital. With the help of a wagon, which went about announcing my noonday street meetings, I began to

draw enormous crowds. Of course, the people came
to hear a bandit story—that was my bait. But they
remained to hear my say about certain officials. I
kept strengthening this part of my campaign. I
gave names and facts. I made statements daily
which, if untrue, would have laid me liable to charges
of slander. Even the friendly newspapers dared not
print all I said. Once I heard that the grand jury
expected to indict me—for slander, I suppose. I
bored in deeper than ever—and the grand jury never
acted.

The machine went out after me, not only secretly
but openly. They tried to get up opposition meetings within a block of my crowd. This proved a
failure; everyone flocked to hear the bandit. Once
I was speaking to three thousand people at California Street and Broadway, when two machine men
stood up at another corner and tried to entertain
two hundred people. They carried a life-sized picture of a masked robber holding up a train. "This
is the man who is running for county attorney
against a decent citizen," read the legend. Someone
reported that fact to me—while I was speaking. I
stopped to say that you'd never get those men any
nearer a bandit than his picture. "But I promise
you one thing," I said. "If I am elected you'll
see a string of officials and politicians taking

a trip to the institution known as the penitentiary."

A day or so later, as I came out of the elevator at the state bank building, I met face to face a Democratic politician.

"Hello, Al," he said, in an insinuating way, "I hear you're going to send me to the penitentiary. How would you advise me to proceed? I understand you've had experience." His pals, standing around him, laughed.

"Friend," I said, "you're safe. I believe in prison reform. I wouldn't contaminate the horse-thieves with your presence. In two days you'd steal the hinges off the prison gates."

We haven't spoken since.

On the eve of the primaries my friends calculated that I was a winner by two thousand votes. I didn't feel so sure. I knew that the election law in Oklahoma was admirably formed for corrupt uses, and that the gang controlled the election machinery. However, the early figures showed me leading by better majorities than I expected. Then the returns slowed up, and the Jennings vote dwindled. It was more than a week before I could get my certificates, which showed that I had won by a majority of 590 votes. Afterward a machine man, in a position to know, said to one of my friends:

"The damned hound was nominated by 2,500, and

346

we tried to shove him out. But we couldn't. The majority was too much for us."

As soon as my nomination had become a certainty Mr. Foster, of the *News*, hunted me up.

"Al," he said, "the regular proceeding now would be for you to lie down, stop muckraking, make your peace with the machine, and let them carry you into office. I hope you won't do that!"

"You bet your life, Foster, I won't!" I said.

However, I had my temptations; and they came not only from the other side, but from my friends. If I would keep still for the time being, some of my supporters said, the machine would think that I'd been muckraking only to get the nomination, and would stop opposing me. When I got into office I could start my prosecutions according to program. I disagreed with that view. I had stirred up the plain people by my exposures. If I quit it would appear to them that I was abandoning the fight, and they wouldn't support me. Besides, such a proceeding seemed dishonest to me. It would be obtaining office under false pretences. I whirled into the canvas, practically without support of my own party, and continued to whack both sides.

My campaign for election differed but little from my campaign for nomination. There were the same street-corner speeches, with the citizens and small boys coming to see me as a show, and remaining to hear my say about public officials. Some of my friends think that I played the bandit line too heavily in the last stages. I disagree with them.

However, my record, as I expected, became the strongest argument against me. With the more conservative and respectable class it proved especially effective. Oklahoma City couldn't afford, said the machine, to have an ex-convict representing it before the world. I had defended many whiskey peddlers. The machine made the most of that. Unofficially several church organizations declared against me. The Law Enforcement League, formed to prevent illicit liquor selling, wrote me a formal letter, asking where I stood on prohibition. I replied that I'd enforce the law, and I'd begin on the officials who permitted Oklahoma City to go wide open under their very eyes. Many such people went to my meetings skeptics and came away convinced. For example, Professor Evans, of the State Normal school, had dinner in town one night with a party of eastern schoolbook salesmen. They looked through the restaurant window, and saw the crowd gathering for one of my meetings.

Professor Evans says that he told of my campaign with a kind of shame for the city. The others agreed that to elect such a man would be a blot on any

community. When I appeared they joined the
crowd out of curiosity; but, after I had finished,
they shook my hand, and wished me well. Professor
Evans campaigned for me to the end.

The strength of my position was the strength
of truth. I had told the worst about myself, and
I had no reprisals to fear. Yet they labored to
catch me in a misstatement, or to find some bit of
scandal worse than train-robbery and two terms in
prison. The author of my campaign circulars
wrote carelessly that I was a graduate of the University of Virginia. That happened to be a mistake; the truth is that I went to the University of
West Virginia, and didn't get a degree. However,
the slip seemed to me so unimportant that I took
no pains to correct it. My opponents telegraphed
to the University of Virginia, found that no student
of my name had ever been enrolled there, and made
much of the fact. The rumor grew that, on the
morning of the Chickasha robbery I had brutally
and grossly mistreated the wife of the section boss.
Among other brutalities—I learned to my surprise
—I had kicked her in the stomach. Certain machine men sent for this woman, hoping to get a sen-
sational statement. She told the truth, which made
her useless for their purposes.

I have related before how Louis, an old postoffice

burglar, nursed me back when I was sick in the Ohio penitentiary, and how, by robbing the prison pantry to get me proper food, he risked all his privileges. I believe that he saved my life. In the very heat of my campaign I received a telegram from him. He had been arrested at Tulsa, Oklahoma, and carried to Madill, charged with robbing the First National Bank. I dropped everything and went to see him. Ten minutes' talk convinced me that this was a case where the police grab the first burglar in sight and try to saddle him with the crime. As a matter of fact, Louis had been in the Lee-Huckins Hotel, at Oklahoma City, on the night of the burglary. He remembered that Cliff Walker, the hotel detective, looked him over carefully. I returned home, saw Cliff Walker, found that he had actually made an entry in his notebook describing this man with the prison look. Further, he had called the attention of ex-Lieutenant-Governor Bellamy and Captain Phelps to Louis—and they remembered. I took back with me to Madill a letter from Mr. Bellamy, and I got Mr. Walker and Captain Phelps to accompany me in person. On the strength of this evidence I had the charge dismissed without trial. Then I took Louis home with me for a week's visit. He is a gentleman; my wife and sister-in-law said that they never had a guest whom they liked better.

REHABILITATION

That visit rose up against me. A clergyman started it by saying that he would not vote for me because I had harbored burglars. This report went from mouth to mouth, until I was forced to meet it from the platform. I told the people exactly what Louis had done for me. "I haven't harbored a burglar," I added, "but I have entertained one. I found him more mannerly and honest than most of your county and city officials."

Still, as the campaign drew to a close I fought without much hope.

My friends said: "It's a walkover."

"On public enthusiasm, yes," I replied. "But remember how the primaries went. They simply can't afford to let me win."

I was in the midst of things, declaring nightly my intention to put certain officials in the penitentiary, when a chance remark called back to my memory the tailor shop at Fort Leavenworth, and made me realize what I was doing. I'd thought, in the penitentiary, that no imaginable crime deserved my fate. And here I was, promising to administer just such punishment wholesale! I mentioned this to my crowd next day. "Even after I've convicted the truly guilty," I said, "I'll get down on my knees to ask mercy of the chief executive. I don't want vengeance on the grafters—I want to clean up this

351

state. What I propose to do is administer the law, shutting my eyes to the remote consequences. I am out to show the people of Oklahoma, for the first time, that a man who betrays the public trust is more guilty than the man who steals a horse. Only one thing would test my strength or weakness —to prosecute some poor devil who, driven by hunger and want, had stolen to feed starving mouths and clothe naked forms." On that note I closed my campaign.

Though the county and district were electing some twenty officials, including a member of Congress, my race for district attorney had become, I suppose, the feature of the campaign. On election night, they tell me, the crowds before the newspaper offices paid little attention to anything except the returns for county attorney. I received the bulletins in my office, of which I had made a political headquarters for the past three months. The early returns exceeded our expectations. From two thousand the forecast of my friends grew to twenty-five hundred. I began to think, for the first time, that perhaps I should squeeze by.

At about eleven o'clock the returns suddenly stopped. I waited fifteen minutes, twenty minutes, half an hour.

"That settles it, boys," I said finally, "I'm gone!"

REHABILITATION

At last the returns came straggling in again. They showed a great slump. The morning newspapers declared that, although they had not received full returns, they could announce my defeat. Eight or ten days passed before I got complete figures. Many ballot boxes were turned in late; mostly they had been "hidden out."

I had not the money, nor yet the influence, to make a contest. I let it stand. But I ask any man acquainted with American politics this question: When a State is tied up by a corrupt bipartisan gang of politicians, which controls the machinery of election; when an independent candidate arises who threatens, if elected, to put most of those politicians in jail; and when that candidate, after a campaign which seems all in his favor, is defeated by 500 votes in a total of 12,000—isn't he really elected?

The reformer who declares that he works for wholly altruistic motives is posing. The best of them have mixed motives. Besides the desire to right the wrongs in the world they are·driven also by hunger for fame or position or admiration. I freely admit that I ran for county attorney with two ends in view. I wanted the job—not so much for fame, position, and power as for rehabilitation. But I also wanted to waken the people of city, county and state to their public condition. Since

BEATING BACK

I am convinced that I was elected, I consider that I gained my first object. The people proved to me that an ex-convict, by playing the game straight, and without concealment, can come back.

Also I achieved something of my second object. I woke the people of the capital; I helped wake the people of the state. The legislature which met in 1913, less than a year after my campaign, showed a disposition toward political reform. They overturned our election laws; they investigated by commission our public institutions; they even got some indictments. It does not matter that the net caught the lesser offenders and let the greater go by; this happens generally in the dawn of reform. The point is that Oklahoma made a beginning. I opened that fight; and I have not by any means finished fighting.

Anyone who has taken the trouble to read this story can draw the moral, I suppose. Ex-convicts can come back if they take the right method. "Grasp the nettle and it will not sting," is an old saying, but a true one. The man who goes out of prison with his record on his sleeve may expect the best, not the worst, of humanity. People will give him a chance. Only he must be genuinely reformed. If he keeps up any of his old practices he is only.

preparing for a harder fall. The man who conceals his record, on the other hand, is riding to his doom. Sooner or later it will either rise up to overthrow him or it will break his heart. My way, I believe, is the only way.

And this applies not only to prison convictions, but to other disgraces as well. In nearly fifty years of varied experience I have observed many scandals of many kinds. I have seen men and women crushed and killed by the disgrace. I have seen others outlive scandal, and make successes of their lives, by the process of facing it down. The greatest power in the world, I suppose, is the power of truth; and next is the power of not being afraid.

THE END

qp

www.ingramcontent.com/pod-product-compliance
Lightning Source LLC
Chambersburg PA
CBHW050450270326
41927CB00009B/1679